suppressed:

Confessions of a Former *New York Times*
Washington Correspondent

ROBERT M. SMITH

LYONS
PRESS

Guilford, Connecticut

An imprint of The Rowman & Littlefield Publishing Group, Inc.
4501 Forbes Blvd., Ste. 200
Lanham, MD 20706
www.rowman.com

Distributed by NATIONAL BOOK NETWORK

British Library Cataloguing in Publication Information available

Library of Congress Cataloging-in-Publication Data

Names: Smith, Robert M., 1940- author.
Title: Suppressed : confessions of a former New York Times Washington
  correspondent / Robert M. Smith.
Description: Guilford, Connecticut : Lyons Press, 2021. | Includes
  bibliographical references and index. | Summary: "A former Times White
  House and investigative correspondent, Robert M. Smith, discloses how
  some stories make it to print, some do not, how the filters work, and
  how the paper may have suppressed the most important U.S. political
  story of the day-Watergate"— Provided by publisher.
Identifiers: LCCN 2020052271 (print) | LCCN 2020052272 (ebook) | ISBN
  9781493057719 (cloth) | ISBN 9781493057726 (epub)
Subjects: LCSH: Smith, Robert M., 1940- | Journalists—United
  States—Biography. | Attorneys—United States—Biography. | Press and
  politics—United States—History—20th century.
Classification: LCC PN4874.S5655 A3 2021 (print) | LCC PN4874.S5655
  (ebook) | DDC 070.92 [B] —dc23
LC record available at https://lccn.loc.gov/2020052271
LC ebook record available at https://lccn.loc.gov/2020052272

For Cathy and Clarissa, who—with constant good humor—experienced these events with me. They tolerated the hidden oddities and biases of journalism, the fashion-conscious trials of law, and the occasional frustrations of mediation.

AND

For those nearly 450 journalists around the world killed, held hostage, or imprisoned while pursuing an independent, neutral version of the truth in 2020, according to Reporters Without Borders. (The group ranked the US 45th in the world in freedom of the press in 2020.)

We are all looking forward to the next Watergate movie focusing on the extraordinary reporting of the New York Times.

—Arthur Gregg Sulzberger, publisher of the *New York Times*, on the *New Yorker Radio Hour*, December 22, 2017

The media should be embarrassed and humiliated [by the 2016 election results] and keep its mouth shut and just listen for a while.

—Stephen Bannon, the *New York Times*, January 26, 2017

The truth is hard.
The truth is hidden.
The truth must be pursued. . . .
The truth is under attack. . . .
The truth is more important now than ever.

—Full-page ad the *New York Times* felt obliged to run in its own paper, February 27, 2017

CONTENTS

contents

contents

INTRODUCTION

To some, these events will seem quite natural; to others, all but incred-
ible. But, obviously, a narrator cannot take account of these differences
of outlook. His business is only to say: "This is what happened," when
he knows that it actually did happen. . . .

—ALBERT CAMUS, *THE PLAGUE*

The biased coverage of the *Times* and other media outlets is both a symptom and a cause of the dreadful divide in America. The divide would
normally welcome the healing role of a neutral press. But we are in a
moment when the White House—correctly—could not trust the *New
York Times*. And the *New York Times*—correctly—could not trust the
White House. And when a lot of the public says—correctly—they just
can't trust either one.

The unhappy result is a terrible wound that journalists have imposed
on themselves and us: They—and especially those at the *New York Times*—
have arranged things so they can have no helpful role in the crucial effort
to bridge the divide.

I was an investigative reporter and White House correspondent for
the *New York Times* in Washington and learned what everyone who reads
newspapers or is tempted by clickbait to absorb their content should
know: The suppression of news is alive and well, even at the *New York
Times*. From a painful dentist's chair in the slums of Boston through the
forced assimilation of Harvard Yard and, later, the top ranks of the Carter
Administration, this book is also the tale of what makes reporters want to
be reporters and why they're cynical.

Since I thought it would be interesting and useful to see things from
the inside rather than the outside, I became a senior figure in the Justice
Department of the Carter Administration. What I learned is also set out
in this book. Among other things, I learned that even a Cabinet minister
is powerless to stop obvious government waste.

As a lawyer, I loved to talk with jurors. Unlike most folks in this society, I believe jurors usually get it right. Fancy lawyers can't always work their magic when their clients have no right to prevail amnesty. I became so smitten with the law that I went on to become a barrister of the Inner Temple in London and to teach a course at the Law Faculty in Oxford.

I found similarities between the skills required to report stories and practice law. Both careers involved listening and observing. And after covering protests, desegregation, Congress, the CIA, and the White House, I heard and saw more than my share of the important, the odd, and the bizarre.

While these experiences may prove interesting, I hope they will show how newspapers like the *New York Times* went off their track when confronted with the challenges to objective journalism presented by Donald Trump. I think my different careers have informed one another and allowed me in this book to take a critical look at the media landscape as it was when I worked at the *New York Times*, and analyze the nature of it now, how the *Times* lost its impartiality when confronted with the challenges to objective journalism presented by Donald Trump.

In my day, there was a powerful cast of characters, in both Washington and New York, at the *New York Times*.

The paper was led by a much-hated Abraham Michael Rosenthal, a cerebral and highly political Max Frankel (who bragged about his ability to get Henry Kissinger, the national security adviser, to take his phone calls—both were from families that had fled Nazi Germany), and the demigod James B. ("Scotty") Reston. They shaped, to a very large extent, the way the world saw itself.

But below them were the working soldiers—the reporters and the editors who are chronicled in their various adventures and misadventures in the pages that follow. Among them was my direct boss, the news editor of the Washington Bureau, Robert H. Phelps, proud of both his purported Native American heritage and the pink dot in the center of his pale stomach. Phelps, diligent to a fault, compulsively used dental picks to tidy up his teeth. But he proved immensely, and lamentably, less diligent in having reporters follow the story of the century, when I presented it to him the day before I left the paper for the first time.

The story was Watergate, which this book deals with, in part. In particular, its suppression by the *Times*—until the paper could no longer turn a blind eye because of two upstarts at the *Washington Post*, one of whom I interviewed to be a reporter for the *Times* and strongly suggested he not be hired.

It was a world then of lies and deception—think of the Pentagon Papers, the odd story of which is also told in this book. (I was assigned to find out who had leaked the papers to my colleague, Neil Sheehan, at the *Times*!)

I won many awards while at the *Times*—given to me by the paper for what it saw as especially good reporting on especially interesting stories. I also have the distinction of having quit the paper and been rehired by the paper (before I left it again). In a sentence, this is a story of when innocence meets reality, and when bias makes its way into the most respected of journalistic temples. That bias continues today.

PROLOGUE

The Leak

Journalism, as concerns collecting information, differs little if at all from intelligence work. In my judgment, a journalist's job is very interesting.

—VLADIMIR PUTIN, RUSSIAN PRESIDENT

Secrecy, being an instrument of conspiracy, ought never to be the system of a regular government.

—JEREMY BENTHAM, ENGLISH PHILOSOPHER

WASHINGTON BUREAU, THE *NEW YORK TIMES*, AUGUST 1972

The elevator performed its ritual ping at the eighth floor as I ran across the hall and into the newsroom.

Good, Bob Phelps was at his desk. Phelps was my editor. He was short, slight, gray-haired, and taciturn. He rolled a miniature wooden dental stake around in his mouth, working away at his teeth during one of his habitual dental stimulator sessions. Shortly after he had eaten lunch, his custom was to part his shirt carefully between the buttons and look with care at a red dot on his small white stomach. He would also take out the trusty wooden pick and diligently stimulate those pesky gums.[1]

"Let's go to your office right now," I said. I picked up a reporter's notebook, handed it to him, and told him to bring a pen.

Bob's idea of showing emotion was to smile slightly, showing the well-stimulated incisors. He didn't smile. No doubt he thought, *the kid's acting up again, but . . . it's his last day*, and it was. I was thirty-one and had been a reporter at the *Times* for four years, but I was leaving to go to Yale Law School. Except I'd just gotten a scoop and I couldn't walk away from it.

I dragged him to the small office he had next to Max Frankel's big office. Frankel was bureau chief at the *Times*. Along the way I picked up a desk-size tape recorder. Once we were inside, I closed the door. He sat at the edge of the small print couch. I paced. Someone came through the door. Bob dealt with whoever it was.

I closed the door again and Scotch-taped a Do Not Disturb sign to it. I started the small tape recorder, made sure the tape was whirling, and urged Bob to take notes in the spiral-bound, tan-covered notebook I had handed him.

I was sputtering. "You cannot attribute this to the source," I warned, "but I just had lunch with Pat Gray and. . . ."

I told him the story of my afternoon when the gray-suited man with enormous cauliflower ears walked through the door of the posh French restaurant and spotted me, his young lunch companion, seated on a red banquette against the wall. Louis Patrick Gray III, the acting director of the FBI, waved off the maître d'. Tall and unassuming, with inviting nonchalance, he headed for the table. I knew Gray was naïve for a Washington official, a former submarine commander turned lawyer. He'd invited me to lunch. He sat down, lanky legs tucked under the white tablecloth, and greeted me warmly. I was dressed as usual in chinos that could stand a pressing and a Harris Tweed jacket left over from college.

He wasted no time telling me that the attorney general and the president were involved in a crime. This was August 1972, just two months after the burglary in which five men had broken into the headquarters of the Democratic National Committee at the Watergate office complex. He was telling me this in a restaurant filled with diners, not in an underground garage.

Gray seemed oblivious that what he was saying, openly, in a crowded power restaurant might be overheard. He used no code names, no secret handshakes, and made no effort to sugarcoat. There was just the bright Washington sunshine streaming in through big windows and steak frites on our plates, just a casual lunch between the acting director of the FBI and a *Times* reporter. This was months before Woodward and Bernstein's revelations on Watergate and a cover-up that led, the director disclosed that day, through the attorney general to the White House.

I struggled hard to remain stony-faced in the French restaurant and likely failed awfully. I managed to say nothing, but must have appeared to Gray, and any other diners who happened to look, shaken, or, as the French say, *bouleversé*—turned upside down.

That day Gray told me—and I told Bob—about a guy later identified as G. Gordon Liddy, an FBI agent until a decade earlier and chief operative in the scandal, and about Donald Segretti. He named Segretti. When he intimated over the entree that the wrongdoing went further, I leaned against the wall behind the banquette. I looked at him and asked in astonishment, "The attorney general [is involved]?"

He nodded.

"The president?" I asked.

Gray looked me in the eye and made no comment. In other words, confirmation. I slumped back, appetite gone. He seemed to me to be a stand-up conservative submariner turned Republican politician, if naïve in a way not typically permitted in Washington, DC. I couldn't imagine why he was telling me this. I couldn't take my notebook out—at least I thought I couldn't. Too many people would have noticed the acting director of the FBI with some youngster taking notes. So I struggled to remember names: *Segretti—spaghetti.* Mnemonics are the last refuge for those with notebooks secreted in pockets.

We finished eating. On the pavement in front of the restaurant, I told Gray I was leaving the *Times* for Yale Law School the very next day. He hadn't known, and he seemed more shocked about my leaving than I was about the story he'd just told me. Or perhaps he just didn't try to mask his surprise the way I did.

I hurried back to the Washington Bureau to brief Phelps, the news editor.

"Bob," I remember beginning. "This is incredible." And for the next half-hour—like a jumping bean, unable to contain myself—I told him everything Gray had just told me. Pacing the length of the small room, I tape-recorded our session, and I gave Phelps the tape so he would have the details his notes might have missed.

I left the *Times* on August 17, 1972. For the next few months at Yale Law School, I read the *Times* every day, and I was certain I would see the story. It didn't appear. I assumed the paper hadn't been able to confirm it, even though I'd given them Segretti's name.

Then, beginning in October 1972, I watched as the *Washington Post* began drubbing the *Times*. New York called me: *Come back.* I said no, but offered to make a phone call. I called Gray. He did not call me back.

CHAPTER ONE

Pain: The Penalty for Poverty

There is no birth of consciousness without pain.

—CARL JUNG

ROXBURY, 1948

One of the first important lessons I learned in childhood came when I was eight years old in 1948. I was sitting in a chair at my dentist's office on Blue Hill Avenue in the Dorchester section of Boston, near my home in Roxbury. I wriggled in that 1940s chair and looked up at the light poised ominously above me, then at the Old Brown Jug tavern across the street in the Black-Jewish ghetto of Boston. I had a cavity, and my parents had taken me to a second-floor dentist's office. I was terrified.

The American Dental Association's website says that "The administration of sedation and general anesthesia has been an integral part of dental practice since the 1840s," but not that day—not in Dorchester. That dentist wanted $1 for Novocaine, and my mother didn't have a dollar, so I got the drill without blandishment and never forgot it. Decades later, with remarkable chair-side manner, one of my dentists in San Francisco told me that the dentistry without anesthetic had made me "a dental cripple." I don't know about that, but it did help make me a liberal who believed people shouldn't be tortured because they didn't have a dollar.

It was that dental treatment that also led me to, and through, investigative reporting in Washington.

CHAPTER TWO

Kids' Stuff

I cannot think of any need in childhood as strong as the need for a father's protection.

—Sigmund Freud

Anyone who hasn't experienced the ecstasy of betrayal knows nothing about ecstasy at all.

—Jean Genet

ROXBURY, 1948

The reporter in me who began to ask those questions of the rich and powerful was born in a shabby red-brick apartment building in the middle of Roxbury. In that apartment, the intercom on the wall looked like an old-fashioned telephone, except it didn't have a crank, and it had a marvelous crackle-black finish. The earpiece hung on a hook on the box, connected by a piece of fabric-coated wire. There was a beguiling silver button that sat in the middle of the box. This was the call button that rang the bell on the other one of the pair of 1940s walkie-talkies.

When I was seven, my parents relented and gave me this splendid device that I so yearned for. Dad hung one crackle box in the reception hall of our ghetto apartment and the other in my bedroom. When it was time to test out the boxes, a pal of mine was at our place, and Dad said he'd go into the bedroom and take my pal with him. I thought that sounded fine, but I insisted he not let my friend take the first call.

"I'll call you, Dad," I said, and off they trooped to the bedroom.

I yelled, "Ready?"

"Ready," Dad yelled back.

I reached up and pushed the wondrous silver button and heard the other box ringing through the bedroom door. Then I managed, on tiptoes, to reach up even higher and took down the round black earpiece.

"Hello," I yelled into the microphone—just little holes in the black spackle of the box.

"Hello," came the response, but it was not my dad. It was my former pal.

I threw a tantrum over this betrayal, but father quelled it, first with shouts, then laughter. He thought my upset was funny, but that deception stayed with me, a life-long memory like the scar I had on my forehead from a rock someone had thrown at me one morning in a routine Roxbury fight.

My father was a letter carrier, a job that required little of his agile mind and left him free for a succession of hobbies, from woodworking to amateur radio. My mother was a housewife until her forties. Then she became a secretary in a government office. Our apartment house was three floors high, in the middle of the Black and Jewish ghetto. Everyone who lived in our building was white except for the nearly blind janitor, Percy, who left us without heat and hot water when rum proved more enticing than shoveling coal into the furnace. No coal shoveled, no heat in cast iron radiators.

To economize, my parents nailed metal taps to the leather heels of my shoes, and with the cathedral radio playing big-band music in the living room, I could—like a spinning Sufi dervish—tap dance wildly on the blue linoleum. Maybe they imagined I'd become a star one day, but thousands are grateful I gave up tap dancing early on. My late wife, Cathy, though, was a huge fan of Fred Astaire, and she might have liked to see me dance—though I don't believe Astaire ever did it on linoleum.

My father's parents emigrated from Europe in the 1880s—she from Vienna, and he from what I think was Vilna Gubernia. When just three years old, they had both fought for a crust of bread on the ship en route to Boston Harbor, or so they told me. They never explained how my grandfather's name became Joseph Smith. They learned English. He got an official Minor's License (No. 37326) from the City of Boston and delivered newspapers, rolled cigars by hand, and finally owned a pool parlor in Roxbury.

My father managed the pool hall, and, as a toddler, not tall enough to reach the tops of the tables, I waddled unsteadily around. Years later, when my father visited me at Dunster House at Harvard, he dazzled my fellow students with his pool playing at the basement tables.

The pool hall patrons were nearly all Black. But in neighboring Dorchester, mostly Jewish patrons frequented the "Ultra-Modern, Ultra Fine" G&G delicatessen with homemade pastries and knishes, corned beef, tongue, hot pastrami, and special "frankforts." The neighborhood also had a few synagogues, or "shuls," as people said, though my memories of boyhood religion are slim, comprised of little more than two stories.

Synagogues were visited during the Jewish High Holy Days in the fall. In those days, the boys would stay out in the yard of the shul during the services and play games. One of the most popular was soaking a handkerchief in vinegar and flogging the hands of the other boys. Standing in a circle, we were all compelled to extend our palms and risk a stinging swat. Red were the palms of those not blessed with quick reflexes. During school days, I received part of my religious training—such as it was—by waiting at a bus stop across the street from the Temple Mishkan Tefila.

I went through my bar mitzvah, my coming of religious age as a Jew, at Mishkan Tefila. I am obliged to say I'm neither observant nor a true believer, although I'm now a member of a Reform synagogue in San Francisco. Neither of my late wives was Jewish, and I belong to the unhappy group that sees religion as a disappointingly divisive force in the modern world.

My father, dressed in a double-breasted blue suit with padded shoulders, went to the temple on holidays, although the experience did not make him happy. My mother was more observant. My grandparents kept a kosher household. I still can't bring myself to have milk with meat.

Our Roxbury was not a safe place. Besides rock fights, there were thieves, one of whom crawled in through our bedroom window while we were home, searched the room, found my mother's purse, and made off with it through the same window. Both my mother and father took the theft placidly; they knew the neighborhood.

Our building was on a slight hill, and the back of the property sloped down sharply. In the back were uninviting "piazzas." They were iron painted black and had open grills, suitable for neither high heels nor anything that might drop from pocket or purse. They surrounded a concrete courtyard that sported a black drain and led to an unkempt, trash-strewn hillock with cars parked randomly and, in the winter, a snowy slope for wooden sleds. In our Roxbury ghetto, Blacks and Whites did not fight; they just did not mix. The scar on my forehead from the rock fight was from a wound caused by another Jewish kid's expert fling—uphill at that. It was generally safe to walk, in daylight, to the kosher butcher, the baker of hot, crusty kaiser rolls—and the Rexall drugstore.

The drugstore sold African-American magazines like *Ebony* and *Jet* as well as the *Saturday Evening Post*, *Life*, and *Look*. I didn't really care about the magazines. I cared about the soda fountain. The soda fountain had hot fudge sundaes with real hot fudge (not Hershey's syrup!), whipped cream, nuts, and (at least one) long-stemmed cherry on top. It cost twenty-five cents and was my occasional wondrous treat from my grandmother, who looked on carefully as I hauled myself onto the red vinyl stool and waited greedily as a long silver spoon was placed in front of me. Talk about Proust and his madeleine: *An exquisite pleasure had invaded my senses, something isolated, detached, with no suggestion of its origin.*

When I was a teenager, my family followed the many middle-class Jews who had fled from Roxbury to, first, Dorchester and then to Mattapan. Alfred Kazin would perhaps characterize us as only a little better off than his "*urime yidn*, poor Jews."[2] My first job in high school was at a small photo-finishing plant in Roxbury. We turned photo negatives into prints and sent them back to the drugstores where the customers would pick them up. I remember when a belt on one of the machines snapped. My coworkers scratched their heads. We had to order a replacement belt, but what size? I said, with a swollen (and empty) head: Just thread a string around the wheels of the machines and measure the length of the thread. That was done. When the new belt arrived, it was too short. It was thicker than the string and didn't fit as deeply into the wheels as the string had. What had seemed to be a common-sense fix was wrong.

The question raised nowadays would be: How many white-collar (not to mention red-tie) news anchors would have gotten the length of the blue-collar belt right?

It was not the harsh streets of Roxbury that schooled me and led me to Harvard. It was the prestigious Boston Public Latin School, more than three centuries old with teachers brandishing a didactic method little changed from English public schools of that same time. At the free but high-pressure Latin School, I was made to study Latin, French, German, English—and Math. At football games, we would chant to our Wolfpack team, which wore the purple of ancient Rome: *Pursue them, pursue them, make them relinquish the ball!* We were taught relentlessly, and what we were taught, we were taught well, though lessons did not have anything to do with enjoyment, entertainment, or imagination.

In those days, only one in three Latin School boys graduated. I may have appreciated going to Rexall's with grandma so much because my mother used to give me lunch in a paper bag to take to school. As I jealously watched the slim, black-haired Italian-American kid from the North End who sat in front of me unwrap his long roll stuffed with provolone and mortadella, I looked at my peanut butter and jelly on Wonder bread. And dreamt of the Rexall sundae.

I didn't have the quarter for lunch in the school cafeteria, and one of the important things the boys learned at Latin School was that the student lockers were not invulnerable to mice. The mice were not fussy—peanut butter and jelly was fine.

I remember coming home from school one day white, weak, and perspiring. I didn't know why, but it was a lack of food. Grandma rescued me with a hastily prepared hot turkey sandwich smothered in a salty mushroom gravy. I can still taste it.

Some of my teachers—whom we called "masters"—made future editors, drill sergeants, judges, and angry and self-absorbed adversaries in a mediation child's play for me, so they served me well. When I finally left Boston for Rewrite at the *New York Times*, I carefully stored all my most valuable memorabilia—including diplomas and awards from Latin School and Harvard—in a large wooden sea chest with sturdy planking and thick twisted wooden ropes at the ends.

While I was in New York, my father moved the prized box, untended and unprotected, to the floor of the unoccupied garage adjacent to, but separate from, the house. By the time I came home, rodents had eaten all items that I cared about, but I never received a word of apology or explanation about the loss. This betrayal seemed like the first one, the betrayal of the intercom. I always understood that these betrayals did not begin to compare with the beatings, incest, and other true horrors many children suffer, but they did inflict pain and left me with a sense of not having been well loved. Still, whatever else those may have done, the betrayals and unreliability gave me a sense of skepticism and suspicion suited to working in an environment where people were lying to one another—and you—most of the time.

CHAPTER THREE

"You're Already a Communist":
Harvard and Power

In the . . . heydays of the early 1950s, Senator Joseph McCarthy called Harvard a "smelly mess" where students risked "indoctrination by Communist professors." He called it a "privileged sanctuary for Fifth Amendment Communists." In fact, Harvard cooperated closely with the FBI's anti-communist witch hunts.

—AMY GOODMAN, DEMOCRACY NOW

HARVARD UNIVERSITY, SEPTEMBER 1958

In high school, I applied to only three colleges—Harvard, Brandeis, and Massachusetts State Teachers College. I was giving myself some leeway and felt sure that at least Teachers College would accept me. Harvard was a stretch, I thought, but it made sense to study there since I could commute by taking the MTA's public transit to Cambridge. On the sunny afternoon when the letter from Harvard came to our apartment, I opened it quickly and saw that they were offering me a scholarship of $1,800 a year. Tuition was just $1,200. I was sure they had made a mistake. With an innocence that dogged me for a long while, I immediately called the Harvard Admissions Office. I told the secretary they had given me too much money.

Without missing a beat, she said, "No, we didn't. We want you to live here."

I'll never know whether the admissions people at Harvard were acting out of a benevolent impulse to take in poor kids from public high schools or if they just wanted to show the posh preppies from Andover and the bastards from Exeter (that's what the Andover grads called them) what a fellow from the slums of Boston looked and sounded like, but that day I didn't care. I just knew my life was about to change, and I was going to have a chance to move out. My parents beamed.

That fall, they drove me to Cambridge.

As a youngster in Roxbury, I watched a leather-aproned man with huge tongs bowing under the weight of large blocks of ice he delivered for ice boxes and the gas man walking his rounds at dusk with a short ladder to light the many gas lamps on the black street posts of Roxbury. I did not see this in Cambridge.

I sat down to my first breakfast at Harvard's Freshman Union. It seemed a wooden behemoth—solid, traditional, impersonal, not the least welcoming. I stood in the cafeteria line and the server behind the counter ladled out something I had never seen, let alone eaten. When I left my tray to get a napkin, I stuck my fork in. The fork stuck straight up in the congealed yellow mass. I asked a guy sitting nearby what the yellow stuff was, and he told me they were hominy grits. At lunch, when I innocently asked someone where the soda machine was, the boys sitting around me exploded in laughter. I quickly understood that they were used to milk, or iced tea, maybe, but never soda.

I was one week into Harvard, when my mother declared her conviction that I had been brainwashed.

"You're already a Communist," she said.

When she told me this, I could think of nothing to say. I reached for the bundle of laundry my father was holding and, in exchange, handed him a bag of dirty clothes. It seemed pointless to debate. Bolshevism aside, it was these laundry runs that allowed my parents to see the Harvard they were so proud their son had gotten into.

I don't know whether my father shared my mother's fears. The closest he got to politics was when the FBI asked him what letters a certain "progressive" institution on his mail route was getting. Generally, Ma kept to her friends, and Dad to his hobbies. The shared activity was the Sunday drive to other parts of the city or near suburbs or to Franklin Park Zoo, where I had paraded in a sailor suit during World War II. Much later in life, like so many from Roxbury-Dorchester-Mattapan, they fled the snow to a middle-class enclave in Florida.

To supplement my scholarship during my first year, I worked in the dining hall at Dunster House. After first year, Harvard students are divided into residential houses, each with its own dining hall and library. At dinner I was busy scooping very, very frozen ice cream out of cardboard containers to serve to House residents and their beautiful dates. My starched white jacket was soaked with perspiration.

I also earned money by fetching books for patrons of Widener Library. I did have a girlfriend, a leftie from Brandeis who made bold to display the antediluvian allure of black stockings and garter belts. That meant my schedule was not like one most of my classmates had. My study, jobs, and girlfriend left me little time to imbibe any alcohol except sherry. I thought sherry was a type of wine, only one step down, or up, from Manischewitz, known for its low-cost Concord wine. Roxbury's dinner-table carbonated "tonic" gave way, unbidden, to sherry in the Master's Lodge at Dunster House. Polished wood and crystal replaced my mother's floral tablecloths and our family's cheap blue-banded tumblers. Before I went to Harvard, I had once tasted a martini. I was eighteen (and underage) at a cocktail party-cum-news conference in Boston when I tried it. I hated it.

But at Harvard, an acquaintance with sweet Spanish 18 percent alcohol by the thimbleful was part of Dunster House life. Quaffing it felt evil but did not taste delicious. The preppies (Exonians, those from Andover, and other habitués of the traditional J. Press clothing store) were used to the harder stuff. If my mother ever had known that Harvard turned me into not only a Communist but a tippler—well, I'm not sure which she would have thought more sinful.

Another problem was my accent. It was 1959, and John F. Kennedy was soon to become president. The way those Kennedys spoke was the way I understood I was supposed to, but during my first two weeks at Harvard, people laughed every time I opened my mouth and my Roxbury accent emerged. Within two weeks, I'd lost it. Gone. Standard American replaced it. The southern kids kept their accents—with pride, I think. What Bull Run and Chancellorsville had over Lexington and Bunker Hill, I had no idea. It turned out that eventually, when I was doing one-minute segments of breaking news on WQXR, the *Times* radio station, that pressure to lose my unacceptable accent probably helped me.

When my parents visited, my father had a habit of pulling the modest family car into Harvard Yard and parking in front of my freshman dormitory, Hollis Hall. Once when he did this, Harvard retaliated by locking the gates to the Yard. My parents were in the perilous custody of the tippling Commies, and they weren't happy about it until a cop with a Boston accent appeared. Boston-accent to Boston-accent. Dad and cop worked it out, and the heavy black metal gates swung open. Geographic separation again reinforced the psychological separation I had long felt, even back in Roxbury.

In the meantime, at Dunster House, I heard through the thin walls the exchanges of my prep-school-trained neighbors and learned about their ingrained, reflexive anti-Semitism. These and other contrasts with Roxbury were befuddling. At Harvard there were anti-Semites, almost no African Americans, and not many poor kids. Still, the ethos—it was practically in the air—was liberalism, though the culture innocently promoted self-entitlement, based in part on merit and achievement, in part on money and family background. Immersed in that world, I began to look back at the way I—and everyone else—was treated in Roxbury. I compared it to the way folks were treated at Harvard. When I did, I saw a discriminatory, class-ridden Boston society with tentacles of racism, classism, and anti-Semitism reaching into every room in Harvard's dormitories.

I had no idea what Final Clubs were, and it took me months to understand they were Harvard's exclusive social clubs. (One of these, The Porcellian, sounded, at the least, precious.) They did not have branches in Roxbury. I determined that I would never again be treated in the Roxbury way. The Roxbury way was: no power, little money, no autonomy, no respect, islands of social division; second-class—no, third-class—treatment, just like the treatment on those ships my great-grandparents had boarded. Never articulating it, I determined to try to help those who continued to be treated that way.

What was the alternative? Let some bastard continue to drill teeth without Novocaine because he needed another house in upper-class

Newton? Investigative reporting sprang without thought from a comparison of my life and ghetto life.

So I decided to become a reporter. The two-mile walk home at night from the MTA station took me over urban roads and bridges. I was obviously too poor to be worth robbing. In particular, the walk took me past Simco's by the Bridge. I didn't have the money to buy a hot dog or lime rickey at the world-famous (well, Roxbury-Dorchester-Mattapan famous) Simco's. But the walk did give me time to dream of not only becoming a reporter, but of becoming a *Times* foreign correspondent.

In 1958, when I began at Harvard, I had no idea that I'd be covering riots there as a *Times* reporter, or that the illustrious Scotty Reston would intervene to kill an interview with Nathan Marsh Pusey, the president of Harvard. All of that was impossible to envision, but what I did see—on every level, at every corner—was a world utterly different from Roxbury. It was the contrasts of those two worlds that came to shape me and my reporting. It gave me a sensitivity to authority and oppression, and to power and its abuse.

Back then I didn't know the power of the *Times* or its limitations. As Jimmy Stewart and Frank Capra demonstrated in *Mr. Smith Goes to Washington*, it turns out that naïveté can sometimes prove surprisingly helpful.

CHAPTER FOUR

Shotgun and Cookies; One-Arm Drivers

I always tell the truth. Even when I lie.

—AL PACINO

The worst part about being lied to is knowing you weren't worth the truth.

—JEAN-PAUL SARTRE

THE *BOSTON GLOBE*, 1961

When I was a teenager taking that quiet two-mile walk, I did dream about being a *Times* correspondent. But it was a *Wall Street Journal* scholarship that initially put me on the road I eventually took. In 1959, I saw that the *Journal* had a posting at Harvard's Student Employment Office offering $500 if you could get a job, even at no salary, as a reporter somewhere, anywhere. But you had to be a *reporter*. So I opened the Yellow Pages and called every paper, big and small, and explained that I needed no salary at all. No one would take me, even though I was free. Finally, the *Boston Globe* offered me a job for the summer of 1961. It would call me a *reporter*. It even insisted on paying me the bottom of the Guild scale, in addition to the $500 I was getting from the *Journal*.

A shotgun. A spit of land jutting into the Atlantic. A lighthouse. A struggle with the Feds. A nice cuppa. A pretty young woman. And the *front page!*

In telegraph-ese, I have just summarized the experience of the first story I ever wrote as an eighteen-year-old working for the *Globe*. The federal government claimed it owned part of a spit of land that led to a federal lighthouse. A white shingle house sat on that part, and the Feds had said to the owner, "Get out." But the owner refused to go.

When I showed up near the lighthouse with a photographer to do a piece about the recalcitrant owner, I was greeted by a man on the porch. I thought he had a shotgun. With desperate speed, I followed the photographer's lead, opened my car door, ducked, and began to scream, plaintively, "Press!"

After just a few minutes, the man invited us inside. He offered us a cup of tea and some cookies. He also introduced us to an attractive, shy young woman—a Vassar student. Since I had just finished my first year at Harvard, my objectivity was immediately challenged. Had her father really had a shotgun?

After a half-hour or so, the photographer and I hastened back to the paper, where I sat down to write the story. I quickly learned that writing a story in the middle of the din of fifty rattling typewriters was a challenge. I repaired to the cafeteria and wrote the story in longhand. Then I carried the draft back down to the newsroom and copy-typed it. Two hours later a copy boy dropped the latest issue of the paper, ink still wet, onto my metal desk, and to my surprise, there was the story about the misplaced house, *on page one.* I had learned my first lesson: No one can resist the lure of a story that includes danger, conflict, a rebel, and a lighthouse.

One cheerless summer afternoon, I was in the *Globe* newsroom, and nothing was happening. Phones were silent. Typewriters idle. There were only three reporters in the room. So why was a woman reporter putting on her cloth coat and leaving the building with a photographer? It was past lunchtime, not yet cocktail hour. And why did she return five minutes later and sit down nonchalantly at her desk? And why had the reporter in the row in front of me—the only other person in the room—begun batting away on his typewriter?

When the copy boy dropped the ink-wet next edition on my desk, the headline proclaimed knowingly in eight full columns across the paper: Registrar Declares War on One-Arm Drivers. Under the headline a photo, taken through the rear window of a car, showed the reporter who had left the building earlier. She was sitting in the front passenger seat with someone's hand draped over her shoulder.

I was stupefied. No one had called, no one had entered the room, no news releases had been dropped off. Where had this story come from, and who had interviewed the registrar of motor vehicles? All I could think was that I didn't understand this journalism business at all.

I leaned toward the reporter in the front row who had written the story with amazing speed and said, "Lenny, I didn't hear you interviewing the registrar."

Lenny Lerner, with an attitude that would have made Chicago's late front-page journalist Ben Hecht proud, said dully and without turning around, "I didn't."

"You didn't?" I repeated.

Then he did turn around. He rolled his eyes. "Look, do you think the registrar minds the publicity—or has a thing for one-arm drivers?"

The scales fell from my innocent eyes, and I understood Lenny had created the harmless banner story to give panache to a news-less day. All we needed in the Athens of America was a roll-top desk, Chicago, and Ben Hecht.

What we had was a news culture that was three decades behind Hecht's Chicago. Much earlier, Ben Hecht had persuaded the *Journal* in Chicago to print a report that there had been an earthquake in Chicago. The evidence consisted of a trench Hecht and his photographer had dug in a park. He also offered the *Journal* a photo of his landlady surrounded by broken dishes.

Hecht, meet Lenny. Lenny, meet Ben. Bob, meet Innocence Lost. I had just started Harvard the fall before. Almost all of what I remember about the summers I worked at the *Globe* was Lenny's prank and dinners at Howard Johnson's with Bruce McCabe, a reporter who later would become the paper's film critic.

Bruce was on the evening shift with me. We went out to dinner almost every night at a nearby HoJo's. There we regaled each other with stories, real and fantastical, about the *Globe*—its newsroom and its personnel, especially the editors. I remember red plastic booths and dinners that left us both, literally, weeping with laughter. We seemed to have misread Ecclesiastes, since our dinners were both a time to weep *and* a time to laugh. The waitresses without doubt thought we were mad, and maybe we were. All these years later, Bruce remembers our near-insane laughter at HoJo's but, like me, he recalls nothing of what we were laughing about. I can only chalk one up for the laughing gas of journalism—the kind I could have used at the dentist in Dorchester many years earlier.

CHAPTER FIVE

Does the Trenchcoat Fit?

Feather-footed through the plashy fen passes the questing vole.
—WILLIAM BOOT [THE FOREIGN-CORRESPONDENT
HERO OF *SCOOP* BY EVELYN WAUGH]

UNIVERSITY OF TÜBINGEN, 1963

It is not often that Howard Johnson's provides an appetite for Europe. But with my goal of entering the exciting precincts of foreign correspondence, I began to read books like *Deadline Every Minute: The Story of the United Press.* Another was *The Man Who Could Grow Hair, or Inside Andorra* by William Attwood, who wrote for the *Paris Trib. Inside Andorra* gave me an alluring, hilarious, but—of course—wrong, view of foreign correspondence.[3]

Remarkably, Attwood later became an ambassador—but not to Andorra (to Guinea). I continued on as an autodidact in the trenchcoated academy of foreign correspondence. In 1963 I became a Fulbright Scholar at the University of Tübingen in southern Germany when I was twenty-two. I had a two-month vacation from Tübingen and decided to spend the holiday in Barcelona. There, I tried to soak up Spanish and the city's culture. This involved developing an intimate acquaintance with tapas, rough red wine, La Rambla, and Gaudi's perpetually unfinished Templo Expiatorio de La Sagrada Familia—and a young British woman, who was a fellow student.

In Barcelona, I stayed with a family. At the dinner table were—in addition to the British woman—two Germans who wanted to be journalists, a French woman, and a Spanish accountant. The Germans, apparently required to learn a foreign language, had chosen Spanish. The setting meant that my dinners were spent interpreting from French to German, German to English, and—as best I could—English to Spanish.

I was on my way back home from the German university and had five weeks in which to write up notes for a United Nations conference on economic development that the UN had me attend as a *rapporteur* in Geneva. My next stop was graduate school in foreign affairs. Those evenings in Barcelona also brought to my almost comedic Jamesian innocence an exposure to foreign ways. One night after dinner, still at table, the Germans began sharply criticizing America (and—I felt—by implication, me) in German. For what? For the fire-bombing of Dresden.

I was astonished but managed, unproductively, to ask: "Who began that war?" and "What about London, Coventry, and Manchester?"

It seemed hopeless—and, worse, unworthy of the victims—to try to mention to these purblind young men the inexpressibly obvious: the murder of six million blameless people by a horrific blaze so wickedly set, and so mercilessly stoked and tended by the German state—the Holocaust.[4]

The German youngsters said nothing.

CHAPTER SIX

Investigative Reporting at the Automat. Excuse Me, They Do Explode

To explode or to implode—said Qwfwq—that is the question: whether 'tis nobler in the mind to expand one's energies in space without restraint, or to crush them into a dense inner concentration. . . .

—ITALO CALVINO

There are three sides to every story: your side, my side, and the truth. And no one is lying. . . .

—ROBERT EVANS, FILM PRODUCER

COLUMBIA GRADUATE SCHOOL OF JOURNALISM, 1964–1965

The training of the Journalism School took. It changed my perspective. I was hooked. Investigative journalism plopped itself, with a loud thud, on my desk.

I decided to go to journalism school because the best way to be trained as a reporter is to get a first-rate editor. And not just an editor, but someone who, in a crowded newsroom, is willing to take the time to teach you to become a good reporter. At Columbia, the professors and instructors are paid to do that. Also, the school only took nine months—and I got a scholarship.

The 1962 romantic comedy *That Touch of Mink* featured the Horn & Hardart Automats. These were eateries in Manhattan where machines with slots for coins took the place of waitresses, and pies beckoned fetchingly through plate glass. When I was a graduate student at Columbia in the School of Journalism in 1964, I went into an Automat near Times Square. I happened to look at the bottom of a water glass there and read, "Duralex, Made in France." Why, you might ask, is a two-bit—sorry, four-bit—place like the Automat serving drinks out of French glassware? And who the devil is Duralex? That's what I asked myself. In those days, there was no internet. Here's what the internet now tells you:

> Duralex was founded in 1939 and has been manufacturing tempered glassware for over 80 years in La Chapelle-Saint-Mesmin in the heart of France. The original tempered (or toughened) Picardie glasses are still produced in France and . . . feel extremely comfortable in the hand. They're also suitable for hot or cold drinks . . . microwavable, freezer- and dishwasher-safe, impact and chip resistant and the perfect weight.[5]

It continues:

> . . . In 1945, the Duralex brand was registered, and the Gigogne model of the Duralex line is apparently in the collection of the Paris Musée des Arts Décoratifs.

My adventure with Duralex began in the Automat when I sneaked into the kitchen—where I had no right to be—and asked a dishwasher why they were using French glasses. He told me he didn't know, but he assured me the glasses were good—until they exploded.

"Sometimes they just explode after the dishwasher," he said, pointing to the large metal machine. "What do you mean explode?" I pressed him, and he told me that on occasion when they were sitting on a shelf, they would just break into pieces and fly all over the place.

"They break into pieces and fly all over the place when they're sitting on a shelf. Just sitting on a shelf?"

"Yep."

"No one touching them?"

"Nope."

"You been hurt?" I asked.

"Not yet."

That afternoon I called the Manhattan office of Saint-Gobain, the owner of Duralex at the time, and asked them about this phenomenon.

"They don't explode," I was told.

"I have a dishwasher telling me they do," I said.

"They *implode*," the speaker told me.

"Oh . . ."

Implode, I was told, means: "To collapse violently inward."

Oh. . . .

I shouldn't have been in the kitchen. A similar lurch into the impermissible nearly got me kicked out of journalism school, but that day in the kitchen and my phone call—well, they help to explain the kind of journalist I was hoping to be.

Lenny Lerner and the others had not prepared me for the solemn Columbia Graduate School of Journalism. It was the spring of 1965, hay fever was in the Upper West Side air, and graduation from the one-year program near. At an Upper West Side tavern, Jimmy Breslin—hallowed be his name—had already given me the key to success in journalism: "Kid," he said, leaning on the bar, "Don't write anything, not even a postcard, without getting paid."

I am tempted to say, like Jess in *When Harry Met Sally*, that Breslin is the reason I became a writer. That wouldn't be true. As I mentioned, I became a reporter because of the escapades recounted by Attwood in *Inside Andorra*.

At Columbia, we had a course in Metropolitan Reporting taught by George W. Barrett, an assistant editor on the Metropolitan Desk of the *Times*. We thought George was a man of exquisitely, painfully formal style to the point of stuffiness. He always seemed in a parade-ground posture, even down to the trim mustache.

He drove a 1929 Rolls-Royce roadster and was said to bring a tranquil panache to the *Times* as both an imperturbable rewrite man and, later, as a gracious editor. We never could have guessed he had served as a seaman on tankers and covered the Korean War. George—Mr. Barrett to us—would send us journalism students all over New York City to various posts of interest like the UN, the Police Department, and City Hall.

I know the giddiness of spring is no defense, but that spring I decided we would shake the stolid Mr. Barrett up a bit, maybe get him to give the *Times* Metropolitan Desk a tip they wouldn't forget. I asked all my fellow students to phone from wherever they'd been sent by our student city desk at the Journalism School at noon and report: *A Red Chinese submarine has been sighted in the Hudson River.*

I chose the most unlikely, fantastical event I could think of, one that would invite journalistic frenzy. At noon sharp those calls began to pour in. The phones were all ringing with reports from the various beats about the Chinese sub.

What did George do?

He listened. And did not bat an eye.

Those of us at the campus newsroom watched carefully. George did not call the *Times,* and more importantly, the J-School did not expel me (although it was clear who the culprit was).

The Red Chinese sub had presented hazards—and not just to Manhattan. A more important hazard: The one thing you could be kicked out of the Journalism School for, even if you were, like me, near graduation was—a hoax. This was a hoax, if ever there was one. I must have been mad, and, worse, I had somehow persuaded many others to join in the madness—for example, the student-reporters covering City Hall, Police Department Headquarters, the United Nations, and so on. Maybe the school did not want to expel so many students. Maybe Maestro Barrett turned two blind eyes. After all, I did intervene just as he was about to call the Metropolitan Desk at the *Times.* To be honest, I thought that would have been something to see! Oh well, these serious students would go on to important jobs in journalism with at least one prank behind them.

Perhaps George didn't blow the whistle because he was of the old school of rewrite. Here is Gay Talese's description of the genre:

> *The very best late-breaking stories went to the man who sat in the first row on the aisle—he was known as the dean of rewrite, and he was unquestionably the most trustworthy and imperturbable under deadline pressure. . . .*

In an ironic turn, I later became a rewrite man at the *Times*. I learned that the other rewrite men used to get good stories, if they took place when Mr. Barrett was out to the dinner he often had, after two J&Bs-with-water, at Gough's Chop House. The desk could always reach George—still impeccable in his carefully pressed suit with dimpled pocket handkerchief—if something big occurred.

CHAPTER SEVEN

Candide Arrives at Rockefeller Plaza, But Only the Seven Sisters See It

Innocence is a kind of insanity.
          —GRAHAM GREENE, *THE QUIET AMERICAN*

I am slow to pick up on anything.
You know, that is one of your sweetest qualities,
you are very naïve.
Oh! Thank you.
          —WOODY ALLEN, *CAFÉ SOCIETY*

TIME MAGAZINE, 1965

My first full-time job was a fluke—the product of innocence. The editors should have been warned because when the job began, the innocence continued. When I was a student at Harvard, I needed money. I saw a sign in the Harvard student employment office that offered $500—$500!—from the *Wall Street Journal* for getting a job, any job in journalism. I had leapt at it.

Later, in the employment office of the Graduate School of Journalism at Columbia, *Time* magazine offered an even more splendid $1,000 for writing three essays—the first an "intellectual autobiography." I leapt again.

I didn't have much to say—and come to think of it, I still wouldn't. But it turned out that *Time* was fibbing. They didn't want essays from university students for research materials. It was a recruiting gimmick. That should have told me something. But, of course, it didn't.

Dick Clurman, *Time*'s chief of correspondents, summoned me. I rode up to some high floor in Rockefeller Center, clutching my essay and my heart. While I waited, I saw a photocopy of my essay on the receptionist's desk. It had "A+" in the top right corner of the first page.

Clurman was an impressive guy, lean and energetic, dressed in shirt-sleeves and wearing horn-rimmed glasses. The view from his office seemed to roll out to California, or at least Chicago. Later he would become administrator of Parks, Recreation and Cultural Affairs for Mayor John V. Lindsay, and later still chairman of the New York City Center. But back then he already lacked neither self-confidence nor boldness. He impressed, in a vaguely Kennedy-family way. He is said to have held dinner parties at which he would tap a spoon against a glass, and announce a topic he expected guests like William Buckley or Barbra Streisand to proceed to discuss.

Clurman wanted to hire me as a correspondent. I didn't want to work for a news magazine, and I certainly didn't want to work for a conservative one. That night, I asked my roommate, a student at Columbia Law, for his advice.

"Start at the top," he said. "If you don't like it, you can quit."

I started at a non-journalist's view of the top. And soon, I discovered the Seven Sisters. The Seven Sisters are, or were, prominent women's colleges in the Northeast. They were the schools from which *Time* hired its researchers. All were women. All were bright. All were pretty. When I finally worked up the courage, I asked them serially—yes, one after another—to go out. They *all* turned me down. And one told me why: I was two years younger—and far less experienced of the world than she. She had that right.

On Tuesday November 9, 1965 at 5:27 p.m., the Great White Way and just about all the rest of New York City went black. Totally black. I grabbed a notebook and flashlight and headed down thirty-five flights of Rockefeller Center stairs to see what was happening. After all, I was supposed to be a correspondent. But I was the *only* correspondent who left *Time* that evening.

Later, I found out that editors, correspondents, and researchers not only stayed behind. They opened the liquor cabinets. These were overflowing with alcohol to celebrate the weekly closing of the magazine. Then they made themselves at home on the couches. Meanwhile, I was calling back to the Bureau with my notebook lit by the rear taillights of new cars in a Manhattan auto dealership. I left the showroom to find food hoarders lining up in delis barely discernible against a black sky.

I thought Harvard had prepared me for a lot, but the Sherry Hour at Dunster House did not prepare me for the weekly Saturnalian, post-deadline throwing open of *Time* magazine's large wooden liquor cabinets and the boozy social interchange of reporters, researchers, writers, and editors. I wondered if I were working at a magazine or an advertising agency.

Thanks to a public relations man, I was assigned to do a *Time* human-interest piece about a multimillionaire inventor/businessman with a small castle in New Jersey. Out I went to the castle, and there was the business-man sitting at the head of an enormous wooden banquet table. There were also the PR guy and a buxom blonde thirty or forty years younger than the businessman. The PR man described her to me as the inventor's secretary.

After the interview, I went back to Rockefeller Center and wrote the story straight—that is, naïvely. For example, I mentioned his secretary. The editors thought the story was superbly satirical. At the time I couldn't fathom satire any more than I had understood who the secretary was. My file—as our reports at *Time* were called—was a smash hit, widely read, carried home to the New York and Connecticut suburbs to be the delight of the cocktail hour.

There was one rub. I persisted in trying to be an investigative reporter. I did careful research and found that the lord of the mini-castle was a convicted criminal. I don't remember whether he had a small cell in the fortress castle of some New York State prison. As I recall, he had been found guilty of patent fraud. I was writing about a millionaire who had been a felon.

I called the PR guy for comment, and he spent a lot of energy attempting to walk back his suggestion that we cover the story. He was successful. Baron and Blonde were spared the *Backward Reels the Mind* prose of *Time*speak—the effort by the magazine to animate its prose by inverting sentences.[6]

In 1966, there was a twelve-day transit strike in New York. I lived in Washington Heights—about seven miles from *Time*'s Rockefeller Center headquarters. Taxis were impossible. For those employees deemed "essential," *Time* had an arrangement with a limousine company. So a long black limo showed up in front of my middle-class building. I slinked furtively and sheepishly from the front door to the limo door, under the unbelieving eyes of my neighbors assembled outside the front door, trying collectively to puzzle out how to get wherever they needed to go for work.

"Look at him," one of them said, pointing with an incriminating finger, "A kid."

Right, and still wearing my (only) worn red-striped, brown Harris Tweed jacket left over from college. My reporter's notebook stuck untidily out of one of my pockets. I had unfashionable horn-rimmed glasses, badly cut hair, and looked as if I might use a good meal. I refrained from ducking down. Reporters—even editors—should not ride in limos, I thought. Not even *Time*'s cadre of Westchester Republican writers and editors. They should use their New York, New Haven and Hartford commuter tickets from Westchester County to Manhattan and then walk the fourteen minutes from Grand Central Terminal to Rockefeller Center!

I didn't enjoy the ride, watching through tinted glass a parade of envious walkers heading south with briefcases, lunch bags, and, probably, bunions, corns, and calluses. I should have gotten out and interviewed them. I didn't. For a year I benefited from Henry Luce's corporate largesse. Later, I also had a virtually unlimited expense account at the *Times*. I did not use it to rent a limo. I did use it to pay a $1 parking fine in a North Carolina town (incurred—I am compelled to add—by the photographer on the assignment).

CHAPTER EIGHT

Adam Clayton Powell, Miss Ohio, and the Bali Hai Effect

Sometimes New York would send me a rocket [a cabled request for more information]. Once, I had just landed at Fiumicino [Rome's airport], and got a rocket. I needed to use the men's room. The rocket was put to good use [for hygienic purposes].

—JAMES BELL, LONGTIME BUREAU CHIEF FOR *TIME*

And chase hard and good and with no mistakes and do not overrun them.

—ERNEST HEMINGWAY, *ISLANDS IN THE STREAM*
(A "SEA TRILOGY," THE FIRST SECTION OF
WHICH TAKES PLACE IN BIMINI)

TIME MAGAZINE, BIMINI, 1966

I have confessed my heart's desire. From the start it had been to become a foreign correspondent. However unlikely the fulfillment of that dream seemed, it came true. The path began in the Caribbean when I had my first full-time job as a reporter for *Time* magazine. (*Time* even called me a *correspondent*—shades of those dream-filled evenings when I was walking home from Mattapan Square!)

This was in 1965. *Time* sent me to the Caribbean Bureau in Miami, and from there to the island of Bimini. The trip to Bimini was not hard. It is just fifty miles from Florida, the most western of the Bahamian islands. North Bimini is about seven miles long and seven hundred feet wide. Yes, seven hundred feet. Its main settlement is Alice Town, a collection of shops, restaurants, and bars on a road known as The King's Highway.

My assignment was to find Congressman Adam Clayton Powell, chairman of the House Committee on Education and Labor. Powell was reported to be on Bimini with his mistress (a former Miss Ohio). Finding him seemed possible, given the geography.

Despite a high absentee record in the House, Powell's accomplishments were many. According to Thomas A. Johnson's article that appeared in the *Times* in 1972, the congressman once said: "You don't have to be there if you know which calls to make, which buttons to push, which favors to call in." The committee authorized more important legislation than any other: nearly fifty major pieces of social legislation, accounting for more than $14 billion.

I guess Bimini had telecommunications in 1966. I don't remember. What it was said to have, though, was Powell's congressional receptionist, Corinne Huff, who had hopped down there with the sassy, effective, devil-may-care legislator from Harlem. When the congressman was criticized for having taken a trip with two women at government expense, he said, "I wish to state very emphatically . . . that I will always do just what every other Congressman and committee chairman has done and is doing and will do."[7]

My assignment was to find Corinne and Adam and—I suppose— interview them. About what, I wasn't sure. Bimini was supposed to have been the site of the original Fountain of Youth, but that didn't seem germane. Maybe it was. But first things first: I had no notion how to catch up with them even though I, repository of so many dreams about great foreign correspondents covering great continents, was on a *tiny* spit of land for two or three days.

The results of this island assignment were:

1. Incredibly—*shamefully*—no trace of the couple;
2. A hotelier who assured me my appearance since arrival had gone from "near death" to "healthy color." That was apparently what Biminites called sunburn;

3. A lasting love of the Caribbean and its soft sand;
4. Discovery of Rum Punch.

Thank you, Corinne and Adam. And, thank you, *Time* for not firing the kid who couldn't find a celebrity on a small, sparsely populated spit of land. At the time I was not yet a war correspondent, but, as my (literary) pal Joe Liebling once observed, "There is an old proverb that a girl may sleep with one man without being a trollop, but let a man cover one little war and he is a war correspondent." I would come to learn that the foreign correspondent does not always end up on sandy beaches.

My mentor was Evelyn Waugh. In his novel, *Scoop*, Waugh wrote:

> "But it's going to be a tough assignment from all I hear. Cutthroat competition. That's where I envy you—working for a paper. You only have to worry about getting your story in time for the first edition. We have to race each other all day."
>
> "But the papers can't use your reports any earlier than ours."
>
> "No, but they use the one that comes in first."
>
> "But if it's exactly the same as the one that came in second and third and fourth and they are all in time for the same edition . . . ?"
>
> Corker looked at him sadly. "You know, you've got a lot to learn about journalism. Look at it this way. News is what a chap who doesn't care much about anything wants to read.
>
> "And it's only news until he's read it. After that it's dead. We're paid to supply news. If someone else has sent a story before us, our story isn't news. Of course, there's colour.
>
> "Colour is just a lot of bulls'-eyes about nothing. It's easy to write and easy to read but it costs too much in cabling so we have to go slow on that.
>
> "See?"
>
> "I think so."[8]

Later, the *Times* decided to send me to Biafra to cover the civil war. There were reports of rabid dogs on the prowl. I checked: Waugh did not offer advice about how to deal with rabid dogs. I asked the *Times* doctor for rabies shots. No, he said, they would take too long and be too painful. He advised me to carry a pistol.[9]

I hadn't needed a pistol on Bimini. It was there that I discovered the Bali Hai effect. This occurs when you are standing on a glorious tropical shore, having a high old sun-comforted time, and suddenly you see through the shimmering tropical air the next island. Without pause, you say, "This island's great but that one might be even better." You buy a boat ticket, more sunscreen, and more sunburn ointment, and toss a few more tropical shirts into your bleached traveling bag.

CHAPTER NINE

A Woman Deposits Herself in a Bank; Depression Is Its Own Reward

There was no pretense to objectivity; 'Time' had a partisan Republican point of view, and if it was one not shared by many of its gentrified Ivy Leaguers, few felt the compulsion to quit.
                    —JOHN GREGORY DUNNE, LITERARY CRITIC

I guess no true Bostonian would trust a place that was sunny and pleasant all the time. But a gritty, perpetually cold and gloomy neighborhood? Throw in a couple of Dunkin' Donuts locations, and I'm right at home.
                    —RICK RIORDAN, THE SWORD OF SUMMER

THE *BOSTON HERALD*, 1966

During my year-long stint at *Time*, I met a lot of bright, well-paid, well-educated folks. But—whatever else they were doing—they were not practicing journalism. The reporters were turning in stories (called "files") that never saw the light of day. They were all rewritten, with or without attention to the correspondents' message.

The writers were rewrite men (yes, men) expected to toe a line when it mattered. And the researchers were expected to make sure the copy was right regarding unimportant facts. The items that mattered included Vietnam.

In 1965, *Time* published an editorial supporting President Johnson's decision to step up the ground campaign: The Right War at the Right Time ran the heading:

Obviously, after overcoming his early hesitation, Lyndon Johnson will not allow the U.S. to be pushed out of Viet Nam. For if that were to happen, Americans would only have to make another stand against Asian Communism later, under worse conditions and in less tenable locations.

Despite all its excruciating difficulties, the Vietnamese struggle is absolutely inescapable for the U.S. in the mid-60s—and in that sense, it is the right war in the right place at the right time.[10]

The "news" articles in the magazine agreed. Twenty years later, in March 1985, David Halberstam sent a letter to *New York* magazine titled "Foreign Correspondents." Halberstam had won a Pulitzer Prize in 1964 for his coverage of the Vietnam War for the *New York Times*. He wrote:

By no means . . . was the problem that the editors of Time *and* Newsweek *faced in their Vietnam reporting during the mid-sixties that of indigenous personnel, i.e., French nationals who, in return for the excellence of their sources, planted pro-French stories . . .*

Rather, it was that of dealing with files that were systematically more pessimistic than was the official version of the war, that went against the assumptions of many of the New York editors themselves, and that made the Johnson administration extremely unhappy. . . .

Newsweek, *to its credit, performed better than* Time, *where the final product was well known as a professional scandal, a product designed to fit the bias of the editors rather than the realities of the story. At* Time, *they not only undercut pessimistic stories on the progress of the war, but also killed vital factual stories that showed the president to be a liar.*[11]

In 1966, I decided to leave *Time*. I couldn't stand it. I was writing stories, all of which were then rewritten, and there was a conservative bias that infected the stories. I rode the elevator down to the lobby of the posh Rockefeller Center building and phoned the *Boston Herald*, where I knew no one. I'd decided it was time to go home. They said come on down. I went.

What I found at the *Herald* did not resemble anything I had been taught in journalism school, but the job was a powerful substitute for a course in journalism history. It was historical journalism, of the 1920s. I even got management experience of a sort.

Fundamental to the job at the *Herald* was training myself to keep my hands in my pockets when visiting the composing room and looking at lead type in cast-iron chases. From 10:00 p.m. to 2:00 a.m., I would go to the composing room—charily—when I had to. I would stuff both hands deep in my pockets, since I'd been warned to touch no type or anything having to do with type. If I did, my bosses warned, the compositors would walk out because of their union rules. I was a scared kid, imagining all those guys in green eyeshades or hats made of folded newspapers abandoning their linotype machines, putting down the heavy steel chases that held the type, and heading for the exits in a ragged, inky platoon. All because a green—no, make that chartreuse—kid with innocently wandering hands had touched their type.

One night a call came in to the City Desk from the switchboard operator who told me, "It's a woman in a bank."

"At this hour?" I asked, confused.

"That's what the woman says."

I picked up the phone at the City Desk and heard a woman on the line telling me she was in the main office of a prominent Boston bank. She had locked herself and her child inside.

"I stayed after they closed," she explained. Later she crawled out from wherever she had hidden. Now she was attempting to communicate with the outside world by phone and by holding notes against the bank window.

She'd done this, she told me, because the bank was foreclosing on her home, and she had nowhere to go. The bank wouldn't talk with her, I guessed, or at least not bend on the foreclosure. I listened, asked her questions, and sent a photographer out to take a photo through the window. The photo showed her thin, petite, and miserable.

I wrote the story and carried the copy to the composing room, and the paper emerged. There it was on page one. Surprise to the editors. Surprise to the publisher. Surprise to the advertising department. Surprise to the bank. I got no reaction from any of them.

After all, they had left me in charge.

Once the story and photo ran, the bank showed the woman some leniency, but no one told me to follow up the next day. It's a story I'll never forget, because for one night at least, I had my own metropolitan newspaper. And for one night, it was a solitary, dispossessed woman who was on the front page of the paper—not the bank.

It speaks to the confusion of my psyche, all these years later, that I also remember that, when I had my own law firm, I represented on the order of three dozen banks and other financial institutions. (But my firm was not in the business of throwing widows and their kids onto the cobblestones.)

But it was more than having every word in my reports rewritten at *Time* and its support for the Vietnam War that led me back to Boston. It was also Judy.

And it was Judy who led me to an institution for the criminally insane.

When I arrived back in Boston, I was twenty-seven and massively depressed. In New York, I had been dating a doctor named Judy. She came from Brooklyn, and was interning at Mount Sinai in Manhattan. There was a marriage proposal on the table. She hadn't accepted by the time I left, although she had applied for a residency in Boston.

Doctors are supposed to mend hearts, not break them. But . . .

I had met Judy while reporting for a *Time* cover story on the "State of American Medicine." I interviewed students from three different medical schools in New York to try to get an idea of why they wanted to become doctors. Columbia sent me an oh-so-black-haired woman of intelligence so apparent that a short, white skirt starched to rigidity couldn't distract from the allure of understanding eyes that jumped from closely observant rest to giggling twinkle.

Judy had arrived.

But what to do? I was, after all, a reporter doing a story. I couldn't date her.

But I wanted to. . . . Did I ever.

Judy was so bright that, when she decided—late—to go to med school, she had studied neither organic nor inorganic chemistry. Med schools required both . . . but you can't take both at the same time. So she enrolled in two different colleges for simultaneous summer courses in . . .

well, you know what. Columbia P&S (Physicians and Surgeons) took her. How could any interviewer not be beguiled?

Judy, I asked, may I do this: I can't ask you out now. But I'd sure like to. Would it be OK for me to call when this story has been written and printed and the magazine is on the newsstands? She said yes.

Story appeared on *Time* cover. Date was made. She said to meet her at her med school dorm room. I did. She said she needed to change out of her white work clothes. I said fine. She began undressing. It was the 1960s, but this was the first moment of the first date. I shyly reminded her—not yet purple as a rutabaga—that I was there and she was undressing. She paused, covered herself, and explained that this is what med students did all the time—repetitively changed clothes, I thought she meant.

The next thing you know, we were sitting in adjacent garden chairs in her parents' backyard in the Flatbush section of Brooklyn (which, for me, might just as well have been the sands of Kalahari, I knew so little of New York outside of Manhattan). And we were laughing, and laughing, and laughing . . .

Is it possible to laugh without pause for an eternity without being in love? Not in my young—or, for that matter, old—life.

Proof of my affection: We once took a holiday to Cape Cod where she decided she wanted to go horseback riding. She had been riding since childhood and had the closest of relationships with a pampered horse in a Brooklyn stable. I came to envy sugar cubes and carrots. (The only horse I vaguely knew had pulled the cart of the iceman in Roxbury.)

So ride we did. I told the stable owner that I had never ridden a horse, but—without telling me—she gave me a horse trained to mimic everything that the horse she gave Judy did: walk, trot, canter, gallop. By the time I climbed off the beast, I was white with exhaustion and fear. I had barely managed to restrain my horse outside the stable when Judy galloped across the bogs. I confess to feeling unkind pleasure when the horse kicked the stable owner as I dismounted.

"Wasn't that great?" Judy asked. "Should we do it again soon?"

For a doctor, she sure didn't notice symptoms of terror, perhaps hysteria.

The inevitable happened. We fell in love.

Judy would roll into my Riverside Drive apartment from her internship at Mt. Sinai at 2:00 a.m., and I would somehow wobble out in time to reach Rockefeller Center by 10 to see what my editors at *Time* had dreamed up for me.

Sometimes Judy and I managed to take a taxi together. I would drop her off at Mt. Sinai, saying things—with unsurpassed stupidity—like "Try not to kill too many today, dear!" as I kissed her when she got out of the cab. Occasionally, I would buy a bouquet at the hospital and stand in the lobby, waiting for my raven Nightingale to come through the locked physician-and-nurses portal so I could hand them to her and watch hospital staff, who were foolish enough to think I had bought them for a patient, wink knowingly to one another and make no effort at all to conceal their chuckles.

I even got to practice medicine once. We went on a hike at Bear Mountain, north of New York City. As we climbed up the path, I noticed Judy's breathing was labored. I felt her forehead—it was hot. "You're sick," I diagnosed. We drove back to the city. She had a high temperature and was coughing.

"Get in the shower!" I commanded. "Stay away from the water, just inhale the steam."

She didn't want to go to Mt. Sinai. The interns worked such long hours, she explained, that if one of them got sick, the others might as well give up the leases to their apartments. And she didn't want her colleagues to see the X-rays of her breasts. I hadn't realized X-rays were salacious.

"You're going," I said.

I got to meet her colleagues, as they trooped through her hospital room. And I showed off my amorously acquired medical knowledge: "No rales." (No clicking or rattling in my sweetie's lungs.)

But then I wanted to leave *Time* and take a job at a paper in Boston. Judy agreed to look for residencies in Boston.

I asked her to marry me. She paused to reflect . . . and reflect. You know the ultimate answer. (Actually, there never was one.)

The doctor had broken my heart.

Now I had moved to Boston where newspapers had been bad for decades, and where reporting was bad. Boston journalism, like San Francisco journalism of the time, had given rise to incredulity and disdain from reporters and editors everywhere. At the *Boston Herald*, poor quality was a constant, with dishonesty making occasional but bold appearances. But bad papers were lax papers, and the upside was that lax papers sometimes gave reporters remarkable freedom. I used that freedom.

This was the opposite of my experience in having every word in my reports rewritten at *Time*. My newfound freedom, coupled with my burdened heart, led me, more or less directly, to an institution for the criminally insane.

As with everyone else, events in their personal lives affect reporters. And what they sometimes choose to write can be a balm—for the reporter, if not for the readers. So I began with a series. I visited Bridgewater State Hospital for the Criminally Insane, where I met a psychiatrist who was remarkably frank and accommodating. I filled a reporter's wide-lined spiral notebook and returned to my little apartment on Beacon Hill, where I sat, frantically typing.

I began writing, and kept writing and writing. By the time I was finished, I had knocked out a three-part series in one long sitting.

The piece began:

The chunky prisoner sat on one of the wooden benches painted a brown as dull as the green of the walls was flat. One pudgy hand lay across the uncomfortable wooden slats that are the cheapest thing devised to let people that nobody cares about set their carcasses on. A shock of unruly black hair was the only thing that gave interest to a puffy face. If the dark eyes spoke anything, they spoke despair.

"All I want is that chain and the handcuffs so that I can go back to Walpole [prison]. I'll make it this time. I can make it this time."

Dr. Lawrence Barrows, one of four psychiatrists at Bridgewater Hospital for the Criminally Insane, listened and moved on.

"He's way off," he told a visitor. "He is in no condition to go back to the prison. He'd never make it there."

The vacant face sank back against the dull green wall. The thick legs in the gray denim uniform sprawled across the swabbed, speckled terrazzo floor. The fluorescent lights, deflected here and there by exposed heating pipes, played across the puffy mask of despair.

> *On benches all around the hall, called a Smoking Room, figures in gray denim lounged. No one spoke. Some looked vacantly at a television set that was the sole ornament of the dull green wall.*
>
> *About 120 men, separate souls, sharing only gray denim cloth, sat from 9 o'clock to 6 o'clock in a world as devoid of meaning as a porcelain basin drained of everything except fly specks.*

When I had finished the piece, my own depression began to lift. The series ran on the front page of the *Herald* and won an award from United Press International. Great sadness had turned into creative triumph. The series led to my becoming an assistant city editor, doling out assignments and phone calls to appropriately bitter reporters with vastly more experience than I had.

The *Herald* proved a way station to the *Times*. I wouldn't have guessed that would happen—mostly because for a long, long time, no one had come out of Boston journalism to go to New York. I had met Judy through journalism, and I healed my unhappiness in parting from her with journalism.

CHAPTER TEN

A Shoebox Leads to Sweaty Palms; Harrison Frowns

His palms are sweaty, knees weak, arms are heavy.
—"Lose Yourself," Eminem
(Marshall Bruce Mathers III)

THE *NEW YORK TIMES* NEWSROOM, 1968

The *Herald* building had an office for the *New York Times* Boston correspondent. He was a short, wiry, brisk, shirt-sleeved fellow with close-cropped hair, and I envied him. I probably got the idea of applying to the *Times* by seeing him. I didn't ask him about it. I just found a shoebox—literally—and filled it with clippings of stories I had done for the *Herald* and probably some reporting I had done for *Time.* I wrote a short, breezy cover letter and sent it to someone at the *Times,* which even I knew as the Gray Lady. I don't remember to whom I sent the box. I sent it after I had done the pieces about the hospital for the mentally ill, but before I had won an award for writing them. It was a longtime fantasy to work for the *Times,* and I was just wishing on an exceedingly faraway star.

I got a call from one of the several assistant metropolitan editors. He asked me down. (A long time later I found out they had made the poor guy read the shoebox.) I was flabbergasted. The *Times* never took anyone from Boston; it was seen as a journalistic sinkhole. I put on my favorite—no, my only—sports jacket and took a bus. A taxi driver made a five-minute trip from the bus station into a half-hour journey, finally depositing me at the *Times* building on West 43rd Street. I somehow got to the elevator, and the enormous City Room. I can't tell you how. My tweed jacket was soaked with sweat. I was breathing, but shallowly. It turned out I was to go—then and there—through a series of interviews with all the principal editors, ten or fifteen minutes at a time. It was a dizzying transit from editor to editor.

I don't know if I met a dozen editors that day. It felt like fifty. The ambulatory ordeal began with Turner Catledge, the executive editor. It went on to Claude Sitton, the national editor. Then it proceeded through the rest of the figures on the *Times* frieze. It ended with Arthur Gelb, the metro editor.

Catledge was tall and stout with slicked-back hair, and he'd tried to relax me by saying he just wanted to get "the cut of my jib." Sitton was a southern gentleman. Harrison Salisbury, the assistant managing editor, was my hero . . . because of garbage.

In 1954, when Harrison came back from Moscow with a Pulitzer in his tweed coat pocket, the *Times*, or some editor, wanted to take him down a peg or two—or three, and assigned him to do a piece about garbage in New York. Harrison pulled out all the stops, or lids, and spent weeks digging up information about New York City's handling of trash. He turned in a three-part series that began:

No city in the world comes within ten million dollars of spending what it costs New York each year to keep clean. And no great city of the world, with the possible exception of a few in Asia, has a greater reputation for dirt, disorder, filth and litter. Why?[12]

As the *Times* wrote in Salisbury's obituary on July 11, 1993:

He braved police threats and a landmark libel suit in exposing racism in Birmingham, Ala., "enforced by the whip, the razor, the gun, the bomb, the torch, the knife, the mob." Six years later, in 1966, Mr. Salisbury courted the wrath of Lyndon Johnson by reporting accurately from Hanoi that Vietnamese civilians were killed by "surgical" American raids.[13]

When it was time to talk to Harrison, I approached him as a teenage girl might approach Justin Bieber. He offered his hand. I shook it.

He frowned. I realized my palm was sweaty. The interview was brief. I was thinking of Mao Tse-tung, Moscow spires, New York garbage. When Harrison gave me the green light, I realized, with astonishment, that I might just become . . . *his colleague.*

It was an antsy Arthur Gelb, the metropolitan editor, who saw me last. Arthur was all business, radiating nervous energy, folding his gangly frame as he mentally moved on to the next half-dozen tasks before we had finished talking. I was to learn Arthur always seemed to be in urgent need of a tranquilizer.

He did make me an offer. But not as a reporter—which is all I was and wanted to be. At better (but not a lot better) than Boston wages—they got me cheap—Arthur wanted me to be a rewrite man. A journalist who never saw the sun or flashed a press pass but rewrote the work of others, or crafted stories from hurried phone reports from real reporters, sometimes interspersed with morgue (library) material.

"Arthur," I said with innocent honesty, "That's not what I want to do."

"Just for a year," he said, "then you can be a reporter. Think about it."

Back I went by bus to Boston, not happy. I approached the *Times* Boston guy.

"What should I do?"

"Take it," he said without pause.

"Maybe I can bargain to get some time to do reporting."

"No," he said, "they'll see that [negotiating] as Chinese water torture. Just take it."

He was kind enough not to say: *you idiot.* I took it.

I packed my few clothes and very few belongings (all portable—including my Royal typewriter), and got back on the bus. With the help of the *Times* real estate ads (ripped off the printing presses before they hit the streets) and a $20 bribe (I mean facilitating payment) to a doorman, I landed an apartment on West End Avenue in the Sixties. I could walk to the paper if I felt like it, have *hamish* meals at Jewish delis, and quickly begin recasting the work of my betters.

Me, a kid from Roxbury.

CHAPTER ELEVEN

The Pied Piper of Queens, and the Man Who Dug President Kennedy's Grave

The greatness of a man is measured by the way he treats the little man.
—MYLES MUNROE

THE *NEW YORK TIMES* NEWSROOM, 1968

My rewrite salary was based on the Boston baked-bean scale (not the Boston Locke-Ober's Lobster Savannah scale). This affected only a little my rewrite dinners. After all, I was young, single, and didn't eat much.

There were two speeds on rewrite—pre-deadline and post-deadline. Pre-deadline was sometimes like the crash car going down the hospital emergency corridor. Post-deadline was dinner at a Brazilian restaurant a few blocks away with another rewrite man (we were all men) or peacefully relishing (as we would have said at *Time*) a hot dog at the huge Nathan's Famous in Times Square.

Not that there weren't emergencies after the first deadline. Like the Russians invading Czechoslovakia in the summer of 1968 to crush the Prague Spring, when there were crash carts banging into one another as soon as they could be rushed to the newsroom. That night Rewrite went into urgent action. I wrote an interpretive piece about the Soviet move that landed on page one. No one at the paper that night knew that, in 1964, I'd earned a master's degree from Columbia's School of International and Public Affairs and had written a thesis on what was then Yugoslavia. My piece survived until James Barrett Reston rushed in to do an interpretive piece for the next edition that displaced it. Even today I prefer mine. That night, Rewrite was not a madhouse, but on most nights, it was.

The rewrite bank lived in a world of gossip, cynicism, sarcasm, and occasional wit—and some combination of all of them. It was a bit like combat, but generally not mortal. A veteran New York newsman and star, Sylvan Fox, suffered a heart attack—not in the newsroom—but clearly, in my mind, because of it. And Shelly Binn's constant crumpling of paper and throwing it toward the ceiling was nothing if not an ongoing release from the torture of several hours of consuming tension.

There were two paladins of reporting at the *Times*—Homer Bigart and Peter Kihss. They occupied the front row of the rewrite bank. They were not part of the bank; it was just a place of honor. Physically, Peter was like a string bean that could twist into almost any shape but preferred to hunch painfully over a manual typewriter. In his obituary in the *Times* in 1984, Bob McFadden, himself a top-drawer rewrite man, described Peter: "[A] tall, stoop-shouldered, baldish man with a nimbus of gray hair, he looked more like an Old-World clockmaker than one of the nation's most distinguished reporters."

With his gangly frame wrapped in a rumpled brown overcoat and a hat straight out of the tumble cycle of a dryer, with a frayed collar and thick glasses that seemed below where they ought to have been, Peter didn't have the scent of trust. He was the Scent. At first sight, people wanted to trust him. In part, the awkwardness demanded it. Kihss was one of the finest reporters the *Times* ever had.[14]

One day early in my career at the *Times*, an assistant metropolitan editor sent me out with Peter to cover student riots at Queens College. The students were protesting the arrest of members of Students for a Democratic Society. The sit-ins went on for four days, and thirty-eight students faced trespassing charges.

I was in awe of Peter. I knew he was, for example, the only reporter *both* sides trusted during the hearings of the House Un-American Activities Committee. I went out to get a cab. Peter waved me away from the curb. "The subway is faster," he said. When we got to the college, I wondered what the hell I should do. There were a lot of angry protesters. Where to begin?

I determined I'd mimic Peter.

But Peter was gone. He had disappeared. For the life of me, I couldn't find him. I went on alone, and saw a large group of protesters, sitting in a circle on the hallway floor of the building. *What's happening?* I thought. I'd better find out.

When I got to the circle, I saw what was happening. Peter was sitting on the floor by himself, in the middle of the circle, lanky legs akimbo, hat still on—if vaguely—interviewing the mob. The mob was well behaved and answering his questions with respect. He was taking nonstop notes.

A Pied Piper, with pad in place of pipe.

There was nothing to do but listen and watch.

This was also the era of the *Herald-Tribune*. It was my paper of choice at journalism school. The *Trib* was better written, and far more interesting. I had met the great Jimmy Breslin of the *Trib*, a self-described "street reporter" who won a Pulitzer Prize. When he died, the *Washington Post* called him bard of the New York streets. It said his "muscular, unadorned prose pummeled the venal, deflated the pompous and gave voice to ordinary city-dwellers." His columns offered a sympathetic viewpoint of working-class people, the kind of reporting lacking today. Here is Breslin's description of the man who dug President John F. Kennedy's grave:

> *Pollard is forty-two. He is a slim man with a mustache who was born in Pittsburgh and served as a private in the 352nd Engineers battalion in Burma in World War II. He is an equipment operator, grade 10, which means he gets $3.01 an hour. One of the last to serve John Fitzgerald Kennedy, who was the thirty-fifth President of this country, was a working man who earns $3.01 an hour and said it was an honor to dig the grave.*[15]

The other fellow on the rewrite bank, next to Peter, was Homer Bigart. Bigart was plump, stolid, phlegmatic—a red-faced, white-haired pumpkin of a man. He was always impeccably dressed and groomed, with round, black-rimmed glasses. He stammered.

It would diminish Homer to say he was a "reporter's reporter."[16] Homer did win two Pulitzer Prizes. More importantly, South Vietnam had expelled him for having criticized President Diem and, after civil rights activists in Mississippi had disappeared, he wrote that opponents of civil rights were "peckerwoods" and "rednecks."[17]

Once, after a first-edition deadline, Homer asked me to join him at an old-school chop house near Times Square. I looked forward to the meal with the great man.

When we settled into our red booth and we ordered our drinks, Homer looked at me and asked without preamble or emotion, "Why did you come to the *Times*?" I noticed that—unusually—he was not stammering.

I had no idea what he was asking. I was thrilled to be at the *Times*. I was thrilled to be having dinner with him. I set down my glass of iced soda.

"What do you mean, Homer?"

He looked at me. "The place to be is not the *Times*."

Stunned, I said, "Not the *Times*?" I was beginning to feel like an idiot. "Well, where?"

He told me: "Television."

Soon the waiter put a hefty steak in front of each of us. Stricken, I was barely able to pick up a knife and fork.

We speed along now in a scary silver bullet train, the train of technology. It has no windows. We can see the track behind us from the rear platform but not the track in front of the lustrous locomotive. In fact, we can't be sure there is a track in front of the speeding train. So it may be comforting to think back just a little.

If Homer and I could have that dinner after the first-edition print deadline today, I'm certain he would take me back to the same chop house. But what would he say about television? And what would be his advice now to a cowed, callow youngster?

CHAPTER TWELVE

Italian Racing Jackets

Almost every man looks more so in a belted trench coat.
—Sydney J. Harris, Chicago columnist and author

A little nonsense now and then is relished by the wisest men.
—Willy Wonka

THE *NEW YORK TIMES* NEWSROOM, 1968

It was a spring day in 1968 when we trooped out, the whole rewrite bank, about eight of us, from the men's room. We were all wearing blue Italian racing jackets, zipped from bottom left to top right. It had a round emblem in white over the heart that read "New York Times Rewrite," and sported a typewriter with wings. I still have mine (though the girth of maturity has made zipping an issue). We took our seats in the rewrite rows at the front of the newsroom and waited, but not for long. There was cohesion among us, the racing-jacket clad cadre. There was plenty of time to talk, and we were all grouped in the first few seats of the newsroom. All we needed for a good, analytic chat was the least item of insignificant gossip.

Abe Rosenthal came out of his office and strode with curiosity and purpose more than fifty feet across the now-quiet newsroom to the rewrite bank.

Stocky, dark-haired Mike Kaufman seemed poised to respond to whatever Rosenthal had to say. Mike went on to be a foreign correspondent in Africa, India, and Poland. Mike had a full mustache, saw humor in almost everything, and couldn't say no to a conversation. He had been born in Paris of Polish-Jewish refugees.

His obituary in the *Times* said he "grew up in Manhattan, a streetwise kid who spoke French and Polish and knew the back-alley shortcuts on the Upper West Side, the con games of Times Square and the pleasures of Coney Island."[18] Mike had begun at the *Times* as a copy boy.

"What does it mean?" Rosenthal asked. We cringed, though it was unlikely the *Times* could fire the whole rewrite bank for wearing racing jackets. We were wearing them as a *cri de coeur*. Almost every night we saved the paper, or some *Times* reporter. On occasion we rewrote prose so mangled it took arc welding to straighten it out. We wrote stories from telephoned notes that may have made sense in the dim coziness of the bar from where they were dictated but made no sense in the harsh light of the newsroom. Phone booths seemed to result routinely in the strangulation of syntax.

We wrote stories that led the paper from the mumblings or ravings of reporters on the phone and from materials in the morgue.

If the paper had a posterior, we routinely rescued it. And, to a man, we felt unappreciated for our nightly accomplishments. Raises were not forthcoming, nor were reporting assignments that might get us off the bank for fresh air and observation (with or without racing jackets). We were quietly protesting, and Kaufman told Rosenthal that.

Abe turned and walked back to his office.

One thing neither Rosenthal nor anybody else could relieve Rewrite or any *Times* reporter or editor of was an artfully crafted Bernstein Barb. Ted Bernstein was an assistant managing editor whose job was to improve the writing and editing in the *Times*. In the 1950s, he had begun issuing a single-paged broadside called *Winners and Sinners*—a house organ of tart wit in which he pointed out successes and failures in the newspaper. You did not want to see your solecism mentioned, however cleverly.[19]

My colleagues on Rewrite were neither *Winners* nor *Sinners*. Truth be told, we were a motley group: Me (sorry, Ted: *I*), lusting to be a real reporter; Long John Phillips, poet of prose; Kaufman, with long hair slicked back and mustache abristle, beating at his typewriter; Larry Van Gelder, a Columbia law alumnus, who seemed so indifferent to his vocational world that I thought he needed a passport to get into the newsroom; and a wafer-thin hippie with dark ringlets whose name slips my mind and whose only connection with Rewrite seemed to be the standard swivel chair he occupied in the bank. The hippie spent most of his time developing rubber stamps with modish sayings and illustrations to expedite messages. I spent some unoccupied time helping him come up with a name for his enterprise. I think I suggested "Stamp-It-to-'Em."

My own relief—physical and psychological—came each evening with my last shriek of "Copy" for the story I had just finished. Breath became possible; I could unzip the racing jacket.

CHAPTER THIRTEEN

Paper Missiles, and Quitting Every Night

I threatened myself with quitting after every movie. But I think everybody does that, right?

—Joaquin Phoenix

When it comes to gathering and reporting the news, it is hard to beat the uncommon sense of legendary journalist Peter Kihss. . . . More than three decades ago, Kihss and I were talking in the old newsroom of the New York Times *when, after a frustrating day of seeing his story mangled by editors, he looked at me and said: Always remember, the job of the editor is to separate the wheat from the chaff—and publish the chaff. . . .*

—Michael Goodwin, *New York Post*, January 2017

THE *NEW YORK TIMES* NEWSROOM, 1969

From one perspective, deadline at the *Times* newsroom resembled bedlam, frosted with absurdity and glazed with madness. I sat in a box seat, in the third row of the enormously long room, right in front of the Metropolitan Desk editors. From there, we rewrite men could hear orders barked at us and were close enough for the copy boys (all males) to pick up the next pages of our story the moment we yelled, "Copy!" and handed them the books. The books held an original on top of a few sheets of paper interleaved with carbons to go to various editors. The bottom copy was for the reporter.

I used to come to work at 2:00 p.m. and leave at 10:00 p.m. or so, with dinner after the first edition at 7:30.

For three hours or more before deadline, the metropolitan editor, Arthur Gelb, a slavish servant of Abe Rosenthal, would whirl around, trying to pulverize every nanosecond to squeeze as much local news as possible into the day's report.[20] The *Times* described Gelb in his obituary as a human pinball machine.[21]

Gelb was lanky and high-strung—whirling without restraint, summoning deputies, reporters, rewrite men, very occasionally grabbing the phone. At least theoretically, he was in charge of the mini-madhouse that produced the city report, though whether he was an inmate or a caretaker I could not say.

Like all of Rosenthal's hand-picked men, he was held first to loyalty to Rosenthal, next to performance. Gelb had begun at the *Times* as a copy boy during the Second World War. He made, or at least approved, the assignments and was supposed to inject thought—or at least rationality—into the report. How he accomplished this in an atmosphere rivaling the Lunatics' Tower in Vienna was never apparent.

As his *Times* obituary pointed out in 2014:

No matter the role, Mr. Gelb, a gangly 6-foot-2, was relentless, fidgety and in your face—whether in passionate response to a potential scoop or in fevered reaction to the whim of a fellow boss, typically the equally relentless A. M. Rosenthal, who had been two years his senior at City College and perpetually a step ahead of him in the Times hierarchy. . . .

Everybody in the Times newsroom had a favorite Arthur Gelb story: about the reporter who, buckling under one more Gelb assignment, collapsed from exhaustion; about another harried underling who stopped speaking entirely, driven to a self-imposed vow of silence; about the time a colleague paged Mr. Gelb at a Times Square pornography theater, where, in the cause of investigative reporting, he and several editors had gone to watch "Deep Throat". . . .

On a foggy July 28, 1945, Mr. Gelb was enlisted to help cover the crash of a B-25 bomber into the Empire State Building. At Bellevue Hospital, he wrote later: "I managed to talk my way into the emergency room to ask the nurses some simple questions. Because of my youth and obvious inexperience, I guess they felt sorry for me, and they gave me a vivid account of their lifesaving efforts. My success alerted me unwittingly to a journalistic virtue: naïveté. "[22]

The journalistic virtue of naïveté. My own career proved testament to that.

Also from the *Times* obituary:

Mr. Gelb himself conceded: "I'm not sure I would have wanted to work for me when I was an editor. I was well aware that not every reporter was eager to chase down the countless (if sometimes dubious) leads I proposed—and some eyed me as though I were some kind of madman." [23]

No—they really didn't. Just manager of the madhouse.

The madhouse had a second shift. At 4:00 p.m. or so, the most important Metropolitan news post migrated to Sheldon—Shelly—Binn, the night city editor. Quick of mind and movement, a little florid, with glasses and a receding hairline, Shelly had two defining characteristics: He sat in his chair—reporters came to him. And he dealt with stress by crumpling up sheets of paper and tossing them high over his head onto the floor around him.

Binn oversaw the coverage that had been written during the day and decided what would get into the paper, and at what length. Like supplicant clergy queuing before the Pope, reporters lined up before him to find out how much or whether they would write. To a person, they respected his judgment, and the man himself. He had served as an anti-tank gunner in Holland, and had been seriously wounded by mortar fire, losing an eye and suffering severe chest wounds. He returned home with a metal plate in his head and a glass eye.

I thought these experiences—as well as the tossing of the crumpled paper and the man's remarkable intelligence—allowed him to remain calm in the cauldron of the newsroom. The only time I saw him flapped was when I came up to him after knocking off a deadline story on rewrite and, just unwinding, reached out to shake his hand. He hesitated for a long moment, then took my hand. I wondered whether he expected a Masonic grasp.

A reporter's editor, Shelly was not just unflappable. He was insatiable. His *Times* obituary said: "He was unconscious for four days after being wounded in the war. 'When he woke up,' his son Joshua Binn said, 'his first question was whether Roosevelt had won the election.'" But it was not Shelly—it was Arthur Gelb—who dealt with the task, virtually a ritual, *after* deadline. This was the continuing saga of the legendary Peter Kihss's threatening to leave the paper.

On Rewrite, we were throwing up tents and hoping they would withstand the winds of the next day. Peter Kihss was building the cathedral of Chartres, every day.

Each night, after the first edition deadline had come and gone, Peter would remain at his typewriter in the first row of the rewrite bank. The rest of us were hungry and went out to eat. Peter remained hunched over at what seemed an agonizing pitch, thick glasses near the end of his nose. His topcoat and battered hat lay on a nearby desk. A manila file folder lay open, next to his reporter's narrow notebook. He painstakingly transcribed his notes and laid each page into the folder. Eventually, he placed the night's folder vertically in the bottom drawer of the metal desk, with all the other folders that held all the other typed notes.

Only when he had finished typing all of his notes for the story would Peter go home. It was, for me, a ritual that seemed at once painful and sacred. No one—reporters, rewrite staff, editors, copy boys—no one interrupted.

After he was finally done, he'd go home to Jamaica Estates, Queens and presumably eat dinner. At 7:30 p.m. the first edition came out. After he saw it, Peter would call Arthur Gelb and quit.

The first time I heard Arthur's side of this exchange, I was thunderstruck. The second time, I was incredulous. The third, I was merely entertained by Arthur's discomfiture. Peter quitting the paper would be like the Pope abandoning Catholicism. Arthur would beg him not to quit, and on and on the conversation would go until Arthur had demonstrated repentance and supplication in ample measure.

Peter quit the *Times* with such frequency for one reason: Some editor had changed, or cut, his copy—however slightly—in a way that made it less than accurate in Peter's view.

This sample of his work reflects the breathtakingly detailed accuracy of his reporting:

Falling Masonry Kills A Lawyer 14 Floors Down
By Peter Kihss

A piece of falling masonry struck and fatally injured a 28-year-old lawyer yesterday as she was walking in downtown Brooklyn. She was struck on the head by what appeared to be a piece of a cornice that plunged from the 14th floor of a building at 66 Court Street, at the corner of Livingston Street.

The 30-story building, decades old, formerly housed the offices of many lawyers. It was converted about a year ago to 104 cooperative apartments.

According to the City Buildings Department, a notice of a violation was issued to the owner last April 7 for failure to comply with a law that requires inspections of building exteriors more than six stories high by a consulting engineer or architect. . . .

The Building Department's records still listed City Heights Ltd. of 630 Fifth Avenue as the owner, but a lawyer, Richard Kent Bernstein, said the company had sold the building more than a year ago. . . .

The Police Department listed as a current owner of the building the Allied Manhattan Development Corporation, of the same Fifth Avenue address, but a man who answered the telephone there said that the concern had only been handling sales of apartments.

The law, Local Law 10, was enacted in 1980 after the death of a student at Barnard College on May 16, 1979. She died when she was struck by falling masonry on West 115th Street.

The victim in yesterday's accident was Mayda E. Alsace, a staff lawyer in the Legal Aid Society's criminal-defense office at 175 Remsen Street.

"She was a lovely person, very cheerful," said Paul J. Madden, the lawyer in charge of the office. "She would sing songs. . . ."

Mr. Madden said that Miss Alsace "was on her way to court this morning, and had left the office, but came back to retrieve her umbrella."

The accident occurred shortly before 10:30 A.M. Kelly Bennett, 19, a platform assistant for the Brooklyn Federal Savings and Loan Association, was walking to a doughnut shop and was going the other way on Court Street.

"It was raining, and I had my umbrella up," Miss Bennett said. "I saw the rock hit her. It looked like it hit her on the side of her head. I ran over and put my umbrella over her head. . . .

. . . . The falling piece appeared to have been a round ball attached to a cornice on the 14th floor, where the nearest apartment belonged to a man who had reportedly been away for about two weeks.

At the Empress Travel Agency in the building, Mark Essner, a travel consultant, said he had heard a noise and, on looking out a window, had seen the victim in front of the door. She was still holding a beige umbrella that the falling stone had penetrated, he said. . . .

Barry Cox, assistant commissioner of buildings, said 8,846 buildings in the five boroughs were subject to Local Law 10. About 60 percent, he said, file reports of the required inspections of exteriors by the Feb. 21 deadline. . . . [24]

Editors are meddlesome creatures in hard wooden chairs whose jobs are to make copy fit the allotted "hole," or available space, educate the grammar, deaden the style, second-guess the whole. And, whenever possible, ruin the piece. The *Times* was, generally, an editor's paper (just ask Peter), while the *Herald-Trib* was a reporter's paper. I happened to end up working in the one place that was the exception: Washington. There the *Times* was a reporter's paper. Because Washington had its own satrap, Scotty Reston.

It is always the reporter, not the editor, who has to see, explain, and perhaps report again on the participants and sources. When things went wrong, I always pictured the editor smugly chortling at his desk.

But back to Peter. Each time he quit, I'd see him the very next day just as rumpled as ever, brown suit hanging limply from his frame, glasses at the mercy of gravity, hunched over his first-row desk, reviewing notebook and files.

CHAPTER FOURTEEN

Not Always New York's Finest:
Reporters Who Carried Guns

Washington—The FBI's use of an undercover agent posing as a jour-
nalist—which led to an uproar in the news media—did not violate
agency policy, a Justice Department review concluded. . . .

—AGENCE FRANCE-PRESSE, SEPTEMBER 15, 2016

The White House revoked the press passes of a significant chunk of the
Washington press corps because they didn't meet a new standard. . . .
Under the new rules, . . . to qualify for the highest level of access . . .
journalists had to be present in the White House for at least 90 days
out of a 180-day period. . . . [V]irtually the entire press corps failed to
meet this new test. . . .

—MATHEW INGRAM, COLUMBIA JOURNALISM REVIEW,
MAY 9, 2019[25]

NEW YORK AND WASHINGTON, 1969–1971

I went on to cover other rallies without Peter, but the memory of his sit-ting inside a circle of protesters stuck with me. His ability to immerse himself in that crowd baffled me. One time when I tried to immerse myself, I discovered the limits of my press badge.

On a warm and otherwise quiet evening in Manhattan, I found myself covering a riot by youngsters in the East Village. I was wearing my yellow police press badge when I saw three of New York's Finest slam a young hippie protester against a door in a dark entryway.

I approached to watch and yelled the protective mantra: "*Times* reporter! *Times* reporter!" It didn't work. My press badge and the power of the *Times* failed. One of the cops, holding his nightstick, waved me off insistently. I backed off and was immediately struck on my right arm by a bottle launched by a protester. Bleeding, I retreated.

I was sitting on a stoop assessing my injuries when a large, young, square-jawed, long-skirted, bedraggled woman took me inside the building to her apartment. She applied an antiseptic and bandage to my wound.

The irony was that at protest rallies the FBI pretended to be reporters and wore press badges on their pressed suits (a dead giveaway, those suits). No one seemed to throw anything at them.

At one rally I covered, I saw the daughter of one of my eminent colleagues, Tad Szulc, protesting, and I wondered whether she knew the "reporters" were G-men. I wondered if I should tell her. Instead, I decided to have fun. Press badge flapping, I walked over to the two agents, stopped a few feet from them, and turned back to face the protesters. I looked at the G-men, made eye contact, and remained impassive. They looked away. Stricken might be too strong a word to describe them. Discomforted isn't.

CHAPTER FIFTEEN

Harlem's History Escapes the Marshal

Happiness is perfume, you can't pour it on somebody else without get-
ting a few drops on yourself.
—JAMES AUGUSTUS JOSEPH VAN DER ZEE, PHOTOGRAPHIC
CHRONICLER OF LIFE IN HARLEM

THE *NEW YORK TIMES* NEWSROOM, 1969

The great reporter and writer Joe Liebling had strong feelings about publishers and editors. He likely tolerated them only because they made possible his inimitable reporting and a style that flowed like intelligent treacle from his chubby fingers. They couldn't flatten the luscious head of random effervescence in Liebling's work. It was like champagne, stream- ing discursively, unimpeded by clichés, always in several directions at the same time. You couldn't calm it—only quaff it. To squelch the stream, you would have had to cork the bottle. And that, even though they owned the presses, no publisher dared do. I loved reading Liebling. He wrote about everything from oysters to the Maginot Line, from true French trencher- men to boxing, from the Normandy landings to the press.[26]

When I was on the *Times* Metropolitan staff, I also had my own paper in one, but only one, sense. I had some freedom. Take this example:

Late one Tuesday afternoon in April 1969, I took a break from Rewrite when the *Times* directed me to walk through the inhospitable heart of 1960s Harlem to talk to one of the saddest people I've ever seen. He was sitting on the stoop of a brownstone surrounded by piles of house- hold goods. I don't know who had called the *Times* Metropolitan Desk, and I had no idea what I would find. I'd heard only something about a photographer. I suspect someone at the Desk thought he'd get the kid off rewrite for an afternoon, and so there I was standing before this man with his solid suspenders buckling, his shoulders and back slumped.

James Augustus Joseph Van Der Zee, eighty-three years old, was being evicted from his apartment in the brownstone. The New York marshal—sheriffs and marshals do this in New York—was putting everything Van Der Zee owned into a large truck at the curb, and not with particular care. The hauling included hundreds—no, thousands—of glass and film negatives. I took an unauthorized peek and saw the history of Harlem. Fifty years of it. Where, I wanted to know, was the marshal carting the treasure?

No one knew—at least James Van Der Zee and his wife didn't know. The Smithsonian described Van Der Zee with his 1922 photograph "Evening Attire" held in their American Art Collection like this:

Van Der Zee began photographing as a teenager after having won an eight-dollar camera as a premium for selling pink and yellow silk sachets.

Beginning in 1916 he worked out of a commercial Harlem studio he opened on 135th Street.

During the 1920s and 1930s, he produced hundreds of photographs recording Harlem's growing middle class. Its residents entrusted the visual documentation of their weddings, funerals, celebrities, and social life to his carefully composed images. . . . [27]

In an interview for his book, Van Der Zee said:

I posed everybody according to their type and personality, and therefore almost every picture was different. In the majority of studios, they just seem to pose everybody according to custom, according to fashion, and therefore the pictures seem to be mechanical looking for me . . . I tried to pose each person in such a way as to tell a story. [28]

James—if I may call him that, given our odd association—and Gaynella, his wife, were being tossed out of their home. All of his images were being tossed out too. Ironically, the eviction came just after his photographs had been featured at the Metropolitan Museum of Art exhibit *Harlem on My Mind* earlier that year.

I can't say James was crying. But his wife was. He just sat on the stoop, looking at the next step down. At first he didn't pay much attention to me, but when I began to ask him questions about his photography, he perked up. I listened, awed by what he had done, scribbling as fast as I could. I hurried back to the newsroom on the subway. I was on deadline. Writing as fast as I could, I threw both religion and patriotism—quite unintentionally—into the story:

Harlem Photographer Sees Lifework Hauled Away

The stocky old man raised his cane. Caught on the rubber tip was a roll of negatives on wide, old-fashioned film. He held it to the light. "Cardinal Spellman at his silver jubilee," he said, and rolled the film into his coat pocket . . .

The photographer, perspiring heavily but with his hat and tie still in place, brushed the wet debris aside. Under it was a tightly rolled American flag.

Mr. Van Der Zee picked up the flag.

"Do what you want to this old gray head," he said, "but spare your country's flag." He chuckled.[29]

I thought the story deserved the front page, but it ran on the second front—the first page of the second section. No matter, the next day, all hell erupted. Museums kicked into action. Charities offered lodging. That same year, James went on to receive the American Society of Magazine Photographers' award. Later, the Metropolitan Museum made him an Honorary Fellow for Life and acquired sixty-six of his photographs.

One theme critics cite as recurring in James's photographs is the emergent black middle class, which he captured in often idealized images.[30] In *Black Stars of the Harlem Renaissance*, Van Der Zee explained that he "wanted to make the camera take what I thought should be there." When personal cameras arrived in the middle of the century, the demand for James's services decreased.[31]

I was proud. Roxbury and Harlem became conflated. So did a Harlem brownstone and the house of the woman in the Boston Bank. I thought I might have had a small part in saving Harlem's history. But a public relations man in Manhattan brought me back to earth the next day. He called me to mock me. "You pulled out all the stops," he chortled. "The Cardinal and the American Flag!"

After I'd written the story, I worried about where the photos and negatives and glass plates were. No one could tell me, including those I thought should have known—like the sheriff and the police. Thankfully, the *Times* did its magic, and the images were somehow saved and yanked back to safety. Later, I got a thank you note from Gaynella and James. As James would say, I had been able to sprinkle a few drops of happiness on myself. James received an award from the man who would become my boss, Jimmy Carter, and Howard University gave him an honorary doctorate.

When I saw James sitting, crumpled, on the stoop as I approached, I didn't cry. It is not fashionable for reporters to cry. But fashionable or not, on two other occasions I came so close to tears that you couldn't have told the difference.

Back at the *Herald*, I was watching a pretty little Black girl, four years old and dressed in her first-day finery, get off a large yellow school bus in South Boston after a federal judge had ordered integration. Large Irish women were screaming in bloody-minded protest. One woman in particular caught my attention. The woman was built like a discarded refrigerator. Her face was scarlet. I could see she had all her teeth, because she was screaming with mouth stretched wide, and at full force. She was screaming at a yellow school bus. It had come to deliver Black youngsters—of primary school age, to Southie—South Boston. As much a part of the sod of Eire as the late blight that caused the Potato Famine.

The Boston School Committee had ordered desegregation of public schools in 1967, and Southie was not taking it lying down. The first battalion of resistance were the middle-aged women, presumably mothers. They were nearly as terrifying as the attack dogs in Birmingham. The objects of their high-volume wrath were the Black kids from Roxbury who were on the bus. The kids had to be there. The mothers chose to be. I was there to cover the two of them. I saw the bus roll up and watched as the door opened. A girl, a kindergartener—at most a first-grader—stood in baffled terror on the last step of the exit, frozen, not willing to forsake her yellow shelter. A woman stood to the left, perhaps a teacher, waiting for her to take that step—or in her case, hop. The girl didn't.

The Southie mother screamed and cursed, cursed and screamed. I was feet from the little girl, clutching my spiral-bound pad. She was immaculately decked out in her cutest dark jumper. I watched, horrified, not able to take notes. Spittle descended from wide-open Southie jaws. Who in the world were they cursing so? City officials? Black toddlers? Police? Reporters? Fate?

The other instance was Kent State.

Like many of the nation's rapidly expanding state universities, Kent State University, until last Monday, was flourishing in an obscurity out of all proportion to its size. In an instant, the obscurity was ended by a volley of rifle fire that killed four students.[32]

That was the lede, or first paragraph, of the story Joe Lelyveld, John Kifner, and I wrote from Kent State right after the shooting. We interviewed a group of students whom we invited to a hotel room. It was another massacre, but right here, on a knoll, on a college campus, in Ohio. The students had been protesting the US bombing of Cambodia.

Twenty-eight guardsmen were reported to have fired sixty-seven rounds in thirteen seconds. The students they shot at were unarmed. These, many Americans felt, are *our kids.*

I was only twenty-nine years old. It was not that much earlier that I had been in graduate school. And at the time, I myself was in the Army Reserve. I was what the Army called a *shavetail*—a new infantry second lieutenant, straight out of the Benning School for Boys (Officer Candidate School). I had been trained in most everything, and knew nothing. I did know that the average time a lieutenant survived in Vietnam was tragically short. First lieutenants suffered the greatest number of officer deaths in the US Army during Vietnam (nearly fifteen hundred).[33] By way of contrast, nineteen colonels died. Seven generals died. Some shavetails were killed by the enemy; some were killed by their own men, who did not want to undertake parlous missions against an incomprehensible enemy in a war that made no sense to them.

I had the good fortune—and I'm probably still alive—because the Army did not send me to Vietnam. I never came under fire, except on the training range, and I was never made to decide whether my platoon should open fire on a village whose residents might, or might not, be hostile. The Army training was useful in helping me to understand and cover the Pentagon when I reported on stories like the My Lai Massacre and fraudulent medals.

I had been trained to command an infantry platoon, bearing the same weapons these National Guardsmen at Kent State had so cruelly used.

I was flattered that Joe Lelyveld picked me for the small team of reporters going to Kent State. Lelyveld was a quiet, thin journalist who often looked as if he was giving something the sober consideration it merited. He later became executive editor of the *Times*. John Kifner, a national, and later foreign, correspondent for the *Times*, was the opposite: not quiet, not calm, and not intellectual. All three of us were young. But it was a terrible assignment that involved reliving, through the students, the massacre. Shades of My Lai.

It was enough to make you weep. I didn't. Remember: Real reporters don't cry. At least not when sober. My colleague, John Kifner, was light-haired, square-jawed, strong, and intense—always the involved professional. But on the plane back to Washington, worn thin, he sat by the window and swallowed a tumbler of Scotch in one gulp. He began to cry. I revisited my diet soda and looked out the window. I wondered what I could find in Washington that might add to the Kent State story.

On October 30, five months later, I found it:

A Justice Department summary of the inquiry by the Federal Bureau of Investigation into the shootings at Kent State University last May 4 differs sharply from the conclusion reached later by an Ohio grand jury that exonerated National Guardsmen on the ground that they believed they were physically threatened.[34]

The woman who imprisoned herself in a bank, Boston's school integration, the Harlem photographer, and Kent State all pushed me toward tears. You notice I don't single out the My Lai Massacre. Or Watergate. Those were horrific stories I wrote, but somehow more remote.

Tears ran for individuals I had to *watch* suffer, write about . . . and not help. Unless readers happened to be moved by my story to help, as some were by my articles about the photographer and the woman in the bank. Marx was right that change comes from action at the societal, not individual, level. And investigative reporting only sometimes yields that. My own misery came from watching the terrified little Black child in Southie and the elderly photographer weeping on the steps of the Harlem brownstone.

Dear Mr. Smith,

Your interview with the Kent State students for the paper of May 11 was just superb. I am very pleased that it has won one of the publisher's merit awards for May. A check for $100 is enclosed.

Congratulations.

Sincerely,

Arthur Sulzberger

CHAPTER SIXTEEN

John Harvard Frowns

If it was up to me, there wouldn't be no such thing as the establishment.
—JIMI HENDRIX

Can we hold him as a material witness? I don't know—he has a lot of friends downtown.
—CHARLIE CHAN, *DOCKS OF NEW ORLEANS*

THE *NEW YORK TIMES* NEWSROOM, APRIL 1969

My pal when I was on the rewrite bank was not Peter Kihss. Nor was it his neighbor, Homer Bigart. It was Long John Phillips. Long John reminded me of Ichabod Crane. Washington Irving wrote of Crane:

> *He was tall, but exceedingly lank, with narrow shoulders, long arms and legs, hands that dangled a mile out of his sleeves, feet that might have served for shovels, and his whole frame most loosely hung together. . . . [His head] looked like a weather-cock perched upon his spindle neck. . . .*
>
> *He had read several books quite through, and was a perfect master of Cotton Mather's History of New England Witchcraft, in which, by the way, he most firmly believed.[35]*

John resembled Ichabod physically and, curiously, also had strong views on witchcraft, Jews, Christ, and the devil. After twenty years, he left the *Times* to spread the word of a fundamentalist God, but during the many days we worked together, he never uttered a word on any of those topics to me. Not a word.

Long John and I went to dinner together often—dare I say, religiously—after the first edition had been printed. I occasionally had a frankfurter at the preeminent Nathan's Famous hot dog emporium half a block away with other rewrite men, but never with John. Nor did John and I succumb to Sardi's, where caricatures of show-business celebrities stared down at journalists and press agents drinking cocktails and enjoying expense-account Continental cuisine.

It seemed a bit rich and celebrity-infested for two rewrite men. Gene Roberts did once nearly take me to lunch at Sardi's, but when the maître d' made us wait while he sorted out our status and gave priority to others, Gene turned on his heels and left.

Instead, John and I often went to a nearby Brazilian restaurant. We sat and had a high old time, talking endlessly about the paper and about the world in general. I would press and press, foolishly, for tips on how I could learn to write better, how to write with style. Long John, you see, was one of the best poets at the paper; for me, he was the poet laureate. He wrote about New York's St. Patrick's Day parade:

The sun was high to their backs and the wind was fast in their faces and 100,000 sons and daughters of Ireland, and those who would hold with them, matched strides with their shadows for 52 blocks. It seemed they marched from Midtown to exhaustion.[36]

... and a ribald parrot:

The Case of the Garrulous Parrot was resolved yesterday in East New York Magistrate's Court.

Mrs. Cecelia Amato, a day worker, had charged that the forty-year-old bird had repeatedly addressed her in "vile and indecent language" as she walked to a subway station in the mornings. But yesterday she withdrew her complaint of disorderly conduct against Sam Maiorana, who pledged to keep his parrot in a private place, out of earshot.

Pete's morning perch had been the back of a chair in front of 1257 Myrtle Avenue in Brooklyn's Bushwick section, where his master lives behind a vacant store. It was from this vantage that Mrs. Amato said the bird had repeatedly anathematized her in the rich argot of the waterfront. . . .[37]

. . . and the death of cheesecake:

What kind of a day is today? It's the kind of a day that if you wanted a slice of cheesecake at Lindy's, you couldn't get it.

There hasn't been a day like it since before August 20, 1921, when Leo (Lindy) Lindemann opened the original Lindy's at 1626 Broadway, an all-night deli destined to occupy a special niche in American folklore.

You would have thought it would last forever, but Lindy's is dead. For some people the world changed a little bit at 1:30 A.M. yesterday, when the big neon sign on Broadway at Fifty-first Street was turned off and the revolving door was locked.

The last dish could have been, but wasn't, a heaping portion of sentiment laced with treacle. . . .[38]

Why had the place gone down? A waiter of long service was asked, and he replied, "A number of things. A cause leads to an effect, and an effect to a cause, and a cause to an effect, and all of a sudden you're kaput. . . ."

To write well, John explained to me, you had to read, and specifically, certain prose writers whose style he admired. These were not well-known authors, and I confess with shame their names have left my memory. At one point, John kindly said I did him proud when I covered riots at Harvard University.

One day in 1969, in the beginning of my career with the *Times*, Gene Roberts, then national editor, sent me back to Harvard (and Radcliffe, then the women's college) to cover rioting by the students. This was my first assignment off Rewrite.

I was twenty-eight, not much older than the rioting students who were striking with the goals of fundamentally restructuring Harvard and protesting against the Vietnam War. The strikes went on for a while. I was running out of the clothes that I had brought with me from New York. Initially, I was supposed to be there for only two days. I called

Gene from Harvard and told him that I needed more clothes. He said, "No problem, just buy some jeans." I told him if I wore jeans, no one would be able to distinguish me from the striking students. He just laughed.

I covered the protests as best I could. When they spread to Radcliffe, the demonstrators crowded into the small office of Mary Bunting, then president of Radcliffe. The students—mainly women or, as we said in those days, girls—were sitting on the floor of President Bunting's office. The office was more than cramped. I worried that the old wooden floor wouldn't support so many people. I was tucked against the wall wearing my blue jeans, watching and scribbling in my reporter's notebook. The next day the paper ran my piece, and I felt proud of myself. I liked the way I'd tried to capture the mood.[39] I especially liked one quotation: "Will you let us girls run one thing?"

Even in that pre-feminist, unenlightened era, that was the quote I cottoned to. I was pointing out a protest within the protest.

My stringer in Cambridge—a part-time reporter who worked for the *Times* on an as-needed basis—was a bright, talented young woman. When I asked her what she thought of the piece, she told me she thought it was good, but she and her friends wondered why I had described what the Cliffies were wearing. It was my first lesson in feminism.

The next day, I covered a trial of a Harvard student rioter who was charged with criminally trespassing after students had occupied a university administration building earlier that month. I was humiliated when the story that ran was cut, with no regard to content. It wound up giving precisely one side of the trial—the prosecution.

I had been seated in the jury box—the case was tried by a judge, rather than a jury—along with the student's parents. They seemed to place great trust, or at least had placed great trust, in the *Times*. Only a few times have I been as ashamed as I was when I saw the story that ran. But, unlike Peter Kihss, it did not occur to me to quit. It was far too late to fight; no one from the paper had called about the intended cut.

Gene Roberts decided to come up to Cambridge to have a firsthand look at the events I was writing about. Someone told me he would be coming and that I would be expected to take him out for a business lunch.

Because I was keen to oblige and impress, I took him to a place I thought would knock his socks off.

It was not to Locke-Ober's for a fine dining experience, and not one of the many clam or lobster houses. I took him to the lunch counter at Elsie's near Harvard Square, where they served up terrific hamburgers on kaiser rolls and wonderful roast beef sandwiches smothered in Russian dressing.

To his credit, Gene didn't complain at all. He took a stool—happily there were two open in a row—and settled in for the hamburger. I thought it was haute cuisine. After we were finished, he turned toward me on his red-leatherette stool and said, "You sure know how to take a guy to lunch." I was naïve enough in those days to take him seriously. I honestly thought that Sardi's had very little on Elsie's.

Unhappily, I did not come to share my colleague Johnny (R.W.) Apple's exquisite culinary taste or his sense of style in prose or nearly anything else, and throughout my career, I remained devoted to Elsie's. I did add to my favorites Chez L'Ami Louis on the rue du Vertbois in Paris. I'm known to the red-cheeked Louis there only because many years ago I bribed him by giving him a California hardwood yo-yo embossed "Special Client Yo-Yo, Law Offices of Robert M. Smith." When I visit, he always puts it on my table, which is named—*sérieusement*—"Gaston."

During the Harvard riots, the president—gray-haired Nathan Marsh Pusey—had gone into hiding. Pusey wouldn't talk with anyone who was holding a pen and notebook, recorder, or video camera, but he was pivotal to understanding what was happening at the school. I pressed, but the public relations office wouldn't budge, even for the purported "power paper."

I decided to take direct action. I kept an eye on the building that housed the president's office in Harvard Yard. One day Pusey emerged from the building, bundled in a dark overcoat. As he made his way across the Yard, I hurried to catch up, identified myself, and asked for his view of the riots. He gave me a quote—not a shocking quote, but a substantive response. Whatever he said was not cataclysmic. He didn't say he would resign. He didn't call for the student rioters to be shipped to Leavenworth Penitentiary. He did not even complain about the difficult circumstances he was in. I was elated and hurried to write the story. I waited for it to appear in the paper.

I still remember two results of my reporting at Harvard—one good, one awful.

When I returned from Cambridge to the *Times* newsroom in New York, Long John Phillips looked at me with a wide grin and chortled, "Let us girls run one thing!" His admiration turned my face tangerine with pride.

The other was about the story I had written from Cambridge that did not run.

Scotty Reston, a journalistic icon and another of my heroes, phoned. For me, this was like being called by Jove on a direct hook-up from Olympus.

CHAPTER SEVENTEEN

Veritas Takes a Direct Hit; Ties to the Powerful

The real rulers in Washington are invisible, and exercise power from behind the scenes.
—FELIX FRANKFURTER, US SUPREME COURT JUSTICE

Organizations, whether they are nonprofits or enterprise, need to be aware that nation-states are coming after them for political espionage, economic espionage.
—DMITRI ALPEROVITCH, A COMPUTER SECURITY EXECUTIVE

WASHINGTON BUREAU, THE *NEW YORK TIMES*, 1969–1972

After brief pleasantries, Reston asked me a single question:

"Are we taking advantage of him?"

He obviously meant Nathan Marsh Pusey.

Taking advantage of him? I thought. Here's the president of a major university, interviewed in plain sight and hearing. "Gee Scotty," I said, "I don't see how."

"He's tired, and under great pressure," Reston said. "Perhaps it's best just to let it go."

And let it go the *Times* did. In one phone call I had gone from Richard Harding Davis, a reporter renowned for enterprise in the time of "yellow journalism," to a hunk of cold lead dropped to the composing room floor. It infuriated me. The power of the academic establishment had called on the power of the media establishment, and presto: Interests were shared, past favors remembered, future favors silently cemented. Power had called Power, and the deal was done. Power was appeased, Judgment prevailed. A good wine would be had later.

Coziness with power reaps warm rewards. I didn't understand much of this then. But what did strike me was how out of place the circumstances made Harvard's motto: *veritas*, truth.

Reston was God for my generation of journalists and for the generation that proceeded us. There is no other way of looking at it. As discussed elsewhere, that view betrayed our own innocence. Reston ran the paper in the late 1960s and won the Pulitzer Prize twice. The first time was when he covered the Dumbarton Oaks Conference in 1945. He had gotten an exclusive about how the delegates planned to set up the United Nations. The second time he won for a five-part analysis on the effects of President Eisenhower's illness on his job in 1957.

We were so crazily reverential about Reston that when he was the first US journalist let into China, we envied his appendicitis attack in Beijing. He did a front-page piece that described how he was writing while being treated for post-operative pain by acupuncture administered at the Anti-Imperialist Hospital.

PEKING, July 25 [1971]—

There is something a little absurd about a man publishing an obituary notice on his own appendix, but for the last 10 days this correspondent has had a chance to learn a little about the professional and political direction of a major Chinese hospital from the inside, and this is a report on how I got there and what I found. [40]

Reston could be quite kind on a human level. When he heard I was getting married, he stopped by my desk, sat down, and congratulated me.

"I thought you might be one of those who are married to this business. I'm glad you're not."

With my ever-present tact, I told him that I was aware of how he had been in Yalta and his wife, Sally, in Moscow when she was giving birth to their first child.

Gay Talese described Reston in his book about the *Times*[41]: "Smoothly, discreetly, rarely ruffling feathers, Reston not only preserved the bureau's autonomy but also increased its prestige within a very few years."[42]

Some people at both the *Times* and the *Washington Post* had a cooperative relationship with the CIA—including the publisher of the *Times*. In his book, Stephen Kinzer, a former *Times* reporter, wrote that Reston was a contact of former CIA chief Allen Dulles.[43] Kinzer said Reston had collaborated with the CIA in Operation Mockingbird, in which the CIA had tried to influence reporting. Others also wrote about this collusion.[44] [45]

Reston owned the *Vineyard Gazette* newspaper. In July 1969, he was summering on Martha's Vineyard when Teddy Kennedy drove his car off the bridge at Chappaquiddick Island. The crash resulted in the death of an innocent young woman, Mary Jo Kopechne. Reston wrote the story for the *Times*.

Reston's original lead was "Tragedy has again struck the Kennedy family." But what about Mary Jo?

John F. Stacks reported in his book that Reston had dictated the first paragraphs of his story, but he did not mention the victim until paragraph four.[46] Reportedly, later in the day, Abe Rosenthal called Sally Reston at home in Edgartown and asked her to advise Reston that there had been a few changes made to his story. The version that the *Times* published led with the real victim.

That story surprised me only because Reston's remarkable accomplishment throughout his career was his total protection of the Washington Bureau from any interference by the editors in New York. Through his closeness with the publishers, the Sulzberger family, and his journalistic power, he decreed Washington an independent island state, misunderstood by New York editors and never to be tampered with by them—either in copy or staff.

I construed Reston's interference narrowly and did not let it keep me from trying to interview Pusey again. When he decided to give his first interview to a television show—*Meet the Press*, I think it was—I installed myself in the studio, behind the cameras. When Pusey walked past, I stood in front of him. This time I knew no one could say I was taking advantage. And this time, without Jovian intervention, my interview ran.

Getting off Rewrite at the end of my year in the thrall of the rewrite bank proved harder than getting the job at the *Times* in the first place. But I used shame, brazenly, on Arthur Gelb. I reminded him that he had promised I would be on Rewrite for only a year. After a short while, I got a phone call from someone who said he was Max Frankel, the Washington bureau chief. Was it really Frankel? I immediately thought of the story of David Halberstam. He hung up on Scotty Reston when Reston called to offer him a job. I decided to listen. "How," the guy asked, "would you feel about coming to Washington?"

CHAPTER EIGHTEEN

More Ties to the Powerful

I am a prisoner of my own pen.

—Anthony T. Hincks

If everyone is thinking alike, then somebody isn't thinking.

—George S. Patton

WASHINGTON BUREAU, THE *NEW YORK TIMES*, 1969–1972

A group mindset is one thing. Being tied to sources who can nourish or starve you with news under their control on your assigned beat is another. You know what they're doing, but it's your rice bowl, and nearly everyone in Washington wants a decent, hand-painted, and preferably bigger, rice bowl.

So, in my great innocence and superb naïveté, Max Frankel and Bob Phelps recruited me to be a general-assignment reporter in the Washington Bureau. I was young, apolitical, and relatively inexperienced. They explained I would have no beat. But, hallelujah!—having no beat meant having no institutional ties and no sources who controlled me. I could write without fear. That was no small thing.

But all these years later, in retrospect, my reactions seem consistent with my naïveté—a naïveté that somehow continued to fuel, rather than be extinguished by, investigative reporting.

Very early on in the Washington Bureau, I began to suffer from professional paranoia.

My discomfort had sources other than Reston. There was, for example, the day I walked into Max Frankel's office and found him sitting behind his large desk. We were talking about some point involving the White House when suddenly, aglow with pride, he said, "Henry [Kissinger] always returns my calls." I said nothing. "As long as I don't call all the time, of course," he continued.

It was an interesting moment. I wasn't sure exactly what to say. Here was the guy who ran the Washington operation of a premier paper bragging about his access to a government official. All I could think about was that he might as well have added, "As long as I don't criticize him . . . or the National Security Council or the White House."

That disclosure shook me, but I said nothing to Frankel. I began to see how playing the power game—buying into symbiotic relationships—gave men like Reston and Frankel the information that the elites and sometimes the public prized. This was a tradition of cozy, tainted relationships. It dated back at least to Reston's predecessor as bureau chief, Arthur Krock.[47] It was a slippery slope about which I wrote a *Times* op-ed after my first year of law school.[48]

Reston won two Pulitzer Prizes. Frankel won one.

When I first came to the Washington Bureau to work as a reporter, I decided to write a piece about the revolving door of Kissinger's staff. It was 1970. Kissinger was in fact bleeding staff—bright, able staff. I don't remember the numbers, but they were noteworthy. I began to interview these folks on the phone about what it was like to work for Kissinger. I asked them why so many assistants left, and some of them actually talked to me.[49] They were quite cooperative and lamented about the way Kissinger treated them.

As was routine, I wrote up a summary of the story for others in the Bureau to see and to be sent to the editors in New York. The summary board happened to be on a ledge in front of my desk. I watched Max read it. When he asked me whether it was warranted, I said yes, of course it was.

Within ten minutes, one of the National Security Council staffers I had just interviewed called me to say what he had said was not true. He went on to detail all the good things he'd experienced while working for Kissinger.

I remember leaning back in my chair and thinking about the import of this. Was Kissinger wiretapping the phone lines of his staff?[50] Had

Frankel had a chat with a source? I listened to the fellow go on and on, but I stuck to my general story. And the *Times* did run it, but things were beginning to become clearer to me.

In general, the *Times* Washington staff was liberal or progressive, and they were also prisoners—prisoners of a mindset, of ambition, of a system, of hypocrisy. As the months wore on, I began to understand that if someone can call your boss to save the Harvard president from his own words and you go along, you're no longer in charge of your own reporting.

If Henry Kissinger doles out his precious calls, can you afford to alienate him? And if you can't, what kind of reporter are you? If you cover the Pentagon and you can't say the Pentagon committed war crimes, are you doing your job? If the Powerful tell you over lunch at a private club that stories about defeat in Vietnam are dunderheaded liberal tripe and dominoes will indeed fall if you report it, and if you accept that view with your crème brûlée, are you a reporter worth anything?

If you accede to all of the above, what else can you call the result other than suppression?

CHAPTER NINETEEN

A Massacre as a Commodity

It is a well-known fact . . . that the house of Rothschild used carrier pigeons in 1815 to be informed of the . . . events on the continent, and thus was able to receive the information of the defeat of Napoleon at Waterloo three days before the English government did, to buy up . . . government stock at [a] depressed price and sell at an enormous profit. . . .

—MORNING POST (LONDON), SEPTEMBER 18, 1884

[The use of news for profit does have a history. But this particular "fact"—however well known—was not true.]

WASHINGTON BUREAU, THE *NEW YORK TIMES*, NOVEMBER 1969

I was exhausting myself getting the information. I was struggling to confirm what seemed an impossible story: American soldiers committing a massacre of unarmed civilians during the Vietnam War. There was increasingly little question that in Vietnam, Americans—our troops—had shot children, women, and old men.

I didn't yet know the awful details: March 16, 1968. My Lai, or Songmy. They slaughtered more than five hundred people, including young girls, women, even babies. They first raped and mutilated some of them before killing them.

US Army officers managed to cover up the carnage for a year before we reported it.

I didn't know that the story would spark a firestorm of such powerful international outrage. And that the brutality and the official cover-up would intensify anti-war sentiment and further divide the United States.

Ridenhour and the Chase

I was chasing the story hard. The chase had led to a Claremont Men's College student named Ronald Ridenhour.

During the spring of 1968, Ridenhour had been a door gunner for the 11th Infantry Brigade, stationed more than thirty miles south of My Lai. Many of his friends who were at My Lai told him what had happened in the village on March 16, 1968. When I reached him, Ridenhour made it clear that he knew about the massacre, but he said firmly that he would give me no information about it. I pressed, and he finally told me he had pledged to Sy Hersh, a freelance investigative reporter, that he would talk to no one but Hersh about what he knew.

I called Hersh to ask him what he was doing tying up Ridenhour. I was going to bawl Hersh out, but I didn't get the chance. As soon as I said the name Ridenhour, he hung up on me.

Frankel and Phelps were standing next to me at the central news desk where I made the call. They watched me as I realized Hersh had hung up.

I was angry and blurted out, to no one in particular: "We'll get this story, and we'll get it for the first edition."

Phelps winked at Frankel and nudged him with his elbow. I knew he was trying to say *the youngster is wound up.*

Word Comes from London

I was making frantic calls when I got a telex from New York telling me that a London paper had just published Sy Hersh's first piece. The article mentioned a Sergeant Michael Bernhardt as having been at the massacre. How could I find the sergeant?

TAG Helps Out, but a Lieutenant Resists

Ironically, the one work experience of my life I disliked—the Army—had taught me how. I knew about the adjutant general, and his keeping track of all soldiers and where we were, by computer. I also knew the TAG office at the Pentagon would have a duty officer at all hours. And I knew how to ask for a current posting—so I hoped to find and interview this sergeant.

I called the Pentagon and—completely bluffing—told the adjutant general duty officer confidently that I had a "TAG" job. Who and where was Bernhardt? The Pentagon computers spun; I sweated.

Click! Bernhardt was—TAG reported—at Fort Dix, New Jersey.

I called the main switchboard at Fort Dix and asked for the company orderly room. I got, of all things, a cocksure shavetail—a self-confident second lieutenant who wouldn't give me the time of day, let alone look for Bernhardt.

"Where is he, Lieutenant?"

"Not here. . . ."

"Lieutenant," I growled, "the Pentagon has told me he's there."

Eventually he, or somebody, got Bernhardt, and I interviewed him.

Yes, he had seen a massacre. Yes, his comrades had killed women and children.

I ran to the far corner of the newsroom, next to the large windows, where there was more open space. The deadline for the first edition had come and gone. They were holding the presses in New York. What was the last decade they had done that in? I felt the weight of the paper—perhaps the weight of a dozen massive Sunday papers—crushing me. I wriggled and hopped onto the estimable typewriter of Tad Szulc, the diplomatic correspondent.

I asked Juan Vasquez, a young copy boy, to hurry over. I couldn't touch type. It was typical of American reporters to hunt and peck. (While British reporters were required to know shorthand and German reporters had to know a foreign language, we weren't required to know anything. It would have likely been a First Amendment violation to require that we could actually type.)

Juan sat next to me in Tad's corner of the Bureau. He read the story hurriedly over the phone as I typed it, page by page, to New York.

They were still holding the presses.

I began to bat away at the machine:

An Army sergeant said tonight that he saw American soldiers gun down "women and children and old men" in a South Vietnam village last year.

Then, with sweat but no pause, a second sentence:

Sgt. Michael Bernhardt said the slayings were carried out by "most of the men" in his company—C Company of the First Battalion 20th Infantry, 11th Infantry Brigade.

I stopped after two paragraphs ("grafs"). I yanked the paper out and handed it rudely to Juan. Juan had an open phone line to Mike Kaufman on Rewrite in New York. Juan read, Mike typed at his end, and screamed, "Copy" after every two grafs. In Manhattan, a copy boy stood in front of Mike, and raced with each "book" of original and carbon-copy "dupes" the few steps to the National Desk, where some editor looked at it and dispatched it to the composing room to be set into type.

I finished my two-graf pages and, exhaling, banged out with battered fingers: *(endit)*. From Washington I imagined I could hear the presses begin to roll. The paper reached the press room doors and the trucks backed into bays on 43rd Street to pick them up, bundle after bundle, with the headline G.I. Says He Saw Vietnam Massacre.

Two things happened—one bad.

I realized I had omitted Sgt. Bernhardt's middle initial. The Times *always* used middle initials. I grabbed the phone on whoever's desk it was and called Bernhardt back.

"What's your middle initial?"

The phone rang on a Washington Bureau main line, and the only editor there—the night guy—transferred it to me. "Pick it up," he shouted across the room.

My shirt soaked, head spinning, I picked the phone up again.

"Great job!" Gene Roberts, the national editor, said.

I didn't say thanks.

"A," I said. "Gene, his middle initial is A."

Gene must have suppressed a laugh.

"A," I heard him yell the essential letter to the copy desk across from him.

My story ran in the first edition on page one.

But the first edition had a bad mistake. Bernhardt said he had *not* fired at the civilians at My Lai. The piece as printed had him saying he had. The second edition fixed that. It wasn't my mistake, but who could blame whoever made it? Some people—often historians—confuse the *Times* with history. It is not; it is journalism. You could tell: We typically didn't wear bowties, and we couldn't type.

I bought a bottle of Pilsner and headed home.

The next day the *Times* sent Joe Lelyveld, earlier a foreign correspondent, to interview Sergeant Bernhardt at Fort Dix for a magazine piece. The Foreign Desk hastened to telex Henry Kamm, a veteran foreign correspondent, a copy of the story in Bangkok. Henry left immediately and was able to find and interview survivors of the massacre.

The next day, I got this note from the publisher, Arthur O. "Punch" Sulzberger:

> *Dear Bob:*
> *I heard that you did the impossible in 50 minutes last night, and I want to congratulate you. It is a source of pride to me that The Times can get a story like yours on the Vietnam massacre, despite all the obstacles that were raised against you. Thank you for a very good job.*
> *Sincerely,*
> *Punch*

I was surprised.

Arthur, with the bearing of the ex-Marine captain he had been, wearing suspenders, and smoking long cigars. Arthur, for whose visits to the Washington Bureau every desktop in the entire newsroom had to be emptied and made to glisten. That Arthur had broken Times tradition and sent me a note before the first of the coming month.

My Mistake

I made a mistake in chasing the My Lai Massacre story after I had written the initial disclosure. I knew Hersh was flying all over—using his credit cards—to interview other members of the platoon. I thought that I had the advantage. The *Times* has a nationwide network of stringers—people who write stories for the paper on an as-needed basis.[51] I gave the list of other members of the platoon and their present location to the National Desk and asked that the editors assign stringers around the country to interview those soldiers.

The stringers failed miserably. Mostly, they couldn't—or didn't—find the soldiers.

When the stringers did manage to find them, the interviews were mostly bad. Hersh asked me why I had done this. I explained, and said, "Sy, I made a mistake."

The Peers Report

When I later learned that the Army's Lieutenant General William "Ray" Peers investigated the massacre at My Lai and prepared a twelve-chapter report about it, I was eager to get it. But, of course, it was classified. You could go to jail for having it, seeing it, talking about it—it was *classified*, like almost everything else worth knowing.

I went to the Capitol Hill office where a copy of the Peers report lay in the office safe. I just had to find a senator or member of Congress or staffer who would show it to me. Of course, that was a crime, for them—and for me. But didn't the public have a right to find out what the Army thought had happened at My Lai?

Eventually, I found a staffer who was not fond of the war. He said I could come and have a look. But how long would I be able to look? Would I be able to photocopy? To make notes? Nothing would be worse than being in the same room as the report and not being able to look at it.

Gene Roberts sent me—unbidden—a Minox ultra-mini camera. Isn't this what spies—real spies—did? I went to Capitol Hill, Minox in sports coat pocket. (This was before the era of metal detectors.)

I didn't get to use the Minox. The staffer just let me read the report and take notes while he stood there, without letting me use Xerox or Minox. The paper ran my Peers Report piece on the front page. Faced with a *fait accompli*, the Pentagon ultimately decided to make it public.

Why had the report been classified in the first place?

Bill Beecher, the paper's Pentagon correspondent, decided to cover that story. The Pentagon briefer set out the Defense Department's authorized version of the massacre. The American public learned what the Army knew: There had indeed been a massacre. But some congressional staffer risked job and jail to tell them, through me. And I risked jail if some federal prosecutor decided to ask me, in front of a grand jury, who had given me the information.

The circumstances resemble a game, but a game with real-world consequences. How, in America, could a young reporter put himself on the knife-edge of prosecution and prison just for trying to tell folks what they had every right to know? This is why government sources put papers on their desks (especially at the State Department) and then left their offices on the assumption you would read the documents. (They could honestly say—and you could say—they hadn't given the documents to you.)

The My Lai story was long and hard-hitting. New York was hanging on every word. The editors were beseeching me for more.

A Tussle Over a Vacation for Me, and a Presidential Pass for a Mass Murderer

When I broke the My Lai Massacre story, I chased it until I thought we had nearly all of the details, then packed to leave for a long-planned break in the Caribbean. (I almost never got to take vacations at the *Times*. When I left the first time, the paper owed me something like three or four months of accumulated vacation time.)

The paper again—this time in the form of the national editor and my pal, Gene Roberts—sought to intervene. "Bob," he insisted languidly but firmly in his North Carolina drawl, "You can't go now. You're my man on My Lai."

"Gene," I pleaded, or whined, "I have tickets and a hotel booked. And the story is in hand, and you have other people working on it."

"Boh-oh-oh-b," he insisted. "We'll pay for all that. Stay on the story."

Shades of what was to come. I enjoyed Dominica, I think it was. I never doubted that the *Times* Washington Bureau—with so many journalistic stars they formed a blinding galaxy—did not depend on little old me.

The outcome of My Lai did not square with naïveté. It did not even square with skepticism. Rank cynicism was called for. An official investigation led to war-crime charges against thirteen officers and enlisted men. Lieutenant William Laws Calley Jr. was the only one convicted. He was sentenced to life in prison, but served only three days. President

Nixon ordered Calley's sentence reduced, and he spent just three years under house arrest.

The lieutenant in charge gets three years under house arrest and then is pardoned? For being in command of a massacre of five hundred unarmed men, women, children and infants. . . .

Perhaps that is war. I don't know, because even though the Army trained me to kill and order others to, it did not send me to the battlefield. But:

Do you think the media stories about My Lai stopped, or even moderated, the massacre of civilians in war after its exposure?

Do you think Watergate made a systemic change? What journalism managed to do was depose, not alter. Look at what has happened in government since.

We have a whole generation of journalism students—perhaps two generations now—trying to unearth the next Watergate. That is not a bad thing, but will it lead to meaningful, even incremental, improvement? Think if those same students had gone on to make a breakthrough in medicine, or science, or astronomy, or cement fabrication, or fish-wrapping, or. . . .

Hersh

Sy Hersh had not been able to commodify Michael A. Bernhardt—or the massacre. But he called and told me I'd stolen the story from him.

News as a commodity. That made me angry. Hersh had the story and was sitting on it, and he had pledged this source—and presumably others—to silence. I broke the My Lai Massacre story at the same time he did. As a freelancer, he flew around the world on credit cards to get the story, and then worked frantically to sell it.

Is news a commodity? I asked him. You lock up your source and peddle the story to anyone who will buy it?

Analysis and opinion, I decided, belong to those egomaniacal enough to think they understand the stories they hear and that they can explain them. What I cared most about is what happened. The idea that a story can be an exclusive, that a journalist would swear a source to secrecy so that he could profit? That never seemed like the function of the press. Sy

Hersh was not just breaking the story first. He was putting the sources of the information in a Swiss vault.

He had an excuse. For a freelancer like Sy Hersh, locking up a source was an economic necessity. He had spent like an intoxicated speculator on chasing the story all over the country and then on finding a British newspaper that would publish it. He was paid no advance and no expenses. He was using his own funds to chase the stories, and he had to pay rent and buy food. So he was marketing the story wherever he could. If Ronald Ridenhour spoke to me, and I wrote the story, what would happen to the credit card debt?

I admire Sy Hersh, but he has had an unusual career. As Robert Miraldi wrote in *Seymour Hersh*:

> *Hersh and Rosenthal began to scream at each other—in Hersh's office, in Rosenthal's office, in the middle of the newsroom.*
>
> *"They fought all the time," Gelb said. Some fights were good-natured; some not, as Hersh would turn red-faced.*
>
> *He regularly called Rosenthal "motherfucker," but also said he was "the smartest cocksucker who ever walked into a newsroom."*
>
> *Hersh called the relationship "complicated" and said he did not really understand it, except to say, "any investigative reporter must eventually end up in total conflict with his editor—or he's not doing his job."*

Miraldi continued:

> *Rosenthal and Hersh were both similar oversized personalities. They could be crude and blunt, as well as charming. Both had big egos and huge ambitions; both came from immigrant Jewish families with modest backgrounds, and both held Pulitzer Prizes.*
>
> *Hersh came aboard the Times because Rosenthal needed a star investigative reporter to match up with Woodward and Bernstein. Hersh gave him that. But he also gave him a headache, all the time. . . .*
>
> *Reporter John Darnton remembers a meeting in New York during which Rosenthal asked his editors: who in the newsroom was trying to make the paper an advocate? Darnton described it as chilling; Rosenthal was trying to root out the liberals.*

But Darnton said Hersh was immune from such pressures. Abe would walk through the newsroom and, approvingly, pat Hersh on the head, saying, "Well, well, how is my little commie today?"[52]

In a way, it worked out well. Hersh broke the story first in London; I broke it in the United States. He collected his wages. I was told that people were wandering around the *Times* building in New York waiting for the next story.

Sometime after that, Max Frankel came to my desk to ask what I thought of Sy Hersh. He was thinking of hiring him. I had always admired Sy as an investigative reporter, and I battled with him for stories. But I also always saw him as an advocate, and in those days at least, I didn't think the *Times* was in the advocacy business. What's the difference between investigative journalism and advocacy journalism? One answer might be that both get you riled up, but they begin from different premises. Advocacy knows at all times where it's going; investigation does not.

So I told Max that.

He walked back to his office, and later that day, he hired Sy. If he had done that with Woodward. . . .

December 22, 1969

Dear Mr. Smith,

Your coverage of the Massacre at Songmy was superb. I can think of no better way in which to express our opinion of it than by enclosing a publisher's merit award check for $100.

Congratulations.

Sincerely,

Arthur Sulzberger

CHAPTER TWENTY

Almost Fired

Billy Beane: I'm not gonna fire you, Grady.
Grady Fuson: Fuck you, Billy.
Billy Beane: Now I will.

—*Moneyball*

WASHINGTON BUREAU, THE *NEW YORK TIMES*, 1970

I was nearly fired from the *Times* twice. I leave it to you, dear reader, to judge whether my misdeeds deserved the guillotine.

In June 1970, I wrote a piece about several congressmen who had allegedly taken bribes in connection with the construction of an underground garage at the US Capitol. A federal grand jury was sitting in Baltimore. The grand jury wanted to hand out what is called a presentment—an indictment that needed the signature of the US attorney in Maryland to become an indictment. The grand jury wanted to indict four representatives, one senator, and one former senator in connection with alleged corruption relating to the construction of the Rayburn House Office Building underground garage on Capitol Hill. An amazing story, no?

But John Mitchell was the attorney general of the United States, and he refused to let the US attorney in Baltimore sign the presentment and convert it to an indictment. I was given the presentment and wrote a story about the allegations and the attorney general's refusal. My story landed on the front page on a Sunday.

I kept the story alive on the front page of the *Times* for a few days, never imagining it might almost cost me my job—or later my ability to become an American lawyer and British barrister. It was a journalistically delicious piece because the *Times* was the only paper that had the presentment. Every other part of the media had to credit the *Times*.

One evening I came home to my tiny (even for a studio) DuPont Circle apartment, exhausted. The phone rang. It was Reston.

"I'm calling about the grand jury story," he said. His tone was businesslike.

I said, "Yes."

"Where did you get the story?" Reston asked.

Keenly aware of promises made, I said, "Scotty, I can't tell you that. I promised not to disclose the source."

Reston answered immediately, with controlled heat:

"I was talking with Lloyd Cutler, and he said that this is quite serious. And it is on the front page of the *New York Times*."

Cutler was a powerful Washington attorney who later served as an advisor to President Carter.

"The reporting is accurate," I told Reston.

"That's obvious," Reston said. "And that's part of the problem."

Figuring what the hell, I asked what Lloyd Cutler, another one of the pantheon of Washington poohbahs, had to do with it.

Cutler was right: Tampering with a grand jury, speaking to grand jurors, interfering with justice, having grand jury documents—these can be crimes. As yet unburdened by knowledge of the law, I didn't know this.

Fired? I could have been prosecuted and landed in a small cell for a long time.

CHAPTER TWENTY-ONE

What Do You Mean, "Do You Have a Lawyer?" Not Jailed . . . and Not Fired: Justice Delayed Is Just Fine

Justice?—You get justice in the next world. In this one you have the law.

—WILLIAM GADDIS, *A FROLIC OF HIS OWN*

WASHINGTON BUREAU, THE *NEW YORK TIMES*, 1970

Having a secret grand jury document in my possession may have been technically illegal, and Reston was speaking from fear. (I did wonder why Reston had consulted Cutler rather than the *Times* general counsel, Jim Goodale—his own lawyer.) Still, I insisted I couldn't reveal my source, and Reston told me that was a bad decision. I was inwardly quaking when I said, "It may be, but it's my judgment. I can't betray my source." I felt every inch a Boy Scout, but a Boy Scout about to be led to ritual slaughter—or wherever bad Scouts end up.

Reston hung up. I sat down on one of the few pieces of furniture in my apartment. I had to think about what had just happened. The phone rang again. This time it was Gene Roberts, the national editor. I told him I'd just gotten off the phone with Reston.

"I know," Gene said.

"He asked who my source was, and I told him I couldn't tell him."

Gene said he had only one question for me: "If they put the US attorney for Maryland on the stand and asked if the story was true, what would he say?"

"If he was telling the truth," I said, "he would say it's true."

Whereas Reston was concerned about whether my story was lawful, Gene was concerned about whether it was true. The paper continued to run the story. I felt entitled to *two* bars of Bit-O-Honey—and hastened to buy them before I was fired and could no longer afford them.

But for me the story didn't end there.

A few days later, on an early Saturday afternoon, I was virtually alone in the Bureau, a place that always felt like the setting for a shop class in an elementary school: tough metal desks, partial white wall dividers, concrete supporting pillars, multi-color accessories (like absurdly heavy metal ashtrays), and a low water fountain. I was sitting at my desk across from the news desk when I heard the elevator ding. A man in a blue business suit walked a few steps into the newsroom. He looked at the editor sitting at the news desk, then at me.

I asked whether I could help him, but he just put some papers on a ledge close to him, near the entrance to the newsroom, and said, "I'm leaving these here." He tapped the papers, turned, and ran for the elevator. It dinged again, and in less than a minute he was gone.

I approached the papers skeptically. I thought they were probably some sort of news release, though I couldn't imagine who would leave a news release on Saturday afternoon in those days. I looked at the papers. They forbiddingly announced they were a restraining order from the US District Court in Baltimore preventing the *Times* from printing the story on Mitchell. The document had a signature block that was not actually signed by the judge, Roszel C. Thomsen. It bore only a typed signature. Were the papers valid? Were they authorized by the judge? Or had they only been delivered by politicians named in the presentment, or their lawyers, to keep the *Times* from printing the story?

In my dunder-headed innocence, what did I do? The very worst thing. I picked up the phone on my desk and called Judge Thomsen's home in Baltimore. His wife answered. I explained who I was and asked whether the judge was around. She said yes and went to get him. When the judge came on the line, I explained that the papers had just arrived but—while they did have a typed name—there was no signature. In all my naïve seriousness I asked, "Did you sign them?"

I'm sure the judge was as surprised as he had ever been in his legal career, but he thought for just a second and said, "Yes." Then he added, "Do you have an attorney?"

I told him I didn't, but I was sure the *Times* did. The judge said, "I suggest you consult with him."

I did not. Nor, immediately, I guess, did anyone else at the paper. Journalists' ovens are fast; they bake tortillas, or maybe matzo, while judges' ovens cook slowly, generally set to roast, not barbecue. Instead of consulting a lawyer, what I did was increase any possible jail time I might have to serve. I immediately added an insert on page one in the story, describing how the *Times* had been served with the temporary restraining order—thus implying we were ignoring it, or you wouldn't be reading this story.

Judge Thomsen did not have a reputation for being easy, or especially flexible, but he was getting old and nearing retirement. He ultimately referred the matter to the Maryland and Baltimore Bar Associations for an opinion as to what should be done. When they released their opinion, they concluded, with—I must say—excellent legal judgment, that there was nothing at that point that would be gained by taking action against the *Times* or me. The judge agreed. Not much later he took semi-retirement.

Why was I not punished by the court, or fired by the *Times*?

Since the *Times* had already printed the facts, there was no longer anything for the courts to prevent. There could only be punishment. I suppose that might have been a warning for foolhardy but intrepid reporters and publishers in a pickle: Run the story and risk marshals at the door.

Short of being jailed, I could have been indicted, charged, even had a criminal record. That record would not have been viewed with favor by the admissions folks at Yale Law School a few years later. Or by the barristers of the Inner Temple in London after that.

Firing me would have been awkward for the *Times*, since what I was writing was incontestably true.

Think about what the story disclosed. Put it in the context of some other country, say Poland: Suppose you had an independent panel of citizens who wanted to indict a number of members of the Polish parliament but were prevented from doing so by the Polish attorney general. Of course, to make matters even more plain, the American attorney general, John Mitchell, the subject of my story, was subsequently indicted for other crimes and went to prison.

The question is: Was the law best served by the *Times* printing the piece or not? Was justice best served?

CHAPTER TWENTY-TWO

Almost Fired Again: Buck Rogers Badges Prove Dangerous

Soldiers win battles and generals get the medals.
——Napoleon Bonaparte

The number of medals on an officer's breast varies in inverse proportion to the square of the distance of his duty from the front line.
——Charles Montague, 1867–1928

WASHINGTON BUREAU, THE *NEW YORK TIMES*, 1970

The second time I got into hot—actually, boiling—water was during the Vietnam War, in November 1970, when I went to Fort Rucker, Alabama. I went because the soldiers who were dying disproportionately in the war were infantry platoon leaders and helicopter pilots. The first were usually lieutenants and the second warrant officers, and I wanted to talk to the warrant officers about their assignments in Vietnam, and about the war in general. The average life expectancy of a Marine Corps lieutenant in Vietnam was two months. During this time, I was an infantry lieutenant in the Army Reserve[53] and could have been called up for Vietnam to be among those slated for death—either shot by the enemy or "fragged" by my own men.[54]

For helicopter pilots, the casualty rate was unspeakable—about half of them were shot down. I thought the "home" of Army helicopter training and pilots, Fort Rucker in the Wiregrass Country of Alabama, might provide firsthand insight into the war.

I was surprised.

I wandered the base, interviewing helicopter pilots. I was about their age, maybe a little older. They had been to hell and back. And what they complained of was—not hell. It was the injustice, not of dying for a war they didn't understand, not of a draft by the accident of lottery, not of setting the 'copter down for one more wounded comrade.

It was the medals!

In the interviews at the camp, I learned that, although warrant officers were often in mortal danger, they weren't getting a lot of medals. At least, they thought they weren't. On the other hand, they told me that a general flying twenty thousand feet over the battlefield would receive a medal for hazardous duty. So, the warrant officers had begun to refer to Vietnam medals as "Buck Rogers badges."

The warrant officers cursed a system that dished out medals that ought to mean something on the basis of rank—not on performance or bravery. An unfair system of recognition for those regularly risking death was not a matter for silence. They had plenty to say, because they were—morally and militarily—seared by a corrupt system that rewarded status rather than sacrifice. This was a mighty grudge, an affront to fallen comrades, and an unnecessary insult on top of daily peril. Their anger came from their hearts, and their unconstrained, emotional language came from the barrack and bivouac, not the military bureaucracy.

One of the warrant officers used a profane or, at least, less-than-polite expression to describe the badges, and I quoted him. I used his language—something along the lines of "These sons of . . . get the medals."

Whatever naughty word he had used seemed understated, not objectionable. It did cross my mind that the quote might jangle the breakfast cutlery, but only for an instant. I was not seeking to provoke. I was just trying to convey what these guys were voicing. It was simple: War is hell, but medals should go to those who earn them.

I flew back to Washington. When I was back in my apartment, Phelps called.

"You're going to get a call from the executive editor. He is going to bawl you out."

Sure enough, the phone rang seconds later. It was Abe Rosenthal. He was angry.

"How could you try to put that language in the *New York Times*?" he practically shouted.

Almost fired for refusing to disclose the source of the pre-indictment to Scotty Reston? And now, for trying to sneak an obscenity into a *Times* news story? Ah, for the day, or rather night, when I could write copy about the woman locked in the bank, hand the copy to the compositor, and wait for the wet paper to come up.

I stood there, gripping the phone.

I didn't understand what he was talking about and asked him. He continued shouting, quoting the language he found offensive in my story. I used truth as an excuse.

"Abe, that's what the pilot said . . . Exactly."

He was not mollified, or calmed.

"We make selections of quotes all the time," he said.

And he got to the point he wanted to make.

"When the decision is made to put that sort of language in the *New York Times*, I'll make it." Why did he keep using the full name of the paper we both worked for?

I responded in my hopelessly naïve way.

"Abe, I think you're overreacting."

One of the good things about being a reporter is you can call your boss by his or her first name. The bad thing is that you sometimes get bosses like Abe.

"Don't characterize my reaction," he snapped.

But, undeterred, I went on.

"Look, I'm sitting down here in Washington. The piece had to be reviewed by the guy on the News Desk in the Washington Bureau and the news editor in Washington. Then it had to be read by the slot man on the National Desk and the editor on the National Desk in New York. Then it had to be read by an assistant national editor and the national editor."

With the boldness of youth, I continued:

"Abe, how could I possibly sneak that, or anything else, into the paper?"

He hung up, and I understood I had made yet another friend in high places. In my naïveté, it had not crossed my mind that I would bump into the rank insecurity of an executive editor who saw my desire to convey the pilots' angry and betrayed disillusionment as something else. He saw it as an unblinking challenge, not to the military, not to generals, not even to the secretary of defense, but to his own power, authority, and control over every word written in his domain. Insecurity had driven him to the top. Insecurity fueled paranoia. It didn't provide me with bureaucratic savvy.

It's true: I probably should have known better. But this wasn't about my disdain for authority—or for the "pallid clerks who control your destiny," as David Halberstam called them.[55] It wasn't even my own insecurity. Ironically, it's what likely made me a good investigative reporter: naïveté, coupled with a desire to pass on what I had heard. To tell my colleagues their place in the Washington salary hierarchy.

And just a bit later, to negotiate like "a son of a bitch" with the folks who ran the joint for the right of a reporter not to have a byline stay on an article that editors had distorted.

CHAPTER TWENTY-THREE

Recruiting: Make 'Em Conservative

In the U.K. we have always had a partisan press that people enjoy and have become acclimatized to. Hyperpartisan news has always been part of our audience's culture—and we do it better in some ways than fake news.

—CHARLIE BECKETT, PROFESSOR OF JOURNALISM
AT THE LONDON SCHOOL OF ECONOMICS

Look at The New York Times *in 1960 vs. 2010. The reportage is more interpretive. . . . One reader's analysis is another reader's opinion. Sixty percent of those surveyed by the Pew Research Center in 2009 believed reporting was politically biased.*

—PROF. JAMES L. BAUGHMAN, UNIVERSITY OF WISCONSIN-
MADISON SCHOOL OF JOURNALISM
AND MASS COMMUNICATION

WASHINGTON BUREAU, THE *NEW YORK TIMES*, 1970

You may think that the *Times* cares not a fig about the political views of its reporters. Not so. And the fact that it does led me into a blunder—a blunder embarrassing to me and to the *Times*.

In May 1970, Bob Phelps approached me at my small metal desk in the Washington Bureau. The Bureau looked like a classroom with its primary colors, rows of desks, water fountain, and cork bulletin board. It was on the top floor of the American Railroads Building at 1920 L Street NW.

Phelps was largely silent. He spent words as if they were doubloons. He was a little less silent when, tilted back in his chair, he negotiated with

New York about space in the paper for the day's Washington news. As the Bureau's news editor, he was unflappable in a job that needed him to be. He was the stone on the grinding mill between New York editors and the Bureau.

"I want you to do something," he told me.

"Yes?"

"New York is looking for a conservative reporter."

I stared at him, but he went on.

"They want a reporter who is politically conservative."

So, I asked how to find one.

"You went to Harvard. Try looking there."

I was sure he was kidding. But I took a break from what I was doing and picked up the phone. I called the *Harvard Crimson*, the student newspaper, and asked for the editor-in-chief.

I don't remember the editor's name, but I explained I was an alumnus of Harvard and a correspondent in the Washington Bureau of the *Times*. I came right to the point.

"*Conservative* reporter?" he asked incredulously. He said no one came to mind, and that was the end of our conversation. But it wasn't the end of the story.

The next day the *Crimson* came out with a story about the search by the *New York Times* for a *conservative* reporter. It noted that it was Phelps doing the looking and my doing the asking.

> *Robert Smith, a* Times *reporter, was discussing the terms of the summer job cordially with one student, until he discovered that the student did not have the political qualifications demanded for the job.*
>
> *He had deliberately asked to interview a "Nixon-conservative" for the post.*
>
> *"This post is new and this is what Phelps [Robert Phelps, Smith's superior in the* Times *Washington Bureau] wants," he said. . . .*
>
> *"What Phelps wants is cross-pollination," Smith said. "After all, we're all a bunch of liberals down here, and this is what the administration has been complaining about all along. . . ."*[56]

When I read the story, I expected a problem; the paper that supposedly didn't slant the news for ideological reasons had been caught out trying to hire reporters with partisan views. I thought the *Crimson* piece would cause a typhoon, but the typhoon did not materialize. Nobody even seemed to notice. Ironically, the hyper-vigilant press did not find it significant that the *Times* was recruiting reporters based on their political ideology. Phelps did tell me about the *Crimson* piece but without comment. As always, he betrayed no emotion.

Despite the widespread belief that reporters' ideologies, perspectives, preferences don't matter, they mattered plenty. The paper's focus was not on unalloyed purity but on getting enough alloys into the mix.

Some people its reporters covered were aware of the *Times's* biases. Indeed, some tried to take advantage openly, reflexively, even innocently, of those biases. One instance that made this clear to me was when I said something mildly probing to Ralph Nader, the prominent activist, for a piece about one of his projects, and he lashed out—accused me of "helping the enemy."

Whose enemy was he talking about? What side was I supposed to be on?

In part to combat my own biases, I made it a point of trying to give fair coverage to those who held more conservative views than I did. For example, I knew the history of the House Un-American Activities Committee and McCarthyism.[57] A minor-league successor to HUAC popped up in 1970. It presented me with a quandary. I was aware of the journalistic treatment of McCarthy. But weren't these people entitled to coverage—fair coverage? I agonized and did a short piece.[58]

When my story ran, these folks must have gone into near-fatal paroxysms of amazement that the *Times* had covered them. Maybe they were fatal, because the committee seemed to disappear.

Like reporters, editors are constantly choosing among competing materials—and a lot of them. They have to choose what stories to cover, which quotes within interviews to use, and finally, what stories to print. When a reporter interviews somebody, the reporter selects the fragments to use. If an interviewee is deliberately brief, for example, concentrating on providing a soundbite, how should the reporter present that and provide context? Editors have to decide also where to place each story—what belongs on the front page? What belongs on the right side (the more important side)?

Every late afternoon on the floor of the *Times* conference room in Manhattan, a group of serious, purposeful people from the various news departments gathered for the solemn occasion of deciding what would be on the front page of the paper the next day. Think of judgment day taking place within the cathedral at Chartres. Their decisions—the "frontings"—were then sent to all media subscribers to the *Times* News Service around the world. The frontings offered their guidance as to what the *Times* thought was important. Editors and reporters nearly everywhere still read the paper, and listeners hear on NPR, for example, stories lifted from that front page. To a large extent, it remains the world's source of news, or the selection of what is journalistically important.

I wonder whether there is anyone past middle school age who does not believe that the biases of reporters routinely tinge their work. As Abe Rosenthal once told me so clearly, a reporter's bias dictates what he or she will choose to write about, whom to interview, and what quotes to use.

CHAPTER TWENTY-FOUR

The Spooks Aren't Talking to One Another (But Some of Them Whisper to Me); the *Times* Attends Germ Warfare Meetings

It seemed to him that the road was thick with spies. Conscious of being continually shadowed, he hid himself behind haystacks, under hedges, and in plantations away from beaten tracks.
—WHEN ROGUES FALL OUT: A ROMANCE OF OLD LONDON
BY JOSEPH HATTON (1899)

WASHINGTON BUREAU, THE *NEW YORK TIMES*, 1970

I loved the poster that advertised the *Times* in my day. The executive editor hated it. The poster was by Edward Sorel. It depicted in a splashy wash of light blue a guy with a Press card tucked into the band of his hat crouching under a table. Three men sat in heated discussion around the table above him. The reporter was scribbling wildly. The poster was large enough to be placed on the sides of *New York Times* trucks—and that was where it was supposed to go. Until Abraham Michael Rosenthal banned it. He thought it portrayed *Times* journalism as unethical.

Sorel was a caricaturist, for Pete's sake, but Abe Rosenthal was not known for his affection for caricature. Whatever cartoons the *Times* might print in its Op-Ed section, it had little interest in comics—a lamentable lapse, and not one Rosenthal was likely to repair.

Unhappily for Rosenthal, one of the most famous pieces connected with him proved him badly in error. He had gotten the tip, assigned the story, and, ultimately, supervised the piece on the 1964 murder of Kitty

Genovese, a Queens woman whose screams the *Times* reported had been ignored by more than three dozen neighbors while her killer attacked her repeatedly for more than half an hour.

That article garnered a lot of attention, and in 1964 Rosenthal wrote a book about the attack called *Thirty-Eight Witnesses*. In 2015, Genovese's younger brother, Bill, said that the police had in fact been called—twice—but had not responded, because they believed the attack was a domestic dispute. He blamed the *New York Times* for bad reporting.

More than fifty years after Rosenthal's reporting—in 2016—the *Times* agreed with him. Shame-faced, the paper called the story "flawed":

> *While there was no question that the attack occurred, and that some neighbors ignored cries for help, the portrayal of 38 witnesses as fully aware and unresponsive was erroneous. The article grossly exaggerated the number of witnesses and what they had perceived.*
>
> *None saw the attack in its entirety. Only a few had glimpsed parts of it, or recognized the cries for help. Many thought they had heard lovers or drunks quarreling. There were two attacks, not three.*
>
> *And afterward, two people did call the police. A 70-year-old woman ventured out and cradled the dying victim in her arms until they arrived.*[59]

The correction came a decade after Rosenthal's death.

Let me be clear: I never hid under a table (although the *Times* did outfit me with a miniature camera). Sources and documents were my default method.[60]

I once got solid information from a source about biological weapons being made and tested at Pine Bluff Arsenal in Arkansas. I called the public information staff at the arsenal and asked for photos of the "igloos" in which the toxic material was stored. The arsenal obliged and mailed me photos, right away. In a way, I couldn't believe it. They sent me photos of igloos with poisonous biological agents.

I asked in plain sight, got the material in plain sight, from people who identified themselves.

There was a Protocol for the Prohibition of the Use in War of Asphyxiating, Poisonous or other Gases and of Bacteriological Methods of Warfare. This "Geneva Protocol" was signed in Switzerland in 1925. It banned the use of chemical and biological weapons (CBW) in international wars, but did not forbid possession or development of chemical and biological weapons.

An inter-agency group was hashing out—or trying to—US policy on germ warfare. I was closely following the group's secret wrangling. After one of my stories had run in the paper, the group had another meeting. Someone asked a Pentagon general for his views. My source told me the general replied, "I'm not going to say. I'll just read about it in the *New York Times*."

When I began to dig into the then-uncovered area of CBW, I bumped into reporting by Seymour Myron Hersh. Sy turned out to be a recurring presence in my life, like a large, occasionally clanging bell. He was both a no-holds-barred competitor saturated with combative energy, and, later, a supportive colleague. With prominent, dark-framed glasses, Sy was a bulky, but not fat, tennis player. He was always aware, scanning the near horizon, and more than fiercely intense.

When the paper hired him, Sy sat three yards from me. On one occasion, when he asked to speak to a government official, a secretary told him the official was tied up. I chortled when Sy suggested to the secretary, *ad alta voce*, "You'd better get a knife and cut him loose!"

I couldn't hear what the secretary said.

CHAPTER TWENTY-FIVE

Shame Comes to a Kid from Roxbury

One is never so dangerous when one has no shame . . . when one has grown too old to blush.

—MARQUIS DE SADE

Shame is a soul-eating emotion.

—C. G. JUNG

WASHINGTON BUREAU, THE *NEW YORK TIMES*, 1971

In October 1971, I was covering a conference for the *Times* on civil liberties. The conference began on a clear, comfortable Friday morning at Princeton. One of the speakers was Lillian Hellman, who was known for her left-wing sympathies and political activism. Among other things, she had written the anti-fascist *Watch on the Rhine* (1941) and *The Searching Wind* (1944).[61] In 1952 Hellman was called to testify before HUAC. It had heard she attended Communist Party meetings in 1937.

Ms. Hellman wrote a letter to HUAC. It said that she was willing to testify about herself and that she did not want to claim her rights under the Fifth Amendment:

I am most willing to answer all questions about myself. I have nothing to hide from your committee and there is nothing in my life of which I am ashamed.

But she went on:

But I am advised by counsel that if I answer the committee's questions about myself, I must also answer questions about other people.

107

I am not willing . . . to bring bad trouble to people who, in my past association with them, were completely innocent of any talk or any action that was disloyal or subversive. To hurt innocent people whom I knew many years ago in order to save myself is, to me, inhuman and indecent and dishonorable. I cannot and will not cut my conscience to fit this year's fashions.[62]

In May 1952, she did testify before HUAC. She answered preliminary questions about her background, but she refused to respond to questions about a specific meeting, claiming her rights under the Fifth Amendment. She referred the committee to her letter and answered only one other question. She said she had not belonged to the Communist Party.

Hellman was blacklisted after her appearance before the HUAC. Although she continued to work on Broadway in the 1950s, the blacklisting caused a drop in her income. Many praised her for refusing to answer questions, but others believed—despite her denial—that she had belonged to the Communist Party.

I did not know this detailed background while I was covering the Princeton conference. I knew her only as an accomplished playwright. I filed my story about the discussion of civil liberties at the conference. A short while later, I got a call from an editor on the National Desk in New York. He instructed me to ask Ms. Hellman if she was a Communist.

"Are you kidding?" I asked him, but he wasn't. I was shaken by the instruction. Don't misunderstand, I was not shy about asking questions. I had, after all, once asked Werner Erhard, the founder of the allegedly transformative motivational course EST, whether it was true he had been an auto salesman. (He had.)[63]

But this was different. I assumed—in addition to being humiliated—I might be castigated by a great playwright if I asked the question. Mortified and petrified, I approached. I told her who I was, and asked the question.

"No," she said, without even a minor pause or hint of objection or resentment. I was nonplussed. This woman was far more than generous, far more than tolerant.

I backed away awkwardly, as if I had been speaking with the Queen of England. I called the *Times* "dictating room" for the filing of stories and inserted into my story:

Asked if she had been a Communist, Ms. Hellman said, "No."

There were moments, I had learned over the years, when I would feel awkward, embarrassed, even shamed by what I had to do as a reporter. The question to Hellman was the worst.

It was far worse than wearing cowboy boots into the Oval Office to meet with the president at an impromptu news conference.

It was far worse than being deliberately introduced to a voluptuous former topless dancer who had run clubs in the Vietnam War theater—with Senate staffers standing around to see how I would react. (I turned raspberry-red.)

It was even worse than something else that produced shame: asking parents for photos of their child who had been killed in an auto accident when they did not yet know of the death.

A photo of a teenager who has just been killed in an automobile crash may not seem important. But when I was young and a reporter in Boston, it was important. It might prove to be an *exclusive* front-page magnet for readers on the run. Reporters were sent to the homes of victims to get a photo from the parents.

I had to visit parents to ask for a photo just once—in Boston for the *Herald.* They did not yet know that an auto accident had taken their child. How to ask for a photo, when I showed up at their door, without telling them about the accident? Journalism school did not teach this.

Their phone rang as I entered. They got the dreadful news. I waited, then asked whether they would like their child's photo in the paper. They said they would. I left the grief-shrouded room, photo in my pocket, still in its frame. I began to understand why some journalists keep—at least used to keep—strong drink within reach.

Put yourself in my muddy, worn loafers. In one sense, this was my exposure to the sad heart of the world.

But it was not respectful—not even to the reader. Also not respectful was sitting next to the corporal at Massachusetts State Police dispatch and eavesdropping—not even knowing what I was trying to hear, what was newsworthy. I was bawled out by the angry corporal, whose personal territory began at the threshold of his open office door—where, he made clear, my right to know ended.

What's the greater shame? Asking parents whose child has died in an automobile accident for a photo for a circulation-driven daily before they even know about the accident, or asking Lillian Hellman for the *New York Times* whether—after all these years and so much painful ignominy—she had been a Communist? The Hellman episode made other embarrassments feel minor. Was I working for the *National Enquirer*?

Perhaps Scotty Reston summed it up in his memoir:

"We deliver a commodity every day like the mail, and . . . like the mail, a lot of what we deliver is junk."[64]

CHAPTER TWENTY-SIX

Why Am I Chasing Daniel Ellsberg? G-Men Are Everywhere They're Not Supposed to Be, and "Mr. Green" Offers Help

Life is full of strange absurdities, which, strangely enough, do not even need to appear plausible, since they are true.
—Luigi Pirandello, *Six Characters in Search of an Author*

You can either read the New York Times *or work for it.*
—E. W. (Ned) Kenworthy, Washington
correspondent for the *New York Times*

U.S. journalists are still not protected by a federal "shield law" guaranteeing their right not to reveal their sources. . . .
—Reporters Sans Frontières [The group—Reporters
Without Borders—ranked the United States #45 in
the world for freedom of the press in 2020.
Norway was #1, France #34.]

WASHINGTON BUREAU, THE *NEW YORK TIMES*, 1971

I was standing next to a Harvard Law School faculty office building throwing pebbles at Professor Charles Rothwell Nesson's window. Nesson was a bit of an odd academic. If he was in the office, he may not have minded the pebbles.

A story in the *Harvard Crimson* reported:

It is 6:30 in the morning as . . . Nesson '60 takes a set of keys out of his pocket to unlock the gates to the Mount Auburn Cemetery. The key to the gate, he says, was given to him by the cemetery so that he could enjoy his morning walk before the cemetery opens to the public . . .

"This place is an arboretum, a bird sanctuary," he continues. "I get up to honor the sun, to feel at one. I feel at one with anyone who feels blessed by the morning."[65]

The solitary morning walks, like so many things Nesson did, had an air of eccentricity. He even caused the occasional controversy. It made national news, for example, when he told the *Harvard Law Record* that he smoked marijuana regularly during these strolls before class.

And there I was, a gentleman from the *Times*, a reporter who had graduated from Harvard, throwing pebbles at Nesson's window to get his attention. I had wound up there on a tip from the FBI. As bizarre as it sounds, the *Times* assigned me to find out who had leaked the Pentagon Papers to Neil Sheehan, my colleague in the Washington Bureau. The Pentagon Papers were a history of US-Vietnam relations from 1945 to 1967.

In 1967, during the Vietnam War, Secretary of Defense Robert McNamara assigned subordinates to compile a history of US-Vietnam relations. The history ran to seven thousand pages in forty-seven volumes and disclosed a record of US involvement in Asia that the government had sought to hide from the American public. The Papers told of massacres and political meddling, and contradicted government assurances that the war was wrapping up.

I had been told who had leaked the papers to Neil. As we all now know, it was Daniel Ellsberg. And Ellsberg was a former State Department employee who got a copy of the confidential report in 1971 and tried to give it to members of the US Senate.

When I found out, the editors told me to go further: They assigned me to find and interview Ellsberg.

Of course, Neil could talk to Ellsberg any time he wanted to. Neil got the leak for the *Times*. His history with the paper was solid. He'd reported well from Vietnam, and that landed him the job. Neil had recognized that the Vietnamese regarded their struggle as a war of national liberation from foreign occupation. His reporting made him unpopular with the Pentagon and the State Department, but like David Halberstam's reporting, Sheehan's made an impact on public opinion back home.

So Sheehan knew who had given him the Pentagon Papers. Why ask me to find out?

That's what I wanted Phelps to explain. Everybody else, Phelps told me, was trying to find out who the source was, and Phelps thought we should try too.

I had to wonder why he didn't just assign me to find Howard Hughes, the billionaire businessman and movie producer who had gone missing (as Gene Roberts later did). Or better still, assign me to find sunken pirate treasure in the Caribbean where I could swig Planter's Punches beneath the setting sun.

I narrowed my list of likely suspects to half a dozen within twenty minutes. One of the half-dozen was Daniel Ellsberg. I called him. Naturally, he took a call from the *Times*.

"Mr. Ellsberg, you were Neil's source, right?"

There was a pause. Then he said with equal straightforwardness:

"You know you're doing the FBI's work for them, don't you?"

Then, quite appropriately, he hung up.

I walked to the News Desk and told Phelps I had found the leaker.

He paused for a moment and then said, "Go find him and interview him."

I walked to a phone booth on Nineteenth Street NW. Using a phone at the Bureau would have gotten Mr. Green, my FBI guy, in trouble since I knew the FBI was monitoring our phones. Mr. Green told me the FBI even had a *Times* employee in our telex room on their payroll. (I told Max Frankel about this, but suggested we do nothing about it, because the FBI could always insert another telex spy if it wanted to.)

Standing in front of the pay phone, I told Mr. Green my problem.

"Know where he is?" I asked, all innocence.

"Cambridge," he said.

He went on to tell me the FBI was trying to pinpoint where.

"Why don't you go to Cambridge and call me from your hotel. Use this number, and ask for Mr. Green."

When I called Mr. Green from Cambridge, they still hadn't found Ellsberg. But I thought I had an advantage the FBI didn't since I could talk to his lawyer—if he'd talk to me. I'd been trying to do that, but Professor Nesson wouldn't take my calls. So I tossed pebbles against his window. No one summoned the Harvard police. On the other hand, Nesson didn't invite me in for sherry, or even for a stroll in the cemetery.

I understood that neither Ellsberg nor Sheehan nor anyone else at the paper was going to help me. I had to think about where to turn. I thought about who else was looking for the guy. It was the FBI.

For a Washington reporter, this was a personal challenge. I would leave the Washington Bureau of the *Times* for the un-bugged privacy of a phone booth. I'd even carry a Minox to congressional offices. I'd hand-carry "hot" copy to New York instead of using the Bureau's "penetrated" telex room. I'd meet with FBI sources in closed hotels and use phony names (like Mr. Green) when calling them on the phone. And that is why, when the *Times* printed the Pentagon Papers, Neil Sheehan took refuge in a hotel room in Manhattan.

When I was chasing Ellsberg, I was asked by Neil's upmarket Washington counsel to sign a paper.

I went to the law firm's oak-and-leather offices. An associate greeted me. He was young, bespectacled, pinstriped, and ever so earnest. He handed me a single piece of paper. The paper announced it was an affidavit.[66]

It proclaimed soberly:

Robert M. Smith, being duly sworn, deposes and says:

1. I am a reporter employed by The New York Times *engaged in writing articles on matters of military, national or international affairs that are published in* The Times.

2. In such occupation, I have written articles which contained information, received from government sources, which I had reason to believe or suspect was classified.

3. It is not an uncommon practice for government personnel to make such classified information available to reporters.

Signed: _____

Date: June 17, 1971

I read it carefully.

Then I asked uncertainly:

"This says that I have gotten *classified material from government sources.* Will I get in trouble?"

"No," he said blandly.

No? I was not yet a lawyer at that point in my life, but I wondered what I might be doing. The government was going after the *Times* for exactly what I was confessing to.

The young lawyer gave me the wrong answer, I think.

And I'm not clear about the ethics of the situation.

The result might just as well have been: Save Neil; toss Bob to the Feds.

I think I could have been dropping myself into a very hot bouillabaisse.

But, thus counseled, I signed.

In this bizarre world, what—at the end of the day—is the real test: Whether Americans were put in physical danger by the "leak"?

If that is the test, why is everything short of that classified in the first place?

Unhappily, I came to be on the other side of this fence. I am shamefaced to recount that I—yes, *I*—caused an inquiry into a leak. Before I explain how that happened, here is how, in an affidavit like mine in the Pentagon Papers case, Frankel explained the grotesque system of government leaks:

> *The Government's unprecedented challenge to The Times in the case of the Pentagon papers, I am convinced, cannot be understood . . . without an appreciation of the manner in which a small and specialized corps of reporters and a few hundred American officials regularly make use of so-called classified . . . information. . . . It is a cooperative, competitive, antagonistic and arcane relationship.*

. . . That is one reason why the sudden complaint by one party to these regular dealings strikes us as monstrous and hypocritical . . .

The governmental, political and personal interests of the participants are inseparable in this process.

Presidents make "secret" decisions only to reveal them for the purposes of frightening an adversary nation, wooing a friendly electorate, protecting their reputations.

The military services conduct "secret" research in weaponry only to reveal it for the purpose of enhancing their budgets, appearing superior or inferior to a foreign army, gaining the vote of a congressman or the favor of a contractor. . . .

High officials of the Government reveal secrets in the search for support of their policies, or to help sabotage the plans and policies of rival departments.

Middle-rank officials of government reveal secrets so as to attract the attention of their superiors or to lobby against the orders of those superiors. . . .

This is the coin of our business and of the officials with whom we regularly deal. . . .[67]

Max should have said some of the officials with whom we regularly deal.

The FBI was watching—carefully. They certainly watched the Justice Department building, where their high command was. I managed to get a copy of my FBI file through the Freedom of Information Act during the brief stint of a relatively open-minded director. And I found out they were watching me, carefully.

Dear Mr. Smith,

It is a pleasure for me to enclose a publisher's merit award check for $200 for the splendid job you did on the stories on the Pentagon for the papers of March 2 and 14.

Congratulations.

Sincerely,

Arthur Sulzberger

CHAPTER TWENTY-SEVEN

The Mafia and Me

The death of former Mafia overlord Joe Bonanno in Tucson . . . was a postscript to the story of the . . . mob in Arizona, a state that Mafiosi historically viewed as a place to retire, hide out or cool off. . . .
"Arizona has always been what the mob considered open territory," said George Weisz, a former organized crime intelligence agent. . . . Bonanno was 97 when he died of natural causes. He had lived in Tucson quietly for more than 30 years after he retired.
—"MOBSTERS NEVER DID CONTROL ARIZONA"
BY CHARLES KELLY, *ARIZONA REPUBLIC*

WASHINGTON BUREAU, THE *NEW YORK TIMES*, 1971

Sources and documents led me to the story of a vicious spat between the FBI and the CIA in the fall of 1971. When I say I had a senior source at the FBI, please trust me: I had a senior source. But I'm still not going to say who it was, other than that J. Edgar Hoover, Director of the Bureau, had complete confidence in him.

My source thought Hoover was no longer fit for the job of running the FBI. Among other things, he thought Hoover was irrational, paranoid, self-aggrandizing, manipulative in the extreme, and a threat to democracy. My source and I developed a working relationship—a wary one on my side—but he showed me documents and provided me with accurate information. I think he may have wanted to provide me with more information than I took.

For example, there was The Willard Caper. The Willard was a proud, old, run-down (now restored) Washington hotel. The hotel brags that some of its notable guests have included Charles Dickens, Buffalo Bill, P. T. Barnum, and Mark Twain.

I never stayed at The Willard, but one day, I was summoned there by "Mr. Green." Mr. Green did not tell me what I've learned since—that The Willard was serving as an FBI training facility at the time. I remember wondering why the dining room was empty except for us. Not risking my status as the chief naïf, I didn't even ask him why we were the only ones in the dining room.

Mr. Green and I sat at a table. No one appeared to ask if we wanted to have something to eat or drink. He carefully laid a bulging manila envelope on the table, then immediately excused himself to use the men's room.

I sat there, with the bulging—no, shimmering—envelope sitting in front of me. *To open or not?* Gentlemanliness—and honesty—urged my hands to remain on the table. The reporter in me urged my hands to immediately open the secret-laden devil. After all, why had Mr. Green left it there? He could easily have taken it with him to the men's room.

The devil coaxed, "Open!" The Boy Scout cautioned, "Sit still."

Mr. Green was away a very long time—twenty minutes or so. But I didn't peek. I thought: Is this a test of my trustworthiness? Or a large, intentional leak?

Mr. Green returned to the untouched—still shimmering—envelope.

In retrospect, the feeling I had then that Mr. Green wanted me to have the information in the envelope was likely right. But I also knew that FBI officials loved using spy-like gimmicks with reporters to give the information they were sharing—and the process of leaking it—a Hollywood glamour, a tantalizing appeal, and impart seemingly genuine value.

Later, it was Mr. Green who led me to this story:

The Federal Bureau of Investigation broke off direct liaison with the Central Intelligence Agency a year and a half ago because the C.I.A. would not tell J. Edgar Hoover who had leaked information from his organization, according to authoritative sources.[68]

The story ran on the front page of the Sunday *Times* and went on for forty-six paragraphs inside the paper. In the fourth paragraph, I quoted the FBI public relations people as saying the story was not true. Oddly, the CIA made no comment. Since I knew there was an FBI spy in the *Times'* Washington Bureau telex room and the Bureau's phones were bugged, I hand-carried my copy to New York.

My fears about phones was not paranoia. Three years later, the *Times* reported:

> *The Internal Revenue Service has secretly subpoenaed and received from a Washington telephone company records of every toll call that was made from The New York* Times *bureau in the capital from June, 1973, to last month. . . .*
>
> *The Telephone records, involving about 2,500 calls made from The* Times's *Washington Bureau to places in this country and abroad, were turned over to the Internal Revenue service on Jan. 14 by the Chesapeake and Potomac Telephone Company.*[69]

Years later, when I got my FBI file, I found that an FBI public relations guy sent his superior a message saying that I had called. He described the story I had asked about—the cutting of liaison with the CIA—and said he had denied it. In the margin something was scrawled in a wobbly hand:

Correctly handled—K.

What followed in the file was a faxed copy of my story as it ran in the *Times*. Next to that was scrawled:

What rat finked on us? K.

It was only later that I realized it wasn't "K." It was "H." "H" as in Hoover.

Only in America would organized crime have a public relations man.

One day in June 1971, I was sitting quietly, lawfully, and innocently at my desk in Washington when the phone rang. It was the PR man for Joe Bonanno, AKA Joe Bananas. Since I had written some pieces critical of Hoover, perhaps the Mafia imagined I had a fondness for things Sicilian.

Despite an arrest record dating back to the 1920s, Bonanno had never been convicted of a serious crime. In 1985, he was fined $450 and held in contempt of court for refusing to testify. He became an inmate in the Federal Correctional Institution in Tucson, Arizona.

The PR man didn't tell me, but I knew that Arizona was a safe haven for superannuated Mafiosi bosses who wanted peace in the last days of their hazardous lives—the reward for survival, I suppose. But Joe complained that he wasn't getting peace. The PR man insisted that the FBI was harassing him. Heartless agents had supposedly even blown up his backyard barbecue!

Should I call Francis Ford Coppola? You have to ask yourself: What's a decapitated horse compared to a decapitated barbecue? The PR man asked me to come out to Tucson for an interview. When PR for the Mafia calls, you tend to pay attention. I told him I would go.

Also, going to Arizona to see what the FBI might be doing fit in with my view of what Washington reporters should do. The FBI referred to Washington as SOG, the Seat of Government. I thought comparing what SOG said and did with things that happened on the same subject out in the country someplace else—almost anyplace else—made sense. Otherwise, I thought we were blind to the real world outside the District of Columbia.

It was hot and sunny in Tucson. For a fellow from Roxbury, it was exotic in a one-story, desert-dust way. I was wearing my warm Harris Tweed sports jacket and chinos, Brooks Brothers collar buttons secure, paisley tie tight, reporter's notebook in hand. I certainly did not look like J. Paul Getty, or even an FBI agent. I didn't know where I was walking, but I saw that I was approaching Tucson police headquarters. Out front stood a stunning dark-haired woman. The curves of her dress matched the swirls of my tie. What a coincidence, I thought.

She looked directly at me and smiled. I would say seductively, if I knew what a seductive smile was. I doubted that ladies of the night were working the desert noon shift and soliciting in front of the police station. I was equally doubtful that I had suddenly become Harrison Ford.

I figured I was being set up—but I didn't know whether it was by the Mafia or the FBI.

Put yourself in my warm shoes.

I marched on to my interview with the Mafia.

When Betty Medsger wrote a book called *The Burglary: The Discovery of J. Edgar Hoover's Secret FBI*, she told NPR: "I think most striking in the . . . files . . . was a statement that had to do with the . . . policy of the FBI. . . . It was a document that instructed agents to enhance paranoia, to make people feel there's an FBI agent behind every mailbox."[70]

That struck home, because my father, a letter carrier, used to tell me (proudly) about an FBI agent's asking him what mail a certain not-for-profit outfit on his route was getting.

That same year, Matthew Cecil, a professor of journalism and public relations, wrote *Hoover's FBI and the Fourth Estate: The Campaign to Control the Press and the Bureau's Image.*[71] If you hang my yellowed press pass around your neck for a moment, you might imagine the Mafia seducing me, but you probably wouldn't believe the FBI would do that. But then, you don't know what else happened between the FBI and me.

There was the battle over *The Investigator*, the FBI in-house magazine for its agents. I knew the magazine had an article, with photos, on *legats*— "legal attachés" who were FBI agents working out of embassies overseas. I wanted to do a piece on legats. Hoover said I couldn't have a copy of the magazine. I pressed hard. He stood firm.

I argued the magazine was printed at government expense and was widely distributed within the FBI. (I was too stubborn to just have an FBI source leak it to me.) I threatened suit (by the *Times*). Ultimately, Hoover relented. I had wrested the magazine from Edgar the Bulldog.

Maybe that's why he refused to let me interview him. I asked for an interview every single week. Every single week Hoover said no. Finally, enough was enough: "Don't write anymore," a spokesperson said in exasperation, "I'll let you know if that is going to happen."

That meant it never would.

After one of my articles about J. Edgar Hoover had landed on page one, I called James Jesus Angleton, head of Counterintelligence at the CIA. It was a long, detailed piece suggesting that some at the FBI thought Hoover might be past his prime.

To my surprise, Angleton took the call. I guess even he didn't see me as a spy. Given the fact that he saw everyone else as a spy, I wondered whether my feelings should be hurt. Where did I fall short?

I had called right from my phone at the *Times* Bureau. I was sure it was tapped, but for this call, who cared?

"See my piece on Hoover?"

"Yes," he said. "And I saw the *Post*'s piece too." The *Washington Post* had also done an article on Hoover.

"What did you think?" I asked boldly.

"The truth lies between your story and the *Post*'s."

Wedge time: "How? Why don't you sit down and talk with me and maybe I'll have a chance to get this stuff about the Bureau, and about intelligence, more accurate?"

He dodged a bit. I pressed a bit. He hung up.

Dear Bob,

I am delighted to enclose a publisher's merit award check for $150 for your exclusive on the FBI and the CIA for the paper of October 10. It was first rate.

Congratulations.

Sincerely,

Punch

CHAPTER TWENTY-EIGHT

Boots in the Oval

I would feel that most of the conversations that took place in those areas of the White House that did have the recording system would... be in existence.

—RON ZIEGLER AKA ZIG ZAG,
WHITE HOUSE PRESS SECRETARY

Where You Should and Shouldn't Wear Cowboy Boots:
They're not business wear unless your business involves cattle or oil. . . .
For the most part we recommend keeping the cowboy boots to "fun"
social events—things that are actively light-hearted, where a little
machismo . . . isn't out of place. Questionable places to wear cowboy
boots . . . include: Political functions of any kind. . . .

—ANTONIO CENTENO, ARTOFMANLINESS.COM

WASHINGTON BUREAU, THE *NEW YORK TIMES*, 1972

The "lid" system guided the correspondents who covered the Nixon White House with me. Whenever the White House had no newsworthy events or announcements, the press secretary, Ron Ziegler, would give a lid and let correspondents turn their attention, even if briefly, elsewhere. A lid was our signal that there were would be no more news for the day.

One weekend, I was at the *Times* cubicle at the White House when the Press Office announced a lid. I was young, dressed in my weekend Dupont Circle best: jeans and cowboy boots. If I do say so myself, the boots were lustrous, tan, artistically tooled. I had bought them while on assignment in Texas. I was sitting at my small desk when a press aide appeared and said, "The president would like to see you in the Oval." I was incredulous. Me?

There were only a dozen other reporters at the White House. As bidden, I lined up with them outside the Oval. One of the women in the press corps turned and fastened on my attire. "What are you, a male model?" she asked loudly and derisively. I stayed silent, but she persisted quacking at me about my uniform until some kinder correspondent told her she had a lid. She stopped, and my blush began to fade.

After a while, we all filed into the Oval and stood before the president, who was seated at his desk. Nixon said nothing satirical or sarcastic about my sartorial choices. *Grâce à Dieu.* Perhaps he recognized it was Sunday and this wasn't church. Or maybe he was respecting regional customs, or just giving the kid a break. Or maybe he was just trying to cozy up to the correspondents on that quiet Sunday, and complaining about jeans and boots might not have been the way to win cynical hearts.

Covering the White House under Nixon was . . . a hoot. Did you know bowling down the aisle with plastic balls was the sport on the White House Press plane? President Nixon did not stay at Mar-a-Lago as Trump does. He stayed on Bebe Rebozo's houseboat, *Coco Lobo II.*

Covering the White House, I came to realize the president sometimes appeared not to be wholly "present." Once, in October 1970, I covered him at a country club on Skidaway Island, one of the most affluent communities in the United States, off the Georgia coast. The audience was behind a rope, and I was the only one in the press area, just to the president's left, also behind a rope. At the end of his speech, Nixon headed straight for me to begin shaking hands with wealthy donors. I waved him off, and he corrected course.

Boats are not my friends. On the way back from Skidaway Island, I got dreadfully seasick. I was dizzy, white, and trembling. But, with remarkable devotion to the *Times,* I somehow managed to type my story about the president's speech. Now I had to file it. I staggered onto the press bus, grabbing the handrail. I lurched down the narrow aisle. I threw my portable typewriter into the luggage rack. With relief, I thrust my copy at the telegraph representative on the bus, and slumped into a seat. I said to the Western Union man, "Jesus, let's get this out."

He said solemnly, "There's no need to blaspheme."

In February 1972, Nixon was vacationing in Key Biscayne. I eschewed Joe's Stone Crab and the Jamaica Inn in favor of doing some enterprise reporting. Ziegler had given us a lid. I learned that the president had a briefing book about China and decided to write a story about it. The piece led the paper that Sunday:

KEY BISCAYNE, Fla. Feb. 12 [1972] —

If President Nixon manages to resist the lure of the sun, sea and Bebe Rebozo's houseboat, Coco Lobo II, he will have a fair crack at answering many questions the Chinese may throw at him during his trip.

The President's visits last weekend and this one to Key Biscayne suggest the quandary of a high-school boy faced with a final exam in Latin next week and fine spring weather this week. President Nixon, fleeing the chill gray of Washington, has come to Florida hauling what one State Department official called "a hell of a lot of stuff" to study for his China trip.

The contents of the China briefing book are so secret that questions about it made a member of the National Security Council staff virtually flee.

According to one official who helped prepare the briefing book, "almost everything imaginable is covered." Asked if that wasn't a tall order for 500 pages or so of material, he said: "No, because the Chinese have been pretty open about what they want to discuss. It is also clear what subjects they are going to avoid because they are embarrassing."...

This weekend's work is described as mainly "domestic"... but once again he has his book bag of China material along. The White House says he plans to do more homework—despite the blandishments of the sun.[72]

When I filed the piece, the guy in charge of the National Desk for the weekend called. He said he liked the piece but thought it was cheeky. He meant I had treated the Prez as a person. And that editor didn't even know about the cowboy boots.

Neither did Ron Ziegler. He hadn't come into the Oval Office. Ron and I had an honest relationship: We barely spoke.

That was not because I thought he wasn't a nice guy, in his way. It was because I didn't think he would tell me anything useful. On his side, I'm afraid Ziegler saw me as the Opposition and worried that I might actually use an offhand remark in a story (and I likely would have). This was before Ziegler's invocation, during Watergate, of his right to delete what he had said: *This is the operative statement. The others are inoperative.*

Ziegler's Secret Service code name was Whaleboat (though reporters tended to call him Zig-Zag). That was because as a youngster, he had worked at Disneyland as a skipper on the Jungle Cruise. His obituary in the *New York Times* described him this way:

> *Ron Ziegler, President Richard M. Nixon's press secretary . . . was known for referring to the Watergate break-in as a "third-rate burglary" and for steadfastly speaking for President Nixon as his presidency crumbled. . . .*
>
> *After leaving the White House, he worked for Syska and Hennessy, Inc., a consulting firm in Washington, and then served as president of the National Association of Truck Stop Operators from 1980 to 1987, then as president of the National Association of Chain Drug Stores, before retiring in 1998.*[73]

Ziegler had attacked the *Post*'s coverage of Watergate as "shabby journalism." But he ultimately treated facts as facts—and later apologized in a news conference:

"In thinking of it at this point in time, yes, I would apologize to the *Post*. . . . When we're wrong, we're wrong."

When he began to add, "But . . ." a reporter called out, "Don't take it back, Ron!"

In 1974, Ziegler made a statement about the White House tapes that won him an award for doublespeak from a group of English teachers:

> *I would feel that most of the conversations that took place in those areas of the White House that did have the recording system would, in almost their entirety, be in existence, but the special prosecutor, the court, and,*

I think, the American people are sufficiently familiar with the record-ing system to know where the recording devices existed, and to know the situation in terms of the recording process, but I feel, although the process has not been undertaken yet in preparation of the material to abide by the court decision, really, what the answer to that question is.[74]

The late Tom Wicker, who covered the White House before me, didn't deal in doublespeak. Tom was a prominent *Times* journalist, for-mer Washington bureau chief, and influential political columnist. He rose to fame after his detailed account of President John F. Kennedy's assassination.

He was unabashedly opinionated, and as a columnist often railed against power—writing, for example, in protest against the war in Viet-nam. He was attacked by conservatives and liberals alike, but nevertheless led a fervent and notable career as a correspondent. When I began cover-ing the White House, here were the Wicker Rules passed on to me:

When the entire White House press corps goes off in one direction, go with them;

When taking an advance for expenses, always take more than you know you'll need, submit your expense account, give New York back a little. They'll be so grateful, they won't ask about the rest.[75]

Tom had covered the Kennedy-Nixon presidential campaign in 1960. Here is what Timothy Crouse wrote in *Boys on the Bus* about report-ers covering the campaign of 1972:

If you stayed away from the campaign for any period of time and then came on again, the first thing that struck you was the shocking physical deterioration of the press corps.

During the summer, the reporters had looked fairly healthy. Now their skin was pasty and greenish, they had ugly dark pouches under their glazed eyes, and their body had become bloated with the regimen of nonstop drinking and five or six starchy airplane meals per day.

Toward the end, they began to suffer from a fiendish combination of fatigue and anxiety. They had arrived at the last two weeks, when the public finally wanted to read about the campaign front-page play every day! —and they were so tired that it nearly killed them to pound out a decent piece. . . .

During the last week, the press bus looked like a Black Maria sent out to round up winos; half the reporters were passed out with their mouths wide open and their notebooks fallen in their laps. When they were awake, they often wandered like zombies.

On one of the last days of the campaign, Jules Witcover walked from the Biltmore Hotel to a rally in midtown Manhattan and had to be repeatedly stopped from sleepwalking into traffic. . . . Bill Greider . . . had a strange habit of placing his arms by his sides, as if wearing an imaginary strait jacket, and walking around in circles. . . . [76]

Today, everyone is yammering on about the press not covering blue-collar workers. But, as you can see from Crouse, sometimes journalists are themselves blue-collar workers. It is just that they tend to cover workers without much sympathy. No one is saying, "These folks have a tough time!" They're just ignoring them. When journalists don't ignore them, you can nearly hear them making remarks—after clicking the mute button on the microphone—that treat workers as ignorant.

Well, I was one—a blue-collar worker, I mean.

Cathy, my future wife, had it right. She identified me as a blue-collar worker when we met. To her, a Washington correspondent for the *New York Times* was a blue-collar worker. After all, we did have a union in the Newspaper Guild. And I ended up wrangling with my boss, Bob Phelps, just the way blue-collar workers often do. And as blue-collar workers often do, I lost.

CHAPTER TWENTY-NINE

Reject Me Once, Reject Me Twice. But a Journalism School Comes to the Rescue, and the Media Queue Up

That's too coincidental to be a coincidence.

—YOGI BERRA

SAN FRANCISCO, 2009

Against my wishes, Bob Phelps went ahead and published his book disclosing the information I'd given him about Watergate. He called his book *God and the Editor: My Search for Meaning at the* New York Times. According to the publisher, the story is about Phelps settling in at the *New York Times* where:

> *Journalism became the religion he had searched for since his adolescence. Over his tenure of nearly two decades, however, Phelps found that journalism's stark emphasis on fact was insufficient to address many of life's dilemmas and failed to provide the sustaining guidance he envied in his wife's Catholic faith.*[77]

Given the possibilities of interpretation and opinion in journalism, this seems an artificial description, but I suppose it provided a theme for the book.

When the book appeared, I called Gene Roberts, a reporter's editor and former managing editor of the *Times*. When Gene became executive editor and president of the *Philadelphia Inquirer*, the paper won seventeen Pulitzer Prizes—and even made money for Knight-Ridder. I told Gene about the galleys from Phelps and asked whether I should finally write what I knew, since Phelps had broken the pledge to Gray. He told me I should. And at long last, after keeping the secret for decades, I wrote the story about what the *Times* had done.

I quickly sent the story to the Op-Ed page of the *Times*. They didn't run it. (To double-check, I tested the submission address. It worked.)

I called Gene and said, "I know it's crazy, but they're not going to run the story." He suggested I put it in a journalism magazine. He told me he would call the editor of the *American Journalism Review*. Gene said that if *AJR* took it, they'd run it online right away.

I felt badly that the *Times* hadn't run it. I decided to write *Times* publisher Arthur O. Sulzberger Jr., and let him know that I had offered the piece to the *Times*. Arthur Jr. is the son of Arthur Sr. (referred to as Punch) and was sometimes, quite disrepectfully, referred to by the staff as "Pinch."

I knew Arthur from my days in President Carter's Justice Department when he was working as a reporter. In fact, he'd once sat in my spacious, wood-lined office across from the attorney general's suite while I leaked him a story. My private line had rung and it was my wife Cathy. I told her I had to call her back. "I'm in the middle of leaking a story," I explained.

I thought about how to approach Arthur. Clearly, by email, but I didn't have his private email address. It took twenty minutes and the use of the old investigative techniques I had learned at the *Times* to find it. I wrote to say I didn't want him to think I'd betrayed the paper by writing about the *Times*'s not having used the Watergate information. I told him I'd given the story to Op-Ed, but they had decided not to publish it—so I had given it to the *American Journalism Review*.

Arthur didn't respond, but the Gray Lady did bustle into action, skirts toppling newsroom trash cans. Lickety-split, I got a call from a fast-breathing Richard Pérez-Peña, the media reporter. When, he wanted to know, was the *AJR* going online with the piece?

Tonight, I said, and I told Pérez-Peña the story.

At points, Pérez-Peña seemed incredulous. I didn't blame him. When I told him I had consulted Kenneth Richieri, the *Times*'s general counsel, for advice, he gasped.

The story ran on May 24, 2009.

Thunderclap.

My drubbing began. The media put me in the stocks. It interpreted the story to make me the villain: I had the Watergate story, and I somehow chose not to run with it.

BBC:

Two former New York Times *journalists have admitted that they let slip one of the biggest stories of all time—the Watergate scandal.*[78]

Radio New Zealand:

Interviewer: Did Phelps and Smith simply not read the Washington Post *and realize they had missed the story, or was it, "Oh gosh, I hope the other guy doesn't mention it, and we'll just carry on."*

[Nathan] King [New York Correspondent]: Seems to me that this was just a case of human error—that these tips were passed on, that there was some preliminary investigation but not followed up. I'm surprised that light bulbs didn't go off when Woodward and Bernstein started sniffing around the story and publishing in the Washington Post . . .

Interviewer: No suggestion that there was any conspiracy here, that the New York Times was leant on?

King: This is a very good question . . . this seems to be just falling through the cracks, but any journalist has to question whether there was some sort of nod and a wink or someone wanted to hide this. . . .[79]

The *Guardian*:

Now, in an admission that must rank among the most excruciating in newspaper history, the former New York Times *journalists have revealed that they knew about the cover-up before their* Washington Post *rivals. But they dropped the ball.*[80]

El Periódico's headline was: *Olvidado En Un Cajón* (Forgotten in a Drawer).[81]

And *New York* magazine wrote:

Woodward seems to have taken umbrage at the Times' *attempt to steal his thunder. "Watergate wasn't about a tip," he told* Editor & Publisher. *"It was about extensive reporting and getting information you can put in the paper. They decided not to do the reporting."*[82]

In other words, that lazy bunch of slackers at the *Times* had the tip, but what they really needed was—a Woodward. (It was unfortunate—as we'll learn—that a while back I had told the *Times* not to hire him.)

The media—at least my less careful pals in the Third Estate—handed me a bum rap. What remained of my naïveté had somehow expected better.

Bob Woodward said only that the *Post*'s reporting had come together from many different pieces. Carl Bernstein called me, asked a lot of questions, but volunteered nothing.

I was once foolish enough to vouchsafe to Bob Woodward, outside of the ostentatious bathroom on the second floor of his Georgetown home, that I had had a pretty good Watergate source myself. Bob ignored my disclosure. Instead, he explained, plainly embarrassed, that he had bought the house from a (presumably quite stylish) hairdresser.

When Bernstein asked me about this exchange with Woodward, he listened, in silence, asking only how Woodward had reacted. I told him: There had been no reaction. I don't think Bob was listening.

Charles Kaiser, a former reporter for the *Times*, called me. I was enjoying the tranquility of the botanical garden in San Francisco but answered my cellphone. Kaiser told me that he had just interviewed Max Frankel. Frankel had told him, he said, that he had full confidence in Phelps.

Kaiser reported my reaction:

You're joking. I'm stupefied. Does he not know now that this was important? He was running the Washington Bureau that got trounced on this story, and he went on to run the New York Times! *How can he say that?*

I also got a call from John Crewdson, who had been a copy boy in the *Times* Washington Bureau, then a cub reporter.

He attacked me as I came on the line:

"Why? Why didn't you tell us about the leak from Gray?"

I was flabbergasted.

"It never occurred to me that you didn't know about it."

"We sure as hell didn't."

When the world seemed to be not so much interviewing me as scolding me, I consulted Sy Hersh. Sy, in turn, consulted his wife, a psychiatrist, and reassured me in his usual robust fashion: "How could anybody think it was your fault? You gave them the story!"

CHAPTER THIRTY

More Secrets: Memories of Playa Girón, Stellar Wind Blows Hard, and Reporter Risen Rebels

I learned long ago never to wrestle with a pig. . . . [T]he pig likes it.
—GEORGE BERNARD SHAW

"The NSA is a very insular community," [a computer-security expert] said. "There's almost no interaction with the outside world, and little interaction with each other. Groups within the NSA don't talk to each other."
—BEN WEITZENKORN, *TECHNEWSDAILY*

WASHINGTON BUREAU, THE *NEW YORK TIMES*, 2000–2006

The *Times* had withheld news from public view earlier, in war and near-war situations. One of these was the disastrous invasion of Cuba.

The irony of that powerful admonitory memory was this: President Kennedy asked General Maxwell Taylor to produce a postmortem on Playa Girón. In April 2000, Taylor's full report was declassified. The *Washington Post* reported:

> *Shortly after the failed Bay of Pigs invasion of Cuba in 1961, a top CIA official told an investigative commission that the Soviet Union had somehow learned the exact date of the amphibious landing in advance, according to a newly declassified version of the commission's final report.*

Moreover, the CIA apparently had known of the leak to the Soviets—and went ahead with the invasion anyway.[83]

Despite the self-imposed restraint of the *Times*, the Russians had known the date of the invasion. Allen Dulles, head of the CIA, did not tell the president this. He did not tell the exile fighters. He ordered the operation to go forward. This resulted in casualties, prisoners, and failure. Kennedy was blamed.

As the *Times* reported, Cuba had been made aware of possible attacks through intelligence and increased dissident activity. The *Times* wrote:

The climate for the invasion—[had been] anticipated and promised by the Cuban rebels for many weeks. . . . Since last Thursday a major wave of sabotage swept Cuba. Saturday, three B-26 aircraft bombed three air bases on the island. Beginning in the middle of last week informants in Cuban groups made it known confidentially that "important events" were to be expected over the weekend.[84]

As David W. Dunlap wrote in the *Times Insider*, put out by the paper: The publisher had his own worries.

"He was gravely troubled by the security implications of the Szulc story," Clifton Daniel said in a speech delivered in 1966, when he was the managing editor. . . . He could envision failure for the invasion and he could see The New York Times *being blamed for a bloody fiasco.[85]*

The *Times* was blamed. So it was not at all surprising when the paper worried itself into paralysis about Stellar Wind, a program that allowed for mass wiretapping without warrants by the National Security Agency. The program had begun in 2001, just after the September 11 terrorist attacks.

The US government had asked the *Times* not to publish material about the surveillance.

James Risen and Eric Lichtblau, both in the Washington Bureau, wrote the story, but the *Times* wouldn't publish it. When I learned that, I heard echoes of Reston, echoes of the Bay of Pigs, and echoes of my days in the Washington Bureau.

It was Philip Taubman, Washington bureau chief, and Bill Keller, executive editor of the paper, who wouldn't let the story run because the government had assured the *Times* that the program was legal. And because the editors apparently thought the piece wasn't ready. Taubman told David Folkenflik, an NPR reporter, that he felt caught between exposing an illegal program and not compromising a tool that a national security official had told him was important. According to the *Times*, President George W. Bush made a personal appeal to Sulzberger.

Depending on your point of view, Risen turned out to be either a bad boy or indomitable, since he covered the NSA disclosures in his book, *State of War*. The *Times* did finally publish the NSA story but denied it had anything to do with Risen's book, which came out in 2006. That same year, Risen and Lichtblau won a Pulitzer for the work they had done for the *Times*. Four *Times* reporters told Folkenflik that the impending book forced the *Times* to publish the piece. Oddly, Taubman was allowed to read the book before it was published, but not to copy it or take notes. Gabriel Sherman wrote in the *New York Observer*:

> [A]uthor James Bamford reviewed Mr. Risen's book in The Times' arts section. "Among the unanswered questions concerning the domestic spying story is why," Mr. Bamford wrote, "if Mr. Risen and The Times had first come upon the explosive information a year earlier, the paper waited until just a few weeks before the release of the book to inform its readers."
>
> According to people with knowledge of the Washington bureau, the publication of Mr. Risen's book was the endnote to a months-long internal struggle between Mr. Risen and Times editors over ownership of the book's contents. . . .
>
> Mr. Risen returned to the paper in June 2005. By September, rumors were circulating in the bureau that the book would contain the N.S.A. material.
>
> Executive editor Bill Keller has said in public statements that the book was not a factor in the timing of the N.S.A. story. But sources with knowledge of the internal debate at The Times said that editors, unsure what Mr. Risen's book might say, pressed to publish the story before the end of the year.[86]

Risen declined to discuss what had happened, but according to NPR, the American whistleblower and former CIA employee Edward Snowden saw what the *Times* had done—or not done. In June 2014, Folkenflik wrote:

> *Snowden's choice was the bitter harvest of seeds sown by the* Times *almost a decade ago. In the fall of 2004, just ahead of the November general elections, the* Times' *news leadership spiked an exclusive from Washington correspondents James Risen and Eric Lichtblau, disclosing massive warrantless domestic eavesdropping by the NSA. . . .*[87]

Laura Poitras was the filmmaker who worked with Glenn Greenwald and Barton Gellman to break the story on the NSA surveillance program. In an interview she said:

> *F]rom conversations I had with [Snowden] after that, I think he had a suspicion of mainstream media. And particularly what happened with The New York* Times *and the warrantless wiretapping story, which as we know was shelved for a year. . . .*[88]

Snowden gave the material—and the Pulitzer Prize—to the *Washington Post* and the *Guardian*. Dean Baquet, the *Times* executive editor, was not happy. He told Folkenflik, "It was really painful."

The *Guardian* wrote that Snowden's material disclosed:

- the NSA's dragnet of phone records of millions of Americans;
- the program code-named *Prism* used by the NSA and its UK counterpart GCHQ to get access to the data of nine large internet companies, including Google and Facebook;
- the cracking of encryption by the NSA and GCHQ that undermined personal security for web users;
- and NSA surveillance of phone calls made by three dozen world leaders.

In September 2016—more than two years after publishing the material that Snowden had given the paper—the *Post* ran a remarkable editorial. The editorial *opposed* a pardon for Snowden for having made the material public. Snowden should come home to the United States, it huffed, and "in the best tradition of civil disobedience" show himself "willing to go to jail for [his] beliefs." (The *Guardian* and the *Times* said they thought the *Post*'s position was wrong.)

In other words, the *Post* got the chance to bite the hand that had fed it. A seemingly shameless canine, bite it did. You have to wonder whether the *Post* was polishing its Pulitzer gold medal while at the keyboard writing that editorial.

Aware of what had happened to Risen, Snowden didn't give the *Times* that chance.

CHAPTER THIRTY-ONE

Cigars Rolled, Pool Hall Closed; Time to Schuss Down the Slippery Slope; Bork and the Bum Rap

I've never been an intellectual, but I have this look.

—Woody Allen

YALE LAW SCHOOL, NEW HAVEN, 1972

In 1972, I decided to leave the paper to become an entrepreneur. I didn't want to roll cigars as my immigrant grandfather had. And the pool hall he ultimately owned had been sold. I decided I should attend Harvard Business School, learn to read columns of numbers, and dive in. I consulted my friend and former roommate, Professor Harvey Goldschmid of Columbia Law School. "Don't go to business school," Harvey advised. "Go to law school—you'll learn what you'd learn at business school and you'll have more options."

So I did. But I hedged my bets severely by applying to only one law school—Yale. This must have been with the subconscious understanding that I couldn't possibly get in and so would remain at the *Times*. Later, a Yale Law dean told me that even if you had a Nobel Prize, you might not be accepted. I took the admissions test, collected my various transcripts, and waited, without expectation.

I got in.

How could I turn Yale down?

I suspected it was time for me to quit the *Times* when the Washington News Desk asked me to stay late to cover a story—past 7:30. I looked at the editor, the talented John Hemphill, and said, "I've got to go home and feed the dog." Hemphill looked at the news assistant and suppressed a laugh. They both smiled—as well they might have. I had come to care less about the news story, and more about my dog.

In August, I was leaving the *Times* Washington Bureau. Max Frankel took me aside. He said: "We need to send you to New York so you can explain to them why we are losing our best people . . . Halberstam, Lukas, Talese, you. . . ."

I felt as if I had just been admitted to the reporters' Hall of Fame, but the Public Latin School taught me that glory is fleeting.

I didn't go to New York. Instead, I had lunch with Pat Gray, came back, and reported that remarkable lunch.

Then I departed, prow pointed toward New Haven.

There's a school of thought, found congenial by publishers, that reporters ought to be poor so that they can better identify with the people they are writing about. But most Yale graduates aren't poor, and they're not naïve. Also, they generally do not come out clinging desperately to the absolutist top of the value mountain rather than sliding gracefully down its oh-so-slippery slope.

When I arrived at Yale, I had a BA from Harvard College, an MA in Foreign Affairs and an MS in Journalism from Columbia. I had done graduate work on the Fulbright in Germany. I'd also spent a few years in the Washington Bureau of the *Times*. I was feeling pretty good about my chops. I thought I'd fit right in at Yale. I didn't think I was a slouch.

I was wrong.

You may recall that I was not enticed to follow up on the My Lai Massacre story after I'd been writing about it for a while. I chose instead to keep the detailed reservations that my weary wife and I had for a long-planned holiday in the Caribbean. Similarly, the Watergate story did not compel me to leave Yale Law School. It was a place that mesmerized me from the moment I arrived.

One of my professors, Guido Calabresi, explained the academic process to first-year students in his Torts class. He said that college or graduate school teaches students to look at both sides of an issue, but Yale would teach us to pick up an issue and look at it as if it were a multifaceted gem. We would learn to look at things from many angles.

This leads to the anguish of weighing the bad against the worse—and, if you are compelled to choose the bad (for example, torture) instead of the worse (destruction of an American city), you have set off down the ethical slippery slope. Goodbye to the comfortable anchor of absolute values. Yale Law graduates are given an analytic framework that can—doesn't have to, but can—address the relativity of values.

Before law school began, I went to Vermont for the weekend and read the first assignment—a case of only twenty pages. I read the case twice, and said, "I've got it."

On Monday morning, I walked into class only to learn I had entirely—*entirely*—failed to understand the points of the case, as explained by Guido. I was humiliated but determined to learn to look at these gems from every angle. I wrote an Op-Ed for the *Times* about this when I finished my first year at Yale. [89]

Bob Bork, my constitutional law professor, told me he had discussed my Op-Ed piece with Elliot Richardson, who had been attorney general—as well as Secretary of Health, Education, and Welfare; Defense; and Commerce. Bork told me that Richardson had said, "Now here's a guy [me] who doesn't want to think."

But Bork didn't criticize the article I wrote for *Student Lawyer* praising him. I wrote that I was "in ulcerous philosophic disagreement" with Bork, and I was writing the piece "not to promote [him] . . . but to defend him." I described Bork as "bearded and plump and bored—oh so bored with teaching law . . . driven to [a] position by his fiercely critical mind, his passion for an organized and principled scheme of the law—which, he admits, may be a chimera—and his conservative values."

Bork was a remarkably honest guy, intellectually. He actually believed there were, or could be, neutral principles in constitutional law. Because of this articulated naïveté and lamentable candor, he was not confirmed as a Supreme Court judge when President Ronald Reagan nominated him in 1987. Although he had been solicitor general, acting attorney general, and a judge on the US Court of Appeals for the DC Circuit, the Senate voted

42–58 against him after his confirmation hearings and the widespread public controversy that followed.

Bork couldn't overcome the animosity of liberals who thought their own *non-neutral* principles were what was required of a justice.

I've always thought it unfortunate that the *Times* did not find that elusive conservative reporter it was chasing and let him or her report on Bork. Bork had, incidentally, won my admiration when, briefly attorney general during Watergate, he refused to use the government limo and instead drove his own car, an old Volvo. Only two of the four cylinders worked, and as Bork explained it, he had to take several runs to get the car up the ramp and out of the Justice Department garage.

Quite apart from my desire to succeed in law as I had in journalism, I was fascinated—no, mesmerized—by what they were dishing up at Yale: They were making me think, or trying to.

It was a remarkable experience and changed the way I thought. As a reporter, I confess I had seen things largely in two dimensions—typically, in black and white. As a law student, I began to see the world in a dubious gray. Yale finished the job of transforming me from naïveté to cynicism, from having clear values to relying on relative analysis, from a hankering for Roxbury's fizzy soda (aka tonic) to a penchant for fizzy champagne.

Many years later, the European Union invited me to give a lecture to lawyers about mediation in Turin, Italy. While I was there, I learned there was a Yale Law graduate practicing in Turin. I called and asked him to dinner. Over black truffles, we both said, simultaneously, "Yale changed the way I look at the world," and that was even before we drank the magnificent Barolo.

After the meal, we left the restaurant and entered the piazza arm-in-arm. I wasn't thinking about Roxbury as we walked. But now, when I remember that walk, it strikes me that back in Roxbury, piazza had an entirely different meaning from what it had in Turin. In Roxbury, it meant harsh, iron-grilled porches in a rear courtyard stacked like barbecue-grill grids. Both the black railings and floor of the porches were open, except for the prison-like bars. Some of them rusted.

The feeling the Italian lawyer and I shared was a fairly standard response to Yale Law School, and it explains why when the *Times* called me during my first term of law school and asked me to come back to continue covering Watergate, I spent just a day thinking about it before I said no. I am not an intellectual, but Yale was a remarkable intellectual experience.

If I were an intellectual, I might be able to explain why I said no to the *Times*, but they said, "Okay, we get that you like it, but come back here and go back to Yale next year and we'll pay for everything," and I still said no. Remarkably, Watergate did not bewitch me the way Yale did. As to Washington—although I didn't yet realize it—I was jaded. As to legal reasoning, I wasn't jaded—I was an optimistic neophyte.

Many people have asked how I managed to sit at Yale Law School during my first semester and do nothing while the *Times* did not print what Gray had given me. I hadn't erased the paper, or the French lunch, from my mind. I had just moved on.

It is a decided weakness that I focus on one thing at a time. One story, one assignment, one career, one learning adventure. Yale was like swimming in the brisk waters of the Upper Nile, headed to take on the riddle of the Sphinx. I was not in Washington, not at the *Times*, not covering a Washington scandal.

I had given the *Times* the entirety of my scoop. I had made the chief editor in the Bureau take notes. I had recorded my briefing for him. And then I had moved on.

Oddly, my unbounded huzzahs for Yale Law School surfaced in a conversation with Bob Woodward during my second stint at the *Times*. Bob asked me whether he—champion of American journalism, worthy hero of film and media—ought to go to law school. I thought for a second, then said:

"Only if you're not going to practice law. What might be good is a year at a first-rate law school. The third year is a waste of time for everybody, and the second is about substantive law—which you won't need. Yep, a year might be good."

Quite correctly, Bob ignored the advice.

CHAPTER THIRTY-TWO

Not-So-Learned-in-the-Law
Steps into a Fairy Tale

Fairytale, *according to Merriam-Webster: Marked by seemingly unreal beauty . . . luck, or happiness.*

In a utilitarian age, of all other times, it is a matter of grave importance that fairy tales should be respected.

—Charles Dickens

WASHINGTON BUREAU, THE *NEW YORK TIMES*, 1975

I left the *Times* Washington Bureau for Yale Law School, spent the full three years, and got a degree at age thirty-four. After that, I had to choose between journalism and law. This was not an easy decision, since I had grown up on journalism since I was eighteen and had worked at the *Times* since I was twenty-seven. It would be only a trifling exaggeration to say I had more affection for the paper than I had for Bit-O-Honey.

Still, I interviewed at law firms and got a few offers in San Francisco, where I had clerked for a summer for a fancy firm (now deceased, with a tombstone that reads *Greed*). Then I approached both the *Times* and the *Washington Post*. The *Times* gave me three offers on that visit: one to run a subsidiary publication, one to be the company's labor negotiator, and one—if I wanted to—to go back to the Washington Bureau.

I wound up reporting again in Washington. I also became, *pro bono*, the shop steward at the *Times* in Washington for the American Newspaper Guild. The Guild was the union for the journalists at the paper, among others. In one of life's ironies, I came to face across the ocean of a bargaining table the man who got the labor negotiator's job I had turned down.

It turned out I retained my naïveté and quixotic idealism. I was at a movie theater in Washington watching *Three Days of the Condor*. Robert Redford indicated he was counting on the *Times* to print his secret information. I turned to my friend and whispered—no kidding, "That's why I went into journalism."

I had had a number of conversations with *Times* executives about coming back to the paper. One of those I visited was Abe Rosenthal. Abe had almost served me a drink from his bar, only visibly catching himself at the last moment and asking instead whether I'd like to make a drink for myself—he had pointed to the bar where he was standing, and thus preserved his power—*faux pas* averted.

I turned down the drink but let him know that I was also talking to the *Washington Post* since I wanted to get away from the low salary the paper had picked me up for when it had plucked me from Boston in 1968. Rosenthal took the bait and asked me what the *Post* was offering. I told him we were still negotiating. I never did get an offer from the *Post*. I abandoned the conversation when I got the offer from the *Times*. Yale had had a practical effect already. I did the *Post* interview and let the *Times* know about it in order to raise the paltry salary that the *Times* had paid me before.

During my interviews at the *Times*, I also talked with Sydney Gruson, an executive vice president of the company who had been the paper's correspondent in Mexico City. He was a confidant of the publisher, I knew, and a bon vivant of the old school. Gruson said, amiably, "Bob, this is a power place. Not a money place." When he said that, I looked at what seemed to be his expensive Savile Row suit, bit my tongue, and did not say, "You had race horses when you were in Mexico City." But I took Sydney's point and listened as he suggested I talk to Jim Goodale, the *Times*'s general counsel—its top in-house lawyer—and the executive I was to meet with next. When I told Goodale what Gruson had said, he laughed.

Having turned over many gems in my sometimes perspiring palms, I reached the Yale finish line. Then I returned to the *Times*. To the

Washington Bureau. Why go back after the *Times* had not used my information about Watergate? In those days reporters were silly—and forgetful—romantics. Why else take the job?

Back in Washington, with my enhanced paycheck, I rented a small brick house in Georgetown—two floors, a fireplace, and a kitchen that opened onto a small garden. One of my classmates from Yale, Max, was working for a fancy Washington firm and had a similar Georgetown house. One Saturday that fall, Max invited me over for dinner and since I liked both Max and homemade food, I said sure.

When I showed up, Max exiled me to the living room. Everyone else was in the kitchen, and Max did not want me to add to the throng. I sat alone on a red chaise longue, occasionally offering to join the group in the kitchen, but Max continued to holler through the door for me to stay out.

At last a woman opened the swinging door from the kitchen and walked into the living room. She was—words still fail me. Tall, yes. Blonde, yes. Absurdly beautiful, yes. With a look of intelligence and kindness. She walked over and sat next to me, and within two minutes we were holding hands. She always maintained I took her hand, but I maintain she took mine. Who knows? Who cares? (All right, she was probably right.)

Unhappily, Max had invited a British academic to be my dinner companion, and the clearer I made it that I existed only for this tall blonde—Cathy her name turned out to be—the more the British academic interposed herself. It wasn't funny. After the table had been cleared, and to escape the clutches of the duenna, I suggested to Cathy that we go out for a walk, and she agreed. I hastened her down the townhouse steps into a chilly Washington night. Unbidden, the British duenna invited herself. She trailed a few steps behind, as Cathy and I trudged, already arm-in-arm, uphill.

When we returned for port, Richard—Max's roommate and a curator at the National Gallery—began to talk about a new exhibit he had just put together. He said he was taking both Cathy and the duenna to see the exhibit the next day. Richard went on and on about the exhibit, and I pretended to be more and more excited about it. Richard was nice, and very bright and elegant, and—it turned out—resolutely obtuse in this regard. The more I swooned over the exhibit—"It sounds really great,

Richard! It sounds like just the sort of thing I'd like to see"—the more he agreed it was, but didn't offer an invitation. It occurs to me only now that I never asked Cathy what she was thinking when finally, unable to stand it, I blurted out, "Richard, could I come along?"

"Sorry, of course. Join us," he said, uttering the magic words at last.

The next day, Sunday, we four assembled outside the National Gallery, and I waited until Richard and the Brit went in and turned to the left before politely escorting Cathy in—and turning to the right.

She looked at the art. I sat on a red banquette and looked at her. She knew it, of course. Finally, I rose from the banquette and said, "Let's go home. OK?" She said yes, and the next day she moved in. We stayed happily together until her death years later.

When I went to the *Times* the next day, the very last thing I was thinking about was journalism. I even forgave the news editor who hazed me by assigning me some complex rewrite piece on deadline my first day, after three years away. (Did you know Smith-Coronas rust from sweat?)

I placed only one call that morning. I had been dating a Senate staffer, a comely Swedish American, and I told her I needed to see her and wondered whether I might take her to a French lunch in Georgetown. She said yes. When I showed up, I said, "I don't know how to tell you this, but I'm a reporter. I'll be direct: Saturday night I met the woman I'm going to marry."

I watched her process this. "You met her Saturday night?" she finally said. "And you're sure you're going to marry her?" I told her yes, and she told me that she was glad I'd told her. Then I ordered profiteroles, certain Cathy wouldn't see this as a betrayal.

That evening when I returned to the townhouse, classical music was playing, the kitchen had the fragrance of my favorite, lamb chops, the door to the garden was open, and the only investigative reporting I was interested in had nothing to do with the *New York Times*. Cathy, incidentally, knew nothing about journalism. When we met, she had placed me in the same status group as truck drivers.

I had suggested to the *Times* that they might like me to have a new beat, of my creation. When I was first assigned to the Bureau, I had no beat—and that thrilled me. As an investigative reporter I could roam without portfolio, and without pressure from government sources. So, when I was assigned to cover the Justice Department, I interpreted it to mean I was covering Justice in the United States. I never went to the Justice Department's newsroom. That would have been a waste of time. The wire services, AP and UPI, could cover any news release the department tossed out, usually for its own purposes.

The beat I proposed now was the intersection of law, business, and government—that is, the intersection of law, money, and politics. This would be virtually the same as having no beat. I argued that the paper did not cover this area. They thought that was a great idea. I never appreciated until now—in writing this book—how much the paper must have trusted me.

Cathy and I were well suited in many ways and alike in this one: She didn't show much interest in politics. Neither did I.

CHAPTER THIRTY-THREE

The Flying Ashtray; Women Reporters Aren't Getting Their Just Deserts

[I]n May of 1097, a mighty host of Christian Crusaders . . . laid siege to [Nicaea]. Sheltered behind . . . thick walls, the Turks . . . were certain that they could hold out. . . . [T]he Crusaders' company of carpenters and engineers went to work constructing their most formidable weapon. Suddenly, huge rocks were sailing through the air, slamming into the walls and towers of the city, terrifying its inhabitants.
— ROBERT HEEGE, WARFARE HISTORY NETWORK

WASHINGTON BUREAU, THE *NEW YORK TIMES*, 1975

My volunteer post as shop steward for the reporters' union in the Washington Bureau promptly led to two problems—both uncomfortable for me and distressing for the *Times*. But first there was the attack by ashtray. This was a result not of union activity but my deficient sense of humor.

I was sitting at my desk when a heavy metal ashtray flew across the room toward me like a blue discus. I didn't have time to duck. It was another day in the Washington Bureau of the *Times*. My desk abutted a concrete pillar, and the ashtray hit the pillar and bounced off.

I realized that I had had the bad judgment to make a joke that did not place feminism on a high enough altar. I thought the joke was harmless (perhaps, silly), but inoffensive. Back then, reporters tended to be irreverent all the time, and sometimes even obscene. Eileen Shanahan, a business correspondent, loosed her outrage at me from across the room in the form of the ashtray. When the ashtray struck the pillar, even Eileen looked horrified by what she had done.

Ironically, as shop steward, I ultimately wound up doing more for women on the paper than Eileen ever could have imagined. It was something that wakened *Times* women with a rude start.

My first union issue with the paper stemmed from the minimums in the contract with the Newspaper Guild. Everyone was paid above the Guild minimum in the Washington Bureau. When a contract was negotiated, a minimum was set for reporters at different levels of experience. In Washington we were all paid above the minimum, and—through individual decisions by management—at different salaries. This meant that no one had any idea how he or she stacked up against anyone else. It also meant that we couldn't effectively bargain. We didn't know whether we were being treated fairly or like the ink-spattered drudges[90] we were sometimes thought to be.[91]

While I had managed to negotiate a significant rise in my salary when I rejoined the Washington Bureau, salaries remained entirely private. I decided to ask the Newspaper Guild in New York to give me a list of reporters' and editors' salaries in the Bureau with no names identified, just a list of the salaries in rank order.

The Guild obliged. When I got the list, I promptly posted it on the section of the Bureau bulletin board that belonged to the Guild. The Bureau went crazy. For the first time, correspondents knew where they stood in the scheme of things, and one of the things that became immediately clear was that the few women reporters were being paid far less than everybody else.[92] This fact was not lost on Eileen. Even putting aside the incident of the flying ashtray, to call Eileen feisty would be like calling a hurricane a strong gust.

She and others immediately took up the cudgels on behalf of women editorial employees. They filed various complaints. One of these was a suit against the paper. At the end of the day, the complaints caused the *Times* to reach a settlement that raised the pay of the women and promised reform.

Eileen had become one of the original plaintiffs in the suit, but by the time it was settled in 1978 for $350,000, she had left the paper.[93]

I might have—indirectly—been the source of her decision to leave the paper. According to her obituary in the *Times,* she had quit in 1977 in anger, when she found out that her salary was far below most of the male reporters.

Eileen never lacked verve. Her obituary reported that as well: "'She yelled at bureaucrats who were uncooperative,' said Richard E. Mooney, who covered economics with her at The *Times.*"[94] Eileen later became an assistant secretary for public affairs in the Health, Education and Welfare Department under President Carter.

A few months later, when Seymour "Top" Topping, deputy managing editor of the paper, came to Washington on a visit, he asked me why I had posted the list. I told him I thought it had been the right thing to do because, otherwise, we were bargaining in the dark. He asked if I'd had the authority of the Newspaper Guild, and I assured him I had. Otherwise I would not have been able to get the information.

He asked to see proof. I said sure and walked to my desk, which was never locked, to pull out the Guild correspondence from New York. It had disappeared. Someone had taken it. At the time the bureau chief in Washington was Clifton Daniel, for whom the term dandy was invented. Clinton was properly outfitted by Savile Row and probably coiffed daily by Vidal Sassoon himself. He was married to President Truman's daughter, Margaret.

Before Top had asked for the Guild correspondence, Clifton called me into his office and asked why I had posted the list. Before I could respond, he said that he had been thinking about taking the sheet off the Guild portion of the bulletin board but had stopped himself because he realized that everyone had already photocopied it.

A while later I was leaning on a counter in the Bureau reading the paper when Scotty Reston came over. He also asked why I had posted the list. "It won't help anybody," he said, puffing on his ever-present pipe. I was taken entirely aback. For a moment I couldn't find the words to respond. At last I told him we were supposed to be in the business of telling people the truth. "What they do is up to them," I said.

Reston was wrong about no one's being helped by the posting of that list. All female *Times* editorial employees were helped. And Reston was also wrong about collaboration, compromise, and accommodation between journalism and power. Still, his words stung, and still manage to sting today.

CHAPTER THIRTY-FOUR

I Didn't Write That—
Don't You Dare Say I Did!

Why are The Economist's writers anonymous? Because it allows many writers to speak with a collective voice.

—THE ECONOMIST

The Newspaper Guild's byline strike at the [Pittsburgh] Post-Gazette is . . . getting harder to not notice. . . . [E]mployees . . . continue to create content but they withhold their names. . . . [T]he union says its members have withheld more than 689 bylines from stories [and] photographs. . . .

—NEWSGUILD

WASHINGTON BUREAU, THE *NEW YORK TIMES*, 1975

My second problem as shop steward for the Newspaper Guild came from the contract negotiations with the *Times*.

First came the strike threat. Lengthy negotiations followed between the *Times* and the Newspaper Guild at Ted Kheel's Automation House, a center for conflict resolution in Manhattan. The Guild had put me on its negotiating team. As negotiations grew more and more tense and the night advanced, *Times* employees began sitting on the internal stairway, crying as they considered what would happen to them, their families, and their houses if they decided to strike. When I saw the scene, I was horrified: It was just what a labor negotiator did not want the other side to see.

But what made me (almost) cry was that the *Times* was yielding not at all—on anything. As the hours dragged on, and the city grew darker and darker, so did our negotiations. The *Times* negotiators kept pleading poverty. Then, deep into the night, a non-economic issue came up. The right of a reporter to not have his or her byline appear on a piece that the reporter thought had been distorted by editing. To my surprise, the *Times* said, firmly, no.

I was stunned and asked why in the world this bastion of Truth and Integrity (all right, maybe without the initial capital letters) objected to doing the right thing. How could it say no to the reporter's right to withdraw the byline if the reporter no longer believed in the accuracy of the story and did not want to be associated with it? The paper had given the job of labor negotiator to Peter Millones after I had said no. He explained it had to do with "editorial control," but I persisted in not understanding what that could mean.

"We cannot surrender editorial control," Peter Millones explained.

He was soft—very soft—in style, but inflexible in position.

I had no cards. If we struck, reporters and editors could not shut the paper. We needed the printers, the drivers, and the others who actually physically produced and delivered the paper to join us or we would surely fail. Would they? Probably, but that was not certain.

At 2:00 a.m. I decided to gamble. I looked at the *Times* negotiators. "You haven't given us one damn thing all night," I said, just as quietly as Millones, but with feigned anger.

> *This is a no-cost item, so you can't hit us again with the poverty routine. As for losing editorial control, in this instance, you're actually emphasizing that control by agreeing in advance to let a reporter follow his conscience.*
>
> *You will be thoroughly ashamed, in the real world, if you force a reporter to let his byline be used.*
>
> *And you'll be ashamed when another publication prints the fact that you've done that.*
>
> *But forgetting all that, I've been reasonably quiet all night. You haven't given us a damn thing. Here's something you easily can—and should—give us. Do the right thing!*

If you don't, I'm going to have to advise my team to strike.

After I'd given my speech, we broke for caucuses, and I walked back down the metal back staircase to go outside for some air. By now, the sky was inkily—no, scarily—black. A few minutes later, the *Times* team came back and announced that we could have the byline control clause in the contract. I could only imagine how they had thought readers and journalists would react when we leaked their not giving us that right. Anyway, that's what I had banked on.

Going forward, I decided I could be reasonable and rational. We averted a strike. People kept their houses. And as far as I know, reporters did not yank names off their articles.

Making the *Times*'s position even more remarkable—if not utterly untenable—is the Berne Convention for the Protection of Literary and Artistic Works. The United States has signed it.

Article 6 bis of the treaty provides:

Independently of the author's economic rights ... the author shall have the right ... to object to any distortion, mutilation or other modification of, or other derogatory action in relation to, the said work, which would be prejudicial to his honor or reputation.[95]

These moral rights are tied to the rights of readers. As the International Federation of Journalists said:

Strong moral rights guarantee the authenticity, quality and integrity of work. There is an indivisible link between moral rights and the ethics and independence of journalism.[96]

I returned to the Washington Bureau. I was working on a piece when my phone rang. It was a senior editor and friend in New York. "Jesus," he said, "management says you were a real son of a bitch!" For one moment I thought about yanking the byline off the *Sunday Week in Review* piece I was writing, but I decided that would be too adolescently rebellious, even for me.

Ironically, the *Times* had yanked my very first byline. I no longer remember what the piece was, but I do remember that when a copy boy threw the first edition—still wet—on my desk in the rewrite bank, I hurried over and scanned the pages. There was the story—in the *New York Times*! *With no byline.* An assistant metropolitan editor explained that for the first byline they needed the managing editor's approval. "We couldn't find him," he said casually, and put a slug of metal type in my hand. That was it: My byline!—*Robert M. Smith.* Well, almost. I still have it. I wonder whether it would make a hole if I kept it in the pocket of the Italian racing jacket.

CHAPTER THIRTY-FIVE

Biz/Fin

In Nevada, where legal brothels have operated since the late 19th century, business is . . . a bit slow. [The] director of the . . . Brothel Owners' Association, said revenue at the . . . bordellos for which he lobbies is down 25 percent to 45 percent. . . . Nevada's brothels [couldn't] advertise outside the immediate areas in which they were located. . . . That law was struck down . . . [Politicians stayed silent.] . . . Nevada is . . . facing a $1-billion budget shortfall. Legal brothels' annual revenue is estimated . . . to be $35 million to $50 million, with an overall economic impact of [40% of the budget].
—CLAUDE BRODESSER-AKNER, *CRAIN'S DETROIT BUSINESS*

WASHINGTON BUREAU, THE *NEW YORK TIMES*, 1975

Biz/Fin, the business and financial section of the *Times*, was a *clos privé*—a private space. A private space it still seems to be today, though it seems to have added a gate or two. Back in the 1970s, when I would write a piece, submit it, or the Washington News Desk would route it to Biz/Fin, that was the kiss of death. Biz/Fin would not run it. It didn't take a lot of guessing as to why, since everything else I wrote ended up in the paper. The reason had to be that my pieces were of a critical bent, or Biz/Fin editors construed them that way. Biz/Fin didn't fancy that.

Truth be told, some of my sources were frustrated, even desperate when they couldn't get their information—despite its accuracy—into the *Times*. One of the first times I encountered this frustration was when a source gave me secret information that the US Comptroller of the

Currency had put many banks on a "problem bank list." I knew that the job of the OCC was to "ensure the safety and soundness of the federal banking system for all Americans." The OCC list included banks that had "aggravated deficiencies in condition and management." I saw nothing wrong with reporting that fact.[97]

The two financial correspondents, Eileen Shanahan and Ed Dale, disagreed. They told me that the list was not meaningful. Reporting about its existence would irresponsibly scare people. And they didn't believe there really were "problem banks." Not believe there really were "problem banks"?

They were the experts, and they wouldn't touch the story. I was still young and new to the game. And I didn't get it. This was a government agency whose job it was to create the list from information that banks had to give it. I argued my point. Maybe the judgment as to what was a "problem bank" was wrong, but, I said, shouldn't we report the Comptroller's view? I listened to Eileen and Ed's points. Then I wrote the story. The *Times* printed the article, but not the list of problem banks.

I was furious. My source had risked a lot to get that list. In my view, it was he—my source—who was the expert, but the paper's business/financial reporters didn't want that list printed. Problem banks—an early hint of things to come decades later—remained protected. A few years later, Ed Dale became a budget spokesman for the Reagan administration.

Dale had gone to Yale, and rumor was that he had been a member of the Skull and Bones secret society. When I later went to Yale, I learned that Bonesmen are supposed to leave the room if the name of the society comes up. It's not my fault if—like many reporters—I was occasionally devilish. One day when Dale walked into the newsroom, I mentioned Skull and Bones. He quickly walked out.

I don't doubt that these two correspondents thought that reporting about problem banks, as I insisted on doing, was wrong, but to this day I don't understand their insistence. I put qualifying language into the story. It ultimately ran on January 23, 1976.[98]

I don't think Eileen and Ed were captives of the OCC, the Fed, the Treasury, and the other agencies. But after years of looking at things through that prism and through those constant institutional biases, wouldn't you see a problem bank list as a not-so-hot-potato and any story about it as—what?—irresponsible and déclassé?

In my mind, Bill Beecher's attitude toward the My Lai Massacre and their attitude toward the bad bank story seem parallel. Bill was the Pentagon correspondent. He sat next to me. A nice man and a good reporter, Bill watched me and listened to my calls through the entire painful life of that story, but he never wrote a word about My Lai. Not one word. He finally wrote about the massacre in March 1970, when the Army held a news conference and released its own report about the massacre, the Peers Report.

Bill was dependent on Defense Department sources. He did one day tell me he had heard about me from those sources. He swiveled his chair toward me and said, "Hey, Bob, you get more with honey than vinegar."

I stared at him and suppressed the obvious retort: "It depends on what you're trying to get."

In other words, cozy up to the Pentagon—or any other Washington institution—and you'll make lots of friends and likely get leaks that your pals want out. Don't cozy up and life may be hard, especially if you are covering just one institution. You'll be punished. The more important question, I thought, was: Would your readers be punished too?

This was a problem not limited to reporters. It included some editors. I've told you about how I could not get some stories into the Biz/Fin section of the *Times*. At all. Period. Let me also tell you how I got bawled out when, in desperation, I managed to place one of those business stories elsewhere in the paper.

One day in 1976, I was leaked a letter that a lawyer for Lockheed had written in longhand to a Lockheed executive on hotel stationery from an upscale hostelry in Switzerland:

Dear Charlie:

Please accept my apologies for addressing you on scratch paper and in my execrable handwriting, but I am in no position to disclose to local third persons the contents hereof and it will be some days before I will be back in the Paris office.

Please hold onto your seat, as what follows may be a shocker to you

. . . [Our agent] states that Gelae [Lockheed's Georgia Company], if it wishes the maximum run for success, must be prepared to go as high as $120,000 per airplane for the cumshaw part. [Cumshaw is a word of Chinese origin meaning present or gratuity.]

He hopes it will be less and will try to keep it less (and I believe him to be sincere in this) but says that such is a nasty fact of life in the arena in which we are trying to off-set the same type tactics by a combination (this time) of both the French and the Germans . . .

[The agent said] there will not again be a face-to-face negotiation between a representative of the "party" and Lockheed representatives but that he will be told, probably by the Antelope Cobbler (get out your little black book—mine is dated October 5, 1965), just how much the "party" demands.

Further, there will be the Cobbler himself and Pun and various others of lesser but highly placed personnel.

In this connection he insists that he will only give names and figures to one person in Lockheed. . . . Actually, he said he wanted it to be me, of those he has been dealing with, because I am a lawyer. (Doesn't that just make you available as a repository for guilty knowledge??). . . .

I really should not be putting even the figures in writing, but I have no choice. . . .

I apologize for the length of this. I hope you keep this letter on a very strict need-to-know basis with respect to your compatriots.

As for the compensation for third persons part, we are dealing with dynamite that could blow Lockheed right out of Italy with terrible repercussions.

Best regards,

Roger

In my story, I let the letter speak for itself, without commentary. I thought it said a lot about American (illegal) corporate bribery overseas, and it was funny, to boot. Biz/Fin rejected it. I assumed it was because they were once again, reflexively or not, looking out for Business.

I was determined to get the letter into the paper. So I did *exactly* the same piece for the *Sunday Week in Review,* and they ran it.[99] And Sunday had a much bigger circulation and readership. The piece was well received. I was content and rolled on with other stories. A few days later, one of the Washington News Desk editors strolled over to my desk to tell me Biz/Fin was not happy. They wanted to know why I hadn't offered them the piece that ran in the *Week in Review.*

Stunned, I reached into the top left-hand drawer of my desk and pulled out a batch of my dupes—the sheet from the multi-ply carbon books that reporters typed on in those days. One copy was for the reporter. I handed him the dupe of the story that had been sent to and rejected by Biz/Fin. The News Desk editor took the dupe, stared at it, and walked away without a word.

One of the reasons I got this sort of piece from sources was that they couldn't otherwise get the material into the paper. They knew I did not do traditional business reporting and I might find a way to get their stuff in.

At the Columbia Graduate School of Journalism, I had been compelled to write two business stories under the tutelage of Joe Lelyveld, later Executive Editor of the *Times.* So, two stories I did. One was on the economics of a hot dog stand in Times Square. The other was on the economics of a bodega—a corner grocery—in Spanish Harlem. Joe gave me an A for both.

One thing I later did enjoy in Biz/Fin was Pulitzer Prize–winning Gretchen Morgenson's weekly column, a refreshing excursion into normal misdeeds of corporate leaders, their accountants, and lawyers. One of Morgenson's columns in early 2017 began, "Deception. Cheating. Shortcuts."[100] The column must make some corporate folks perspire like wayward souls visiting an incense-laden chapel. (Morgenson is now on the investigative team at the *Wall Street Journal.*)

Throughout my stay in Washington, I persisted in my Sunday detour unless the story was breaking news and had to be in the next day's paper. I suppose I could have asked Biz/Fin why I was having a hard time getting them to take my stories. I even thought of going to New York to visit the editor, Dick Mooney. But I didn't think the conversation would do much good. As with Eileen, Ed, and problem banks, this was a mindset issue.

I told Bob Phelps and the Washington News Desk about my problems and continued to use a guerilla approach. I wrote nearly every weekend for the *Week in Review* and developed a habit of going to the liquor store next door to the *Times* on Wednesday nights. I bought a Czech lager—a completely atypical thing for me to do—and settled in to do a seven-hundred-to-one-thousand-word "thumbsucker," or analytic piece.

Sy Hersh's experience with Biz/Fin apparently paralleled mine. I was trying to get pieces like the Lockheed lawyer's unwitting confession into the financial pages and ultimately end-running the section by sending the stories to the *Week in Review*.[101] Sy explains how an editor in Washington showed him a confidential message from Biz/Fin, warning the editor that Hersh was biased against American companies. Sy read the message and headed for the elevator. Sy and I may have taken the same elevator down, just at different times.

CHAPTER THIRTY-SIX

Oxy Threatens My Job; Pursuing the CEO from Hernando's Posh Hideaway

People may expect too much of journalism. Not only do they expect it to be entertaining, they expect it to be true.
—LEWIS H. LAPHAM, FORMER EDITOR OF *HARPER'S MAGAZINE*

WASHINGTON BUREAU, THE *NEW YORK TIMES*, 1975

The paper's power was both an important shield *from* the powerful and could also get you access *to* the powerful. That's why when Armand Hammer, the CEO of Occidental Petroleum, demanded I quash my piece on Occidental's paying bribes in Venezuela, I could stand my ground.[102]

How many people could tell the guy who ran Occidental Petroleum (nearly $18 billion in revenue) to go to the complaint window? I had to be certain that Hammer would not go to Sulzberger, that Sulzberger would back me up or stay out of it—or I had to be even more naïve than I was.

Other correspondents were, for good reasons, afraid that offending those in power on their beats could mean no more leaks, or worse, more leaks to their competitors. But I had no real beat, and I was therefore not so much courageous as insulated. Insulated—unless somebody else saw the brief summary of my story on the clipboard near the news desk that described the stories being written and decided to use the information. For example, someone once called me to say that Kissinger really wasn't a tyrant at the National Security Council, shortly after I had put my summary on the clipboard. Had somebody called Kissinger and given him a chance to intervene?

Similarly, once I had wonderful material about Lockheed paying bribes to officials of foreign governments. Oddly, these stories were the result of a possibly improper journalistic invasion into policy making.

The *Times* business reporter in Washington, Mike Jensen, took me to meet Stanley Sporkin, the head of the SEC's Enforcement Division. During that meeting, Sporkin disclosed, inappropriately, that it was Jensen who had come up with the idea of getting the SEC into the business of policing bribery overseas by American corporations. Jensen had come up with a theory and shared it with Sporkin. The theory was that bribery was a "material fact" that the law required companies to disclose to investors. Jensen should perhaps not have contributed to government policy and enforcement. He was there to watch the SEC and report on it, not push it into novel investigative territory. But that's what Sporkin told me Mike had done, as Mike reddened slightly. Ignorant of journalistic conventions, Sporkin was trying to praise Mike to a *Times* colleague.

That was the route to my stories about bribes that Lockheed was supposed to be paying overseas.

I called the president of Lockheed, but his secretary said no interview. I called again. Same result. So I hopped on a plane to Los Angeles, and there, from the comfort of my elegant room at the Beverly Wilshire at Rodeo Drive (and its Hernando's Hideaway restaurant, which offered up huevos rancheros of renown), I phoned Lockheed's board chairman, Daniel Haughton (known as "Uncle Dan"). He proved a more sympathetic fellow. "I've come out here to Los Angeles," I told him, and "I'm going to interview *somebody*." In the end, I got to interview Haughton. The *Times* Biz/Fin section ran my piece:

LOS ANGELES, Sept. 3, 1975

Daniel J. Haughton, chairman of the Lockheed Aircraft Corporation, which has admitted making payments of at least $22-million to foreign government officials and political parties, feels that the United States Government undoubtedly will adopt regulations restricting such payments.

In an interview Sunday, at the company's headquarters in . . . Burbank, Mr. Haughton was pressed on whether he felt Government regulations prohibiting American companies from making such payments would be a good idea. Mr. Haughton replied that he thought "that's a moot question" because in his view the Government is certain to adopt "rules and regulations and laws" . . .

Mr. Haughton said that he was "not trying to uphold these payments." The point involved, he added, was that "if American companies are restricted more than foreign countries' companies, we are going to lose some business. If we want to pay that price, O.K.". . . . [103]

The anti-bribery campaign got Sporkin, a Yale Law grad, and the SEC a lot of media attention. Sporkin, who resembled a bulldog in appearance, was tough. He was subsequently appointed general counsel of the CIA. Later President Reagan appointed him a federal judge.[104] I later wrote about Sporkin,

Can this chunky, 43-year-old with clothes that look as if they are going to burst at any moment be at the center of a drive to make America's biggest companies embarrass themselves by telling whom, how and when they bribed overseas?[105]

I'm certain now (though I began to understand this only after leaving the paper) that Reston would not have liked my naïve chasing of the hapless president of Lockheed to question him about secret skullduggery until I finally pressured him into an interview by appealing to the chair of his board. And he certainly wouldn't have approved of my telling Armand Hammer where he might lodge his preemptive complaint about a report of foreign bribery by Occidental. (With the publisher.) I must have been fearless, blind to bureaucratic politics, naïve—or all of these. That didn't detract from the professional pleasure of being able to report critically about Oxy and other huge American enterprises, let alone warn that the sun might persuade the president to shirk doing his homework before going to China. This was independence of a remarkable kind—and I took it for granted.

This bulletproof insulation ends when you leave the paper and find yourself, in maturity, facing all the workaday problems you never had to face without the benefit of the experience of having had to face them, the techniques of facing them, or the ability to let them roll off your back. At least, that was my experience.

I couldn't imagine then there would come a time in my life when I would advise corporate boards or travel dizzyingly from country to country managing the lawsuits of a multinational bank. But for now, I was raking muck from the elegant comfort of one of the poshest hotels in one of the poshest neighborhoods in America. That's akin to savoring five-star haute cuisine and criticizing the restaurant's politics. I was using the power and influence—and bountiful expense account—of the *Times* to unearth corporate shenanigans.

CHAPTER THIRTY-SEVEN

A Cosseted Crowd; Kafka Has You in His Embrace; Leaving the Gray Lady Again

If you ever find yourself in the wrong story, leave.
—Mo WILLEMS, *GOLDILOCKS AND THE THREE DINOSAURS*

SAN FRANCISCO, 1975

My decision to leave the Bureau the second time was driven by three motives: fear, cynicism, and restlessness. In a story about me in *Esquire* magazine, Gene Roberts suggested a fourth: "Bob is the world's most traditional and moral man . . . Going to the bathroom probably involves a philosophical decision. He was tormented by his persistence and agonized about going through life as a royal pain in the ass."[106]

I had always felt pity for those *Times* reporters in their forties, fifties, and sixties who were banished to the last rows of the cavernous newsroom to . . . sit. They were guys—generally, guys—who had been shot at covering wars, who had given decades to the paper, but who had been passed over for editors' jobs and had, in Rosenthal's view, passed their expiry dates. The newspaper business, everyone callously insisted, was a young man's game. A young, straight man's game, as "Ms." was not an acceptable honorific in the paper, and "gay" could refer only to cheerfulness.[107]

As with other *Times* people, it was a negative for me that I had been hand-picked by Abraham Michael Rosenthal: I had become one of his elect, an extension of his limitless ego, with its demand for limitless loyalty.

Gay Talese tells this story about Rosenthal:

Bernard Weinraub, a *Times* reporter, was in the men's room one day when Rosenthal walked in and asked Bernie whether he thought he had lost weight. Mr. Weinraub looked at him and said he didn't think so, to which Rosenthal shouted, "You son of a bitch!" and abruptly left the room. Weinraub was stunned and asked Mr. Gelb whether he thought that was the end of his career.

Gelb answered, "I'm not sure."[108]

One day, Phelps called me over to the Washington news desk and told me, "Abe Rosenthal has fallen." I thought he meant Rosenthal had been deposed as executive editor. Actually, Rosenthal had fallen on the sidewalk when he was leaving work. It turned out he suffered from a nerve ailment. Word quickly spread around the newsroom. I didn't hear a word of sympathy.

Phelps told me that, ultimately, I would become the national editor. With my newfound hubris—in rank defiance of the gods—I asked him quietly, "Only national editor?"

"The rest involves chance," he answered. And so I rolled along, reporting in the Bureau, winning a few Publisher's Awards, the paper's merit badges doled out monthly. After a year or so, I wrote Abe Rosenthal and imprudently asked: How about my moving on to be an editor?

The reply was brisk and to-the-point: We don't make editors of reporters who are doing mediocre work. It stunned me. If I was doing mediocre work, how was I winning those awards? My friends tried to calm me down. "It's just Rosenthal," they said.

When I came back, Phelps warned me: "Abe hired you. So you're his guy now." I didn't get that this would mean I would now be an object of his boundless ego, subject to his whims and fits.

My colleagues in Washington advised, "Go to New York and talk with him." That, they explained, is what people did. I thought about it. I decided I did not want to work for this guy. Hell, no one wanted to work for this guy. And I didn't have to.

Rosenthal scared me, but he had recruited me back. I had won awards. And now he was beating me up, or so it felt. It was time to leave. I was also cynical about my future; I had seen the lengths people at the paper went to in order to get ahead, and I didn't want to compete in those demeaning bureaucratic ways. And besides, I was restless. To say I had a short attention span would not give "short" its due.

I also couldn't compete bureaucratically. Whatever the gene for group success is, or the kindergarten training required, I didn't have it—and still don't. Take this example: I didn't give, or host, many social events when I was a reporter. I did host one champagne-laden event in a colonial town-home in Alexandria, Virginia, across the river from Washington. To it, I invited many friends and colleagues from the *Times*. Keeping with my lack of bureaucratic awareness—let alone cunning—I did not invite Max Frankel, on the simple (to me) ground that we were not close.

The *Times* could not—at long last—bear the embarrassing column Rosenthal wrote after management forced him to give up the editorship. He had, at last, managed to snuff out the *Times*'s affection and end the tolerance of the *Times* executives, not to mention their patience. Rosenthal had shown you can be an intuitively gifted journalist without being able to deal in the most rudimentary way with ideas and analysis—or people. Perhaps lackluster led to bluster.

Incredibly, Rosenthal ended up as a columnist for the *New York Daily News*. This was not like crossing Times Square. It was like going down a salacious skid-row alley.

Rosenthal's obituary in the *Times* by Bob McFadden said he was brilliant, passionate, and abrasive:

> *. . . a man of dark moods and mercurial temperament, he could coolly evaluate world developments one minute and humble a subordinate for an error in the next.*
>
> *A gravel-voiced, jowly man with a tight smile, a shock of black hair parted vaguely on the left and judgmental gray-green eyes behind horn-rimmed glasses, he was regarded by colleagues as complex, often contradictory. . . .*
>
> *Max Frankel, who initially lost out to Mr. Rosenthal in the competition to become executive editor but who later succeeded him in that post, assessed his predecessor in a memoir, "The Times of My Life and My Life with The Times," published in 1999, five years after his own retirement.*

One chapter was titled "Not-Abe," a reference to Mr. Frankel's belief that one of his tasks as executive editor was to set a more collegial tone in the news department. . . .

Mr. Frankel added: "His innermost judgments of people depended not just on their value to The Times but on their regard for him and his ideas."[109]

The *Times* obituary did not mention it, but Frankel's book also offered this remarkable ethical view:

Abe Rosenthal left the newsroom with a reputation for brilliant, instinctive news judgment coupled with an intimidating, self-centered management style. Most of his values were admirable, and many of his tactics were therefore forgivable.[110]

You forgive questionable tactics if they are in the service of good values: Ends justify means.

When Frankel replaced Rosenthal as executive editor, a clear part of his mandate was to settle down the newsroom.

But whatever Frankel did, the newsroom was not destined to remain a happy place.

Jill Abramson became the paper's first female executive editor in 2011. In a meeting, she drove one of her subordinates, Dean Baquet, to such anger and distress that he slammed his hand against a wall.[111] When I heard the story, I worried about Dean and called to ask him whether the wall would be okay. He assured me it would.

When Abramson began her lawyer-accompanied swan song, I sent Arthur Sulzberger an email. Then I offered to mediate the dispute. He said they had already tried mediation and it had failed. I asked how it came to be that seemingly difficult people ended up running the joint. Arthur did not respond.

Despite the tyranny of bosses like Rosenthal, there was—and, I assume, still may be—a comfortable aspect to working at the *Times*. The paper's people are cosseted, insulated from everyday difficulties because they work for the *Times*. Some people fear *Times* reporters, some are in awe. So most people working at the paper seldom have to deal with dishonest car repair people, or bad restaurant tables, or undercooked chops.

They are not like President George H. W. Bush, who was forced to admit he did not know how much a gallon of milk cost during a debate with Bill Clinton and Ross Perot. *Times* people know the price of milk, but they rarely have an unpleasant experience with grocers—or, for that matter, vendors of air conditioners or mortgages. These vendors have a fear of negative publicity (which—really—is not likely to result from a spat with a *Times* reporter).

But power, oozing from the paper, forms a protective barrier around its correspondents and editors. People shy away from offending *Times* reporters. They don't want to give reporters something bad to write about them or their companies. No one carried this farther than Henry Kissinger. He used to bug the phones of the professionals who worked for him in the National Security Council—as well as other officials. He reportedly even had a bug in the office of the secretary of defense, according to *Wired.*

But there is less comfort in Washington. Investigative reporters there are in a setting Kafka and Orwell would have had to join forces to describe. The theory is that they are members of a free press, telling the American people what is happening, just as Jefferson Smith did in 1939 when he went to Washington. The theory is that Washington reporters are writing to educate the famous Chicago milkman (a journalist's mind's-eye model to test clarity of prose and presentation).

But if you are serious about journalism and think (a) the society is free and (b) people should know what's happening, you soon learn that no one wants to tell you the good stuff, either because the government has stamped it *Secret,* or because it's just not in the government's interest to tell you. It is this conflict that makes investigative reporters eligible for Pulitzers and then puts them at risk for endlessly polishing and repolishing the Pulitzer Gold Medal in their prison cells.

I think psychiatric residents at the end of their training should be sent, in platoons, to do research on Washington reporters. I am convinced they would find paranoia rampant because reporters spend ten hours a day listening to people lie to them.

The trick was always to be suspicious, to figure out who was not lying to you, but after a while suspicion can turn to paranoia.

Investigative reporters need a few qualities: They must be able to get people to trust them and to open up. Then they have to decide whether what the sources are saying is what the sources think is true. The reporters have to figure out what is the truth. And they have to do this quickly—and without becoming so jaded that they get all or part of the story wrong.

I was once interviewing a lawyer in the State Department about the Middle East. I had already seen the State Department internal cable traffic about the subject I was asking about. I shouldn't have seen the cables, but I had. As I sat across from the man, I saw he was looking at the cable traffic. He said he was reading it to me. And since I'd seen the traffic, I knew he was. I leaned back, looked up at him from my reporter's notebook, and thought: *Why is this son of a bitch telling me the truth?*

The day before I left the Bureau again, I was chatting with Phil Shabecoff, the environmental reporter. Phil was an immensely principled fellow. It was his habit to walk out of a room when a government official tried to take refuge by going "off the record." I must have been complaining about something. Phil looked at me and said quietly, "Do you think *any* of us would be here if we had what you have?" I understood he meant my law degree and the options it afforded.

Cathy and I came to a firm decision. Then we went to an ice cream parlor (which did not have sundaes!) in Washington. I told her we could go pretty much anywhere.

"I have to take the bar exam somewhere," I said. "It can be anywhere."

Our ice creams were melting in the Washington sunshine.

As we licked the sugar cones, I asked offhandedly, "What about San Francisco?"

Cathy said fine.

I quit again.

It is easy to tell that today is your last day at the *Times* because we can hear the sigh of relief from the Justice Department all the way up here in fun city. We also want you to know that we are sighing—but with regret—and that we will miss your intrepid, irrepressible, birddog digging that is the hallmark of the fine, tough reporter you are. We'll miss you bob. Best wishes for a smashing future.

—Roberts, Jones, Slosser, Jenkins, Wark and all the admiring hands on the national desk

(by *Times* telex)

CHAPTER THIRTY-EIGHT

Josie Insists: Piaget or Nothing— Brooks Brothers Gets Dressed Down; Behind the Frosted Glass

The curse of the [New York] Herald Tribune is drink. The curse of The Times is sex.

—New York newspaper adage

A trial in Italy had to be suspended after the judge and jury spotted a pair of court employees having sex in an adjoining room, behind a frosted glass window.
—Nick Squires, *Daily Telegraph* (UK), May 20, 2014

SAN FRANCISCO, 1976

At my first trial, there was no rich paneling, no Oriental carpets, no stained-glass windows, no chandeliers. These luxuries would come three years later in the World Court in The Hague. I'm reasonably sure my first trial took place in a courtroom, because the sign on the door told visitors that it was.

That first trial was a drunk-driving case. I was the prosecutor. I lost the trial. My loss of that *simple* trial almost made me give up law, return to journalism, sell fish—anything but represent someone in another trial. I've wished many times since then that I could re-try that case with just a little more experience than I had in those first days. I should not have lost . . . really, I should not have.

Prosecutors have wide discretion. They don't usually have to take cases they don't believe in, and they don't typically take cases they think they may lose. I was too new to know when—and how—I might lose. Anyway, I had been assigned the case.

The guy on the other side knew what he was doing. That included trying to distract me by talking to me while I was preparing my final argument. This effort got me angry. This was good when I stood up to argue. The passion came right through.

One of the jurors—Josie—was a stunning blonde interior designer from upscale Pacific Heights, and since I was not allowed to talk with her, all I knew about her was that she was stunning. At the beginning of the trial, while the defense lawyer was making his opening statement, she looked at me. She kept her gaze on me and began to smile.

This is not a subject covered at Yale Law School. Lawyers in trial are not supposed to communicate with jurors in any way, and as a rank rookie, I took the rules literally. So I didn't know what to do. If I didn't return the smile, I might offend her and lose her vote, but if I did smile back, I might offend the other jurors and everyone else, including the judge.

I looked down at my yellow pad and began scribbling—I have no idea what.

After I lost and before the jurors left, I walked over to the jury box. Since this was a California state court, not a federal court, I was allowed to speak with the jurors now. I spoke to a few, asking the obvious: "What did you think of the case? Anything I could have done better? It's my first trial, and we don't have any video." Eventually I approached Josie and asked, "Well?"

As Josie began to reply, an elderly woman to her left tugged on her elbow urging her not to speak. I knew something was wrong. But I persisted: "It's okay," I said. "I have to learn."

Josie cleared her throat. The old lady tugged on her elbow again. I stepped between them and tried asking again.

"Well, Bob," she said, converting the name I'd used to introduce myself—Robert—to something less formal.

"Do you see him?" she asked, pointing to my adversary.

"Yes," I said.

"Do you see what's on his wrist?"

"Looks like a watch."

"It's a Piaget."

"A Piaget?"

I might not have been a great trial lawyer, but I was one hell of a straight man.

"It's the world's most expensive watch," Josie said. I unconsciously touched my pocket watch—yes, *pocket watch.*

"And do you see his suit?"

"What about it?" I asked, still not catching on.

"You see how it's tailored? Probably Italian."

Italian? I thought to myself. Brooks Brothers (my notion of high style back then) has failed me.

"Do you see how he is dark, Mediterranean . . . exciting?"

"And me, Josie?" I asked, fearing the worst.

"Bob, you're more mainstream." My God, plain white bread. Harvard, what had you done to a kid from Roxbury of Eastern European extraction?

That's when I realized trials involved sex appeal. I understood that neither the *Times* nor Yale had swept away my naïve belief that courtrooms were chaste. Time to leave the courthouse for the newsroom again?

They didn't teach sex appeal at Yale. Ever since that day I've thought I should one day endow a chair: *The Smith Charisma and Magnetism Chair of Trial Practice.*

Sexual Attraction Chair seems outré.

The trial reminded me of the day I covered my first and only fire, years ago in Boston. I arrived at the fire. The judge and jury were here, just as the flames and firefighters had been. I was very warm at my first fire, and my first trial, and I was thinking the same thing at both: *Now what the hell am I supposed to do?*

Josie's raising so vividly style and the appeal of sex reminded me of the role those two factors played in New York journalism.

The blessing of the *Herald Tribune* was style—style in writing, style in graphics and layout, style all the way around—a pleasure to pick up, like a piece of apple pie topped with cheddar cheese. Beckoning. You knew it would provide a treat somewhere between the front and back pages—maybe several.

The curse of the *Trib*—in lore, maybe fact—was alcohol.

The curse of the *Times*, on the other hand was—in fact—sex.

As the *New York Daily News* reported in September 1999:

Stories of office romance at The New York Times *definitely fall under the paper's definition of news that's unfit to print. . . . [A]ccording to "The Trust," a . . . biography of the Sulzberger family . . . in the '80s, then-executive editor Abe Rosenthal had an affair with "a young Times secretary" whom he later promoted "to an executive position." According to the book, Punch [the publisher] had to intervene to end the affair.*

At the *Times*, sex did not often come up in reporting. I had heard rumors about a woman reporter who later came to Washington and whose inclination toward intimacy with her sources was linked to her success. These stories or rumors, true or not, were so incessant they were hard to disregard. They were trotted out every time her name came up. And, yes, there was the estranged bureau chief whose liaison with his secretary was a staple for a while. And, yes, there was my own likely imprudent liaison with a Senate staffer. But the *Times* was a competitive, serious place, too serious for rampant trysting. (I can hear the howls from my former colleagues: "Naïve! Naïve!")

CHAPTER THIRTY-NINE

My Learned Friend Exposes the Press; Yelling in the Courtroom

*[W]hen an advocate raises his voice in court, people usually wonder
. . . what's gone wrong with him.*
— Keith Evans, *Common Sense Rules of Advocacy
for Lawyers: A Practical Guide for Anyone
Who Wants to be a Better Advocate*

SAN FRANCISCO, 1977

The press can be used to good effect in the courtroom. Jurors can be swayed by its reporting and ramblings. That's why, if the trial is noteworthy, lawyers and judges often tell the jury not to read or watch media coverage of the case.

In 1977, I asked the judge to keep my opponent in a trial from mentioning the press. The San Francisco press had dealt with the issue in the case. The issue was decoy police. Two cops had dressed as Marines and had lain flat—seemingly passed out—on Market Street in the grubby middle of town. Not to be obvious, one had a wallet sticking out of a back pocket. Cops were on nearby rooftops watching over them, and, sure enough, two guys approached. But they were not passersby. They were the owners of a bar the cops were lying in front of. One of the owners kicked one of the Marines/cops. All hell broke loose as cops descended from rooftops and ran from hiding and handcuffed the shocked bar owners.

A local law school dean—a tough, short, wiry, middle-aged woman with gray hair—was defending the bar owners. On loan to the DA's

Office, I was prosecuting them on behalf of—as I intoned as often as possible—the People of the City and County of San Francisco.

The dean's defense was that decoy cops equal entrapment, among other terrible things. One of San Francisco's two major local papers had agreed with her position, at length. I asked the judge not to let the media intrude, not to let the jury know the views of the press, and he agreed: There would be no mention of the media coverage, and so there wasn't. At least not out loud. The dean began to walk back and forth in front of the jury box, slowly, holding a clipboard that faced the jury. From the clipboard dangled a photocopy of the editorial lambasting decoy policing.

Whoa, I objected eloquently.

Right, said the judge.

The dean of a law school no less, I breathed, trying to calm myself. I had to wonder if I'd called attention to the article by pointing out what she was doing, but I'd had no alternative.

I was still very much on training wheels those days. It was my habit to repair to the marvelous Beaux-Arts City Hall Law Library, where I would pore over books on trial advocacy. They were mostly British. In one of those English hornbooks I found a chapter on "Raising One's Voice in the Courtroom." Really? I thought. Barristers shouting at the Old Bailey? I had the impression they lived for understatement. (It did not occur to me, sitting there in the library, that life would lead me to the black gown of a barrister of the Inner Temple, where I did not find understatement underappreciated.) But when I read the passage on roaring in court. I thought: Why not?

So I went back to the decoy-cops trial, and once again the dean was at it. Her trick this time was to have one of the bar owners leave the courtroom while the other testified. She could later argue that their testimony matched, even though they hadn't heard each other.

It came time to begin my cross-examination:

You and your partner see each other all the time, right? This trial is important to you, right? So you have discussed it? Discussed it many times? And so you know what he will tell the jury? And he knows what you are saying, doesn't he?

During the "so" part I began to raise my voice. A little at first. Then a notch more. Then still more. The dean objected that I was yelling at her client. Damn right, you've got me there. The judge seemed amused. He said quietly, "Well, Mr. Smith, you are speaking a little loudly." Sorry, Your Honor.

You got that right, I thought. I glanced over discreetly and found that the jurors were sitting at the very edge of their seats. Even the tubby, sleeping juror in the back row had woken up. I thought: Chalk one up for British nineteenth-century trial training. Silly, immature advocate that I was, I felt I'd become part of a long line, going back centuries, of barristers addressing—or perhaps shouting at—jurors.

Years later, I would walk through the pelting rain in Holborn in the West End of Central London, just past Chancery Lane, to take the examination to become a barrister. Inside the legal building, the examiner greeted me. This was an oral exam, mainly hypothetical questions. I soon realized that the examiner did not understand that I could *understand him*, just fine. He insisted on speaking so slowly that I feared paralysis might seize him at any moment. Finally, the time came for me to answer the first question. I couldn't help myself: I proceeded at a pace slower than a colt urged to come out of the stable at dinner time. Somehow, I was awarded a wig and gown—or, rather, allowed to buy them. (Wigs are so expensive that they are, on occasion, stolen.)

Barristers used to come from the British upper classes, by way of Oxford and Cambridge. They had *manners*. I did not. Roxbury had never quite imparted those, unless you count getting just the right twist on a stone to throw in a rock fight. I regarded the gown that I wore during some meals as a black protective cloak against mustard, ketchup, oil, sauce, and especially red wine. As a reporter, I could just observe, sit on the floor with Peter Kihss, grab a Nathan's hot dog, wear my college tweed jacket forever (by cunningly adding elbow patches), and think an Italian racing jacket was more elegant than Savile Row. But Roxbury had also made me think that places where the rich congregated were enviable and particularly those clubs and groves where the initiates know the code and the best single malt. A lack of refinement, not to say polish, might prove a problem.

So you will be astonished, as I was, that posh clubs like the Bohemian elected me to membership. But you will not be astonished to learn that my Roxbury manners did shine through and did fail to impress. A venerable club on the Champs-Élysées in Paris, The Travellers, also admitted me to membership. When I visited from England, my Anglophone accent in French also failed to impress. But I had one special friend at The Travellers. This was the club cat, the late Poupette, who seemed to understand me completely. Of course, she did have great affection also for the special treats I brought from Oxford.

The club in France has reciprocal privileges with the exclusive Pacific-Union Club in San Francisco. The P-U occupies a polished nineteenth-century Classical Revival brownstone on top of Nob Hill. I sometimes sit on the soft cushion of a red leather couch in front of the gas fire in its wood-paneled and Oriental-carpeted library, sip Earl Grey (they don't have Lipton), and read the *Times*. The P-U does have pool (sorry, billiards) tables that never fail to remind me of the pool hall my grandfather owned in Roxbury. I confess that I am ashamed of still being even a little impressed by the surroundings . . . but the fire is comfortable. And the white-jacketed barman (whose unfulfilled dream was to be a policeman) always sets out on a long, highly polished table popcorn and gingersnaps.

CHAPTER FORTY

The Archaeology of Leaks

Governments are the only vessels that leak from the top. . . . [The leaks included] the central point that the Big Four agreed on practically nothing. . . .

—JAMES B. RESTON, 1946, ON POSTWAR PEACE NEGOTIATIONS

Stopping leaks is a new form of censorship.

—JULIAN ASSANGE

OFFICE OF THE US ATTORNEY GENERAL, WASHINGTON, 1979

I was working during the administration of Jimmy Carter (whom I admire) as special assistant to the attorney general. I'd never been active in politics. But while I was working as a lawyer in San Francisco, Fred Graham, then a television correspondent, recommended me to the attorney general. Crazily, I was hired.

I say crazily because this was the late 1970s, and Cathy and I were (*gasp*) not married then. The president had announced his strong negative feelings about living in sin. When Attorney General Ben Civiletti called to interview me for the job, I disclosed the awful truth about me and Cathy and suggested he consider it before we went any further.

The AG ultimately brushed it aside. Cathy and I decamped to Washington where I became Ben's special assistant and chief spokesperson for the Justice Department. With that move, I was squarely on the other side of my former journalistic colleagues. Still, all along I had wanted to see what things were like on the inside, and I'll tell you now: It turned out they were what they looked like from the outside.

When I served in the Carter Administration, I was given what the FBI calls a Full Field Investigation. They sent agents everywhere I had blown my nose, including the German university town where I had lived. The dreadful result: A landlady in San Francisco wouldn't rent to me again. That was it. Well, I also found the Bureau had caught me entering its domain willfully and wantonly, openly and notoriously, with abandoned and malignant thirst. I was in search of a bottle of Coca-Cola.

I was reporting a story at the Justice Building on Pennsylvania Avenue and was on the seventh floor where the attorney general's office was. This linked through a corridor right to the FBI. This was in the days before the FBI got its own building, of the Brutalist School, with its own morgue, across the street from Justice. It was hot. I was thirsty. A vending machine was on the other side of a glass swinging door in the corridor that linked Justice and the FBI. No one was guarding the door. It was not locked. I could almost feel the frost on those bottles of Coke. I pushed the door. It swung inward a little. There was no alarm. I pushed harder. Entered. Got out my coins—and bought a bottle of the FBI's Coca-Cola.

Bad boy as the FBI duly noted in my—or I guess, its—file. This was one of the subversive activities the Bureau had caught me engaged in. But, if the First Amendment didn't entitle a hard-working scrivener to a tonic, really what did it do?

Of course, Hoover did have a contentious relationship with the press, culminating, I think, in the scouring of his garbage by a reporter for columnist Jack Anderson. Black Label and Irish Mist bottles were important detritus—no Coca-Cola was found. And my relationship with Hoover when I covered the Bureau (as part of trying to cover Justice in America) was adversarial, maybe feisty. For example, I asked him for a personal interview every couple of weeks until the public-information people said stop.

On my very first day in the AG's office, when I opened the center drawer in the big desk in my laughingly large office across the hall from the attorney general, I knew I had a major problem. In the desk drawer was something my predecessor as spokesperson had presumably left behind—a casual remnant of the job. He was a personable and talented fellow, as his subsequent law-firm career showed. At first glance, the piece of paper looked like a diagram of an archaeological dig. On one level, in pencil, was written "on the record," on the next level "on background," on yet another level "not for attribution."

It was a map of levels of disclosure, and closer inspection disclosed layers of leaks to reporters—off-the-record, not-for-attribution, on-the-record. I can't remember the other layers, but there were several. As I studied it, I realized someone in the office had done some extensive briefing on a topic and, to keep things straight in his mind, had constructed a "terms-of-press-engagement" chart.

Leaking was a highly refined art—that much was obvious. I can't—honestly—remember the topic, whether it was a case or policy, but I remember being shocked that it was a detailed portrait of an unauthorized, impertinent leak. I wondered whether the then attorney general had authorized the disclosure. That wouldn't have mattered much anyway—at least in theory—because the leak shouldn't have taken place at all.

Acts 9:18 says: *Instantly something like scales fell from Saul's eyes, and he regained his sight. Then he got up and was baptized.*

I don't know about being baptized, but that day I did come to realize why the twelve-foot, cast-aluminum statue called Spirit of Justice in the Great Hall of the Justice Department Building in Washington holds no scale—and wears no blindfold.

The oddity—and danger—is that, as a Washington reporter, you are invited to work in the White House press room and travel on presidential trips. And you can be arrested by the FBI . . . because well, you are a spy. This is because nearly everything in Washington is classified. I used to think that half of the bureaucracy had the job title "Classifier," and had a standard carousel of Secret/Top Secret/Ultra/Death-to-Traitor rubber stamps on their desks. Now the stamps are computer-generated and probably have even more categories.

It was also on my first day at the Justice Department—in fact, my first morning—when my secretary buzzed to tell me that a prominent Washington attorney who had worked in the White House was on the phone. This was a fellow who spun through the revolving doors between his law firm and various administrations at the highest levels, and he did it with such speed and grandeur that I'm certain the door was fitted with bearings specially greased for him alone.

I picked up the phone. He identified himself and said, "Hi, Bob."

I said hello, and, though I didn't know him, used his first name, feeling we were fellow Democrats. I thought, "Am I now an Insider?" He told me in one sentence what he was calling about. I don't remember what that was, but whatever it was, I immediately told him I was putting my secretary on the line with us. That was not only unconventional; it was likely insulting.

The distinguished in-and-outer said that wouldn't be necessary and ended the call. Whatever he wanted would not tolerate another person's hearing. When my secretary picked up, she found an empty line.

"Should I stay on?" she asked. I hung the phone up.

"It's OK," I said to her over the intercom, and did not explain.

I sat far back in the large leather chair I had inherited, paused, and looked at my predecessor's chart of his levels of discretion, or indiscretion, on the large desk in front of me. My aim had been to stop him, lest I become involved in a conversation that might offend my scruples, as yet untutored by government service in Washington. But. . . .

Was I being paranoid? Was I still suffering from a Washington journalist's mindset?

My paranoia was not without basis. It turned out that my boss, the attorney general, later became involved in a mini-scandal for answering a single question from Lloyd Cutler, the White House counsel. Cutler had asked about whether the president's brother, Billy, was likely to face legal action for making allegedly false statements to the FBI in its investigation of Billy's relations with Libya.

Ben had lied about speaking with Cutler. Billy had registered as an agent of the Libyan government, had received a $220,000 loan from the Libyans, and was accused of influence peddling. After denying any contact with the White House about the case, Ben ultimately disclosed that he had advised the president that if his brother registered as a Libyan agent, he probably would not be criminally prosecuted.

I also knew Ben had been pilloried by the media just for having marched in a parade with President Carter in Baltimore, Ben's hometown.[112] Just having marched.

As I sat there, thinking about what I had just done, I knew I had not made a friend of a powerful member of the administration—and on my very first morning. I decided not to tell the attorney general.

CHAPTER FORTY-ONE

The Guardian Who Turned Out Not to Be; The Cabinet Sphinx

Quis custodiet ipsos custodes? *[Who watches the watchmen?]*
—JUVENAL

You want a friend in Washington? Get a dog.
—HARRY S. TRUMAN

WASHINGTON, OFFICE OF THE US ATTORNEY GENERAL, 1979

Attorney General Benjamin Richard Civiletti had his own definition of his Cabinet job. He was a skilled trial lawyer who had been called at his prestigious Baltimore law firm (behind his broad back) "The Silver Fox."[113] Tall and handsome—a "hunk" as one Justice Department secretary once described him to me—he was not a talker. In 1979, when he was about to become attorney general, the *Times* described him as a leader and prosecutor this way:

> *Mr. Civiletti is not expected to point the Justice Department in new directions or give it a major injection of élan.*
>
> *"At the bottom, Ben is a technocrat," said one senator.*
>
> *Mr. Civiletti, describing himself today, used such phrases as having "no flamboyance" and "little humor."[114]*

I think I saw him chortle *once*—after his argument at the World Court in *U.S. v. Iran.* After the previous attorney general, Griffin Bell, who was flamboyant, Ben's apparent mandate was to make sure the Justice Department caused the White House no problems and provoked little controversy. In this, Ben succeeded superbly. He said virtually nothing to the media. Ben was a placeholder between Griffin Bell and the Reagan Administration's William French Smith. As a placeholder, he was not in office to make difficulties, and he never did.

Being his press secretary was challenging. When a reporter got an interview with him, as Robert Pear of the *Times* did one day, Ben would give amazingly fulsome, winding non-answers and would tergiversate until the listener (and I) had to find inner reserves to stand the formal, nonsensical flow. Imagine Lewis Carroll in a detailed, anesthetic address on the state of mid-nineteenth-century England to members of a dining club after the port has gone round twice.

It took me only a little while—but longer than it should have—to work out that this attorney general did not want to say *anything* to the press. I don't mean he didn't give the occasional interview. He did, and I sat in. But those sessions did not resemble the conventional definition of an interview—a conversation where questions are asked and answers are given. At the end of the day, the monologues constituted nonsensical torture. On his way out of the Justice Department, Pear said to me, with astute practicality, "Bob, just let me know when there is something he wants to say."

Initially, reporters did think I would leak to them, and I knew they wouldn't like it if I didn't. I didn't, and they didn't. After all, I had been an investigative reporter for the *Times*. When a *Times* reporter called, for example, to ask me about organized crime in Nevada, what could I ethically say? I was also a lawyer, and I was caught in the Washington trap. That I was unpopular with my former colleagues is an understatement since in Washington, leaking is institutionalized.[115] And yet, those were the limitations of my job as chief spokesperson for the Department of Justice.

Almost everything I leaked that reporters would actually like to know would be illegal to leak. So leak and break the law, or say very little and alienate the reporters? Reporters can be jailed for reporting; the government spokesperson can be jailed for leaking.[116] Whether either is jailed—or prosecuted—rests in the discretion of whom? Probably the ones whom the leak helps or harms.

Sometimes, even though I wasn't leaking, my naïveté caused me to say true things about the Justice Department that got me in trouble. One time, I told the press that the Immigration and Naturalization Service, or INS, files were scattered hopelessly around basements and warehouses, and INS had no idea where anything was or how it could be retrieved. I was quickly summoned to the principal's office. Corporal punishment was considered but abandoned in favor of humiliation.

But not leaking was not enough. I had to appear not to leak. On one occasion, the late David Rosenbaum of the *Times* Washington Bureau wrote a piece using material that someone in the Justice Department had obviously leaked to him. People pointed fingers at me. It made sense. I knew David, I had worked for the *Times*, I had the information. The attorney general called me into his office. Dick Blumenthal was there. Dick was then US attorney for Connecticut (and currently a US senator). On the speaker phone was the head of the Department's Office of Professional Responsibility, Michael Shaheen.[117] He was the ethical guardian of the Justice Department and headed up internal investigations. I was going to be roasted about the leak that informed Rosenbaum's story.

I turned toward the speaker phone and said, "Hi, Mike." I paused. Then asked, "Hey Mike, why did you leak the piece to the *Times*?"

Mike said he hadn't.

"David Rosenbaum tells me you did," I said. That was a lie; I hadn't even talked with David. I had used an old reporters' trick—pretending to know something I didn't to get Mike to confess. I held my breath and saw the attorney general and Blumenthal focus their gazes on me. Then they both turned to the speaker phone. There was silence. A few seconds went by. Then Mike said softly, "Yes, I did."

Ben may not have been acquainted with each of the four attributes of the Sphinx—to Know, to Will, to Dare, and to Keep Silent—but he rivaled the mythical monster's command of the last. In me, he had found the right person to rely on not to leak. Now on the other side of the journalistic fence, a lawyer and former criminal prosecutor, I was obliged to play the mummy to Ben's sphinx.

Even when I was a good mummy, I was sometimes suspected. For example, I was out of the information loop about an investigation called Abscam, but I was investigated for a leak relating to it anyway.

I arrived back in Washington on Christmas Eve and took the bus to my office. (Ben looked bewildered—the only time I saw him bewildered—when I had first told him I regularly took the bus to the Justice Department from our home in Georgetown.) I went across the hall into the attorney general's office and found him with Philip Heymann, a Harvard Law School professor (now emeritus) who had served in the State Department in a previous administration and had become assistant attorney general for the Criminal Division. I first met Heymann when I had arrived to do my job but had barely seen him since.

That day, Heymann was briefing the AG on some sort of undercover operation. When I walked in, I had no idea what they were talking about. When Heymann left, Ben walked with me toward the large wooden door to his suite. He stopped and, unbidden, said the meeting was typical of Heymann. He was briefing him right before Christmas, Ben told me, so that Ben could never say he hadn't been briefed but also could do nothing to control or stop what turned out to be a highly sensitive undercover sting operation.

The attorney general's view was that Heymann had set him up, manipulating the situation to his ends. Whether Ben was right or wrong about that—and he was one shrewd fellow himself—little love was lost between them, despite the polite conversations.

Personally I didn't care much for Heymann. In my view he seemed ambitious beyond good taste. According to folks on his staff, the distaste was mutual. He thought I was operating above my pay grade and at one point instructed *his secretary* to tell me so on the phone.

The attorney general had told me he distrusted Heymann and suggested I have a look at his own papers about Heymann's time at the State Department. Ben indicated he wanted me to understand what was, in his opinion, Heymann's inclination to bureaucratic manipulation.[118]

Before I stumbled into the briefing, I had known nothing about the Abscam operation. The FBI had videotaped politicians taking bribes from a phony Arab company in return for political favors. Seven congressmen were involved. One, famously, refused to take a bribe. Senator Larry Pressler reported the approach to the FBI. Walter Cronkite called Pressler a "hero," and Pressler said, "What have we come to if turning down a bribe is heroic?"

Some saw the operation as entrapment. Ultimately, this led to the attorney general's issuing guidelines for FBI undercover operations. Someone leaked Abscam to the press, and the AG asked me whether I thought he should investigate the leak. I said yes but soon came to rue my answer.

I said yes because this was no ordinary leak. It threatened to cause dismissal of the prosecution of members of Congress. If we didn't look into it, it might appear to the court and to others that we were somehow behind the leak, supported it, and instigated it. When Ben asked me whether I knew someone to head the leak inquiry, I suggested Dick Blumenthal. Dick had been a fellow student at Yale Law School. He accepted the job and put together a staff.

Dick's team never found the source of the leak. But they did get my back up—to the point where I caused them to suspect me. The fact that I had known nothing about Abscam before the leak was a problem for them. Apparently, Dick told his FBI guys to play tough. One day a mid-career FBI guy showed up in my large office to grill me. He was short, thin, dark-suited, middle-aged, and pugnacious as a lap dog who was in the furious phase of rabies. That was odd. I would have thought we were on the same side. After all, I did not even know about Abscam until *after* the leak.

Perhaps Heymann had given the FBI agent direction as to my interview. Who knows in the persistently self-seeking shadow world of government political bureaucracy?

The agent's attitude also confused me, since I was the one who had—unfortunately and unwisely—told Ben, when he asked, that an investigation into the Abscam leak was not a bad idea. And I had come up with Dick Blumenthal—this agent's temporary boss—to lead the inquiry.

But, anyway, there he was. Foaming may be too strong a way of putting it, but he took it on himself to rearrange the furniture in my large wood-paneled office (across from the attorney general's suite). Not happy with the distance between the guest chair and my desk, he picked it up and moved it to within feet of my desk.

His interrogation techniques proved just as heavy-handed. Since I was never a fan of heavy-handed techniques, he provoked a knee-jerk response of non-cooperation. The agent didn't like learning nothing, but even if I had been of a mind to be cooperative, I had nothing to tell him.

As you may have intuited by now, I was never an easy ally of power. I bristled, and answered his questions honestly, but briskly. Truth be told, I was not actively helpful. But then, I had little to be helpful with. In the end we were both frustrated. I asked him to put the chair back where he had found it.

Dick Blumenthal chastised me later when he saw me in the hall-way between my office and Ben's. "You are making yourself a target," he warned. That warning was quite inappropriate for a number of reasons, both of substance and process.

"Dick," I protested, "are you kidding? I couldn't have leaked it. I didn't know about it."

"Even so," he said.

"Even so?" I thought.

Blumenthal was a Marine Reservist who tried to stay fit for his required annual stint of active duty by running around the small Wooster Square park in residential New Haven. He once told me the story of his crushed thumb. He got it by pointing his rifle other than at the target on a Marine rifle range. A sergeant made him put his thumb in the slide of the weapon and when the bolt flew forward, it crushed Blumenthal's thumb.

I forbore from saying that day in the corridor outside the attorney general's office, "Dick, you're pointing your rifle the wrong way again."

I did not realize, after having been a *Times* reporter, that I was naïve. But I was. That naïveté faded when I took the job of special assistant to the attorney general.

In my first moments on the job, I saw that my predecessor was play-ing the game of leaking for advantage—cultivating, I assumed, important members of the media by briefing them on background or off the record. I had been the recipient of, probably, hundreds of leaks. But should I provide information to reporters that I knew I shouldn't? Put me in the straight-arrow, sandbox category. Inconsistent? For sure.

Some moments, embarrassing to the government or at least the bureaucracy, did not get leaked. Sometimes, I learned, they involved the limits of governmental power even at very high levels. There was, for example, the attorney general's inability (not to mention my own inability) to keep an extraordinarily expensive, nonsensical mutt in his kennel.

Fortunately, no one ever asked me about the hugely expensive Justice Department house hound. I mean McGruff, the Crime-Fighting Dog.

The idea was to *Take a Bite out of Crime™*. As the National Crime Prevention Council described him, McGruff was tall and wore a rumpled trenchcoat. He was to appear in television ads on the scene of potential crimes, with tips on how to prevent them. McGruff was even to make live appearances "to encourage Americans to take common-sense steps to reduce crime."

Some of the dog's more sophisticated messages were to be: "lock doors, leave the lights on when away from home, and let neighbors know when you go on vacation. . . ."[119]

The sponsor of the dog was the Law Enforcement Assistance Administration (LEAA), part of the Justice Department. By the end of the 1970s, during my tenure with the Carter Administration, LEAA was being criticized for wasting money. LEAA had distributed $7.5 billion in thirteen years. While the agency contributed to several criminal justice improvements, the money had not led to a significant reduction in crime.[120] President Carter decided to shut it down. The hound somehow survived the shuttering.

When McGruff first came across my desk, I saw him as a terrible idea. I walked across the hall and urged the attorney general to stop it.

"Ben," I began, "a dog? We are going to spend a million dollars on a dog? When we are being criticized for waste?"

The attorney general sat silent, thinking.

Then he got his secretary on the phone and asked her to have the head of LEAA come around for a meeting.

When Henry Dogin, the administrator of LEAA under Civiletti, arrived for the meeting, I was sitting there. Ben criticized the hound. He quoted me: "Why has LEAA gotten into a campaign that is spending good money on a talking dog?" He ordered Dogin to shut the campaign down, but the ads had already been distributed to the media. There was no way to keep McGruff in the doghouse.

A Justice Department staffer accused me of blindsiding the LEAA. He was probably right. But any inadvertent stepping on toes proved to have no effect.

It is difficult to get a handle on what McGruff has cost the taxpayer since he was born forty-plus years ago. It's also not clear just how many bites he has taken out of crime. Back in 1979, the government gave a $900,000 grant (equivalent four decades later to *$3 million*) to Professor Garrett J. O'Keefe of the University of Denver to assess the dog's impact. With the $3 million, Professor O'Keefe published a sixty-six-page paper. He concluded that "McGruff has had a substantive impact."[121]

More people, O'Keefe found, *left their outside lights on or asked their neighbors to watch their houses when they were away.* "Most significantly," O'Keefe discovered that more of the people he surveyed "became involved in neighborhood crime prevention techniques."[122]

Maybe McGruff deserves a treat. How about a hickory-smoked bone? The government should be able to get one for $50,000.

In the man-bites-dog story journalists live for, the actor who played McGruff, John R. Morales, was arrested in 2011 in Galveston, Texas. Morales was charged with possession of drugs and weapons. The drugs included one thousand marijuana plants, and the twenty-seven weapons included a grenade launcher and nine thousand rounds of ammunition. A judge sentenced him to sixteen years.

In other circumstances, though, a recalcitrant and combative bureaucracy could be brought to heel. This happened when I mobilized the Justice Department—at the expense of the State Department—in an effort to make our best case at the World Court.

CHAPTER FORTY-TWO

Journalism Provides a Soundbite: A Plea in the World Courtroom

When Israel was in Egypt's land
Let my people go
Oppress'd so hard they could not stand
Let my People go

Refrain:
Go down, Moses
Way down in Egypt's land
Tell old Pharaoh
Let my people go
—AMERICAN NEGRO SPIRITUAL

THE WORLD COURT: THE HAGUE, 1980

The blonde Dutch secretary looked up from her neat desk in the American Embassy in The Hague and said, "No." She meant it.

"Are you sure you understand how important this is?" I asked.

"Lunchtime is lunchtime," she said.

I was an appalling failure as chief spokesperson for the US Department of Justice. I admit that. An exception was a case—the *case*—in the World Court. That was not a failure. Even that doesn't support bragging, though, since the hostages remained hostages. But here was a Dutch secretary threatening to undermine even this effort.

Thus nearly ended a saga that had begun two days earlier with a telephone call with the White House about the US hostages being held in Iran and the case about the hostages in the World Court. Fifty-two American diplomats and citizens were suffering in Tehran. Some had been beaten. It was 1980. The World Court let me use journalism and law to make the American argument at the Peace Palace into a worldwide PR exercise. I came up with the idea of the attorney general's arguing the case to the World Court.

Jimmy Carter would lose re-election, largely because of the hostage issue. But in that moment, the entire administration was anguished about how to get the Americans out of Tehran.

Teams were working feverishly on the problem at the White House and the Pentagon, a truly Foggy Bottom (the State Department's nickname), and everywhere else within hollerin' distance of a frowning Lincoln Memorial.

It was Sunday morning and my wife, Cathy, and I were lounging in front of the unlit metal fireplace in our small modern condominium in Georgetown.

In those days, I was always at my twelve-hour-a-day job before sunup, never home before sundown, and typically ate breakfast and lunch with the attorney general in his staff dining room. I was, in other words, the perfect Washington administration staffer whose average professional half-life is eighteen months. They come and, exhausted, they go.

Cathy and I lived in an eggshell-white condominium that was so small the closets were not wide enough to hold a clothing hanger. There was little room for pacing, and that fact and the frenzied work pace made lounging in front of the fireplace on Sunday morning particularly inviting. That morning it dawned on me: The hostage situation was really about public perception. Yet the United States was sending to The Hague a State Department lawyer steeped in the exquisite niceties of practice at Covington & Burling, whence he had come (and whither he would return).

I called the attorney general. I suggested to Ben that the government was sending the wrong guy to the World Court—a fancy-dancy Washington lawyer, as nuanced as his pinstripes. They ought to be sending you,

I told Ben—a trial lawyer, accustomed to courtrooms and judges. What I didn't say was that Ben was tall, broad-shouldered, and handsome. This occasion required someone who would look good on TV worldwide and who could deliver a soundbite. Secretly, I intended to take care of the soundbite. I proposed to Ben that I call my opposite number at the White House, Jody Powell, a laconic member of the president's Georgia Mafia who was suffering terribly in this crisis.

Subtlety has never been my long suit. I pointed out to Ben that the administration was sending a second-stringer when the situation demanded a Cabinet member with courtroom experience (though I omitted the fact that I had no idea what international-law experience this big-firm Baltimore business lawyer had). Ben immediately agreed, and two days later the attorney general stepped into the *Case Concerning United States Diplomatic and Consular Staff in Tehran* in the International Court of Justice at The Hague, Holland. I walked through those broad, round archways with him.

Getting to those archways, with a brief in hand, presented unexpected challenges.

I called Ben's executive assistant and told her that he was leaving the next day. She would have to get airplane tickets for both of us. Also, she had to find him a set of tails—required, we were told, in the World Court. Could she do that on a Sunday?

During the overnight flight, I got my first peek at the brief prepared by the State Department. Legalese to the core. Was that brief going to make anybody passionate about our cause? In the brief, living, breathing hostages had become lost in forests of jurisprudential prose. We were seeking worldwide sympathy and help, not a real ruling from the Court. What was the Court going to do after all—declare that the Iranians had the right to kidnap, hold, torment, and barter human beings? Besides, I needed—right up front—*a soundbite*, to be shown on TV and sent around the world. And I needed something Muslims as well as Westerners could understand, something that bridged entirely different legal systems and cultures.

I sipped Dutch cocoa on the plane while the attorney general and the Justice Department's international lawyer slept. Finally I got it: *Let my people go.* Muslims acknowledge the Old Testament. So do Jews and Christians. So I borrowed those four words from Exodus 9:1—just four words. I thought they would do the job.

This mission to make a plea to the Court was an exercise in public diplomacy. Public diplomacy is public relations writ large. And public relations is journalism stood on its head—propaganda. This was global propaganda. I was trying to give the media a soundbite by casting "Let my people go" as a formidable appeal that would cross boundaries.

I shortened the State Department brief and tried to make plain English of at least some of it. The attentive Dutch flight attendant had made it her mission to cater to the only one in the cabin who was still awake, and working. As I wrestled with the State Department's bramble of legal prose, she served the fourth cup of cocoa. I was just finishing as we neared Schiphol Airport. She wakened the AG and international lawyer.

I realized it didn't much matter what more I did. No one—maybe not even the World Court —was likely to pay attention to the entire brief. I would go with those four words. What luxury: By constraint of time and place, I was reshaping the brief by myself—not a battalion of lawyers, not a department, not even that DC staple—a committee. What more could I have asked?

When the attorney general awoke, he read what I had done and said, "You've lifted the brief right up."

That did not keep the State Department lawyers, caught at the eleventh hour, from feeling resentful. Who could blame them? They had prepared a learned brief and were ready to begin the largest legal assignment of their lives.

They—correctly—blamed me for their being shoved aside and replaced by Ben. But if the change hadn't been so compelling, so obvious, the White House would not immediately have approved.

Still, what seemed the pettiness of bureaucratic vanity showed itself, even in this, the desperate case of the hostages.

I was sleepless, and likely grumpy, by the time we landed at Schiphol Airport. A State Department officer greeted us on the tarmac and announced a *fait accompli*:

"A press conference is starting at the Embassy."

"Who is giving it?" I asked.

"The State Department legal people, of course."

We were still on the cold tarmac. And that's where the exchange continued.

"They'd better not. You have a Cabinet member sent by the president right here in front of you to handle this. You'd better hold the conference until he arrives at the Embassy."

Calling the White House was mentioned. I can't say why I cared about the bureaucratic glory. Chalk it up to time served in Washington.

The Foreign Service officer looked startled. What would we find waiting for us at the Embassy? And when would I get to sleep?

We approached the Embassy. So did the headache that had been hammering at the top of my head since Goose Bay.

State graciously decided to delay the news conference. But someone had unkindly made a point of suggesting to reporters they ask the attorney general what international law experience he had. I didn't understand his answer, but in those days the media did not focus on unintelligible answers.

Enter the Dutch secretary. I now had a hand-scribbled, hand-edited version of a brief for the World Court. For starters, that had to be typed.

I asked for a good, fast secretary. The office manager directed me to a secretary at a nearby desk.

"Please type this right away," I asked. "It's the US brief for the World Court. The hearing is in two hours."

"It's lunchtime," she said matter-of-factly.

I ran for the Embassy staff manager, and begged.

Heaven knows what that State Department fellow had to offer to have the brief typed. As a former shop steward for the American Newspaper Guild in Washington, I didn't want to know. But somehow the brief was typed, and we sped to the imposing portals of the Peace Palace.

The registrar or deputy registrar greeted me. The attorney general, the State Department folks, and everyone else American was placed in an ornate waiting room. The registrar—let's call the nice fellow that—looked, honest, just like a black-robed wine steward. A metal symbol hung from his neck instead of the usual small cup. But what a guy!

When he heard that I had a headache, he fetched a white powder to be dissolved in warm water. What is it? I asked. But Dutch medical remedies were to remain a mystery as he hurried me, time pressing, to the large courtroom. I was sure I would be the first lawyer to pass out when appearing before the World Court.

Head throbbing, following the registrar, I approached the lectern in front of the long, long bench. The bench has to be long to seat fifteen judges. All of them, I noted, would have a clear view if I did pass out.

The lectern was remarkable. It tilted this way, and tilted the other way—in fact, it tilted all ways. It had the usual timing lights to guide the advocate and an earpiece for translation of the judges' questions. (They are called judges, not justices—Chief Justice John Glover Roberts Jr. and crew, take humble note.)

I asked the registrar to brief me on the tilting and translating. He showed me the tilting, but said we could skip the mechanics of translation, because there would be no questions.

"No questions?" I asked, surprised. How did he know?

"No," he said.

"Are you sure?"

"Sure," he said.

Fingering my packet of headache powder, I headed for the grand room and pulled out the attorney general.

"They're not going to ask you any questions," I confided, thinking that would be a relief—since neither he nor I knew a damn thing about the relevant law. I thought he might just have squeaked past suffering ignominy in front of the whole world.

"Oh, too bad," he said. I thought to myself "typical trial lawyer," and quickly reached for the medicine the registrar supplied.

But the State Department had two more arrows in its quiver.

First came this important question: The Court required us to file in, one at a time. But in what order? The State Department arranged that, and its lawyer came first, ahead of the attorney general (without tails—just in a business suit). How come? Because, of course, he had been listed as the person initiating the case with the Court.

I was last, and that was not only *comme il faut* but very good for me. Klieg lights of the type you associate with torture chambers were turned on and aimed at us for the benefit of the photographers and television cameras. Still cameras from around the world sought out equally—maybe not so equally—The Hunk and me, with my unhappy, chalky face. At least, I thought, pained was the appropriate look of the day.

What argument did the Iranians have? None whatsoever, it turned out, because they did not attend the hearing. I am proud and pleased to report, unopposed, we won.

I am also pleased to report that the Dutch headache powder did its work. I survived. There was, though, a tussle about my being mentioned in dispatches. The State Department omitted me from the members of the delegation. Did I care? On principle, yes. I had rewritten the brief, or at best its most important parts.

I placed a phone call to my close colleague and pal, the registrar, who set the record straight. The dispatches appeared with my name engrossed.

A car took us to a hotel after the hearing. The attorney general and the international lawyer from the Justice Department whom I had suggested we bring along were going to dinner in Amsterdam. Ben asked me to go. I hadn't slept since we had left Washington and though my headache was abating, thanks to the magic Dutch powder, it was still intense. I declined. Full of energy, the attorney general pressed. I declined. He seemed baffled as to why I wouldn't go.

He and the international lawyer went out for a fine Dutch dinner, or maybe it was rijsttafel.

I had already heard that "Let my people go" was making its speedy way around the world. Exhausted, I went to bed.

THE WHITE HOUSE

WASHINGTON

June 17, 1980

To Bob Smith

Thank you for your service as a member of the American delegation to the International Court of Justice in US v. Iran.

We are all gratified by the Court's recent decision, and you
should be particularly proud of your role in the preparation
of the argument of the case.

Best wishes to you.

Sincerely,

Jimmy Carter

Mr. Robert M. Smith

Special Assistant to the Attorney General

Department of Justice

Washington, D.C. 20530

Thanks!

CHAPTER FORTY-THREE

The Unreasonable Man Swings from Tree to . . . Tree

Remembering you are going to die is the best way I know to avoid the trap of thinking you have something to lose. . . . There is no reason not to follow your heart.
—STEVE JOBS, STANFORD COMMENCEMENT ADDRESS, 2005

The reasonable man adapts himself to the world; the unreasonable one persists in trying to adapt the world to himself. Therefore, all progress depends on the unreasonable man.
—GEORGE BERNARD SHAW

SAN FRANCISCO, 1982–1998

The defeated, obese man with sparse, matted gray hair and stubble was elderly and ill. My friend, a bankruptcy lawyer to the east of San Francisco, had advised him to go to Brazil—so hopeless was his case. My friend must have been joking—old, sick, with a wife and daughter, and speaking only English? Brazil?

Journalism molded me into an unconventional lawyer. For starters, I did not take individual clients, only companies—and usually just banks. I did this because I did not think individuals could or should pay my high hourly rate. I saw individuals only for free—in the San Francisco poverty law program. I sat on the program's board and sometimes staffed the intake center in the city's largely Hispanic Mission district.

My friend had called and insisted I see this man.

"I don't take individual clients," I reminded him. He insisted.

The sick fellow in the red leather chair in front of me looked disconsolate. He had to travel to a rural hospital for treatment every week. On the last of those trips, his battered truck "was in collision with"—as lawyers and reporters say—a young motorcyclist coming very fast in the other direction. The teenager had just gotten the powerful machine. He was badly injured, almost killed.

"Did you cross the yellow line to get into the hospital driveway on the other side of the road?"

"Yes," he said.

"Did you contact your insurance?"

"No."

"Why not?"

"I didn't pay the premium."

"How long ago did you stop paying for the insurance?"

"A month or so."

"Why did you stop paying?"

He looked down at the Oriental carpet. "Couldn't afford it."

I abandoned my usual practice and said I would try to help him. I asked him to come around the next morning with his ramshackle truck. We were going to take a ride.

I met him the next day on Montgomery Street, in front of my office. We set off. Our ride took us to the suburban office of the multinational insurance company.

My client was as gray as the office equipment on the counters on the other side of the glass partition. I asked the receptionist just inside the door of the modern, sterile building—probably called a campus— whether this fellow could make a payment on his policy. She said, "Sure," and sent us to a cashier. The cheerful, middle-aged cashier was not busy. In fact, there was no line at all. I stepped right up to the counter, client in tow.

"Give her the check," I said. He did. She took it.

"Can I have a receipt?" I asked.

She stamped a piece of paper and handed it across the flat counter.

"Sorry," I asked her, "could I have another receipt?"

The check brought my client current. The cheery cashier had just reinstated his policy. "Thank you," I said, and meant it. Reinstatement meant the insurance company was on the hook for the accident. I guided my client, who did not understand what had happened, to the glass doors and back to his truck in the large parking lot.

"Don't worry," I said to my client. "You will have nothing to pay, except your deductible. Nothing. The insurance company will pay for the accident. And they will pay for a lawyer. They'll give you some choice of lawyers."

"I want you," he said, still not fully understanding what had just happened.

"Well," I said, "I'm flattered—really flattered—but I'm the one lawyer I don't think the insurance company will hire for you."

I was wrong. The company honored its obligation to its insured. And, bizarrely, they hired me to represent him in the court case about the accident. Settlement was reached, peace restored to the family, Brazil avoided. The family—husband, wife, and daughter—visited my old-fashioned office in the financial district—all dark wood, red leather, and polished brass—one more time and generously gave me a wonderful red-leather recliner, in which I could read the *Times* and an obscene mass of legal papers during my weekend catch-up sessions.

I suppose that insurance company lawyers might see my approach to my client's problem as not just unorthodox. They might see it as less than reasonable.

I would disagree. They could easily have required a sworn statement from my client saying he had not been in an accident since the insurance had lapsed, together with another half-dozen pages of restrictions, waivers, covenants—you get the idea.

And if there was an argument between my client and the company down the road, he would not get a judge and jury to weigh fairness; no, all those pages he would have had to sign would require—it would certainly turn out—an arbitrator to decide who would get what. But that approach, the company lawyers would say, is *entirely normal.*

The end of the case required the blessing of a judge.

The judge was ruddy faced and white-haired. With things wrapped up, he leaned over the bench and looked down at my client.

"Sir," he said, "you should thank Mr. Smith."

But my client didn't have to. Some people—a destitute Harlem photographer, a woman locked in a bank, a sergeant who did *not* fire during a massacre, a sick old man in a battered truck—they shouldn't have to say thanks.

We walked out of the courtroom. Someone from the insurance company said some unkind things to me, but the company paid my bill.

The insurance company was wrong if it thought I was unreasonable. But there were times when I was unreasonable. What kid, for instance—and I was a kid—would leave the *New York Times* Washington Bureau? Who would start a law practice in a major city with no clients and hope to build a firm? Who would come into what turned out to be a billion-dollar corporate mediation in London and tell the board chairman of the acquiring company—a lord—that he had to yield his end-of-the-table power seat to the mediator?

Throughout my career, I persisted in combining a large dollop of unreasonableness with more than a pinch of naïveté. For example:

- In being as naïve as I had been when I took the national editor to lunch at Elsie's hamburger counter in Cambridge;
- When I thought Reston knew what he was doing in killing my interview with Harvard's president;
- And when I thought the woman in the castle of the New Jersey millionaire was just a secretary.

It was this same naïveté that led me to believe that, in this society, you *could* swing from vine to vine. This got me into a lot of trouble sometimes, but it allowed me to graft the skills of journalism onto the advocacy requirements of law. And then try to add both of those to the demands of mediation's triad: communication, imagination, and compromise.

Add naïveté to ambition and this odd faith that I could actually move from field to field without a problem—and that's how I followed my heart, swinging from tree to tree just above the rapids.

In 2005, Steve Jobs told Stanford graduating seniors to follow their hearts.[123] I was too old to have heard and heeded Steve's advice, but I had tried to do just that. Is it my fault that I haven't been given a reasonable heart? Perhaps. A senior *Times* editor once described me this way: "You're a pain in the ass, but worth it."

This reminds me of a *Time* news executive, who was hugely frustrated at a time when I happened to be passing through his office. He looked up from a large pile of files (news reports by correspondents) and said, "If you have to choose between hiring a very nice but average journalist and a really good journalist who is a son of a bitch, choose the son of a bitch." Then he looked back down at the top file on the heap and shook his head.

But this I did not do without fear, Mr. Jobs. When I moved my new (for which please read nonexistent) firm to a glitzy, forty-eight-story, cylindrical San Francisco tower in the Financial District, I had to cross a highly polished granite apron from the elevators to the wide steps to the street. For a week I was afraid, as I approached the granite, that I would slip and fall. ("Anxiety-stricken lawyer rolls across lobby and down steps. He is finally stopped by the wheels of a hot dog cart.") Similarly, when I left the *Times* for the second time—an act akin to committing journalistic *seppuku*—anxiety consumed sleep.

After I was a reporter and before I became a mediator, I practiced trial law in California. I tried cases in different settings, but I never did get to try cases as a barrister in the UK. I did oversee disputes in many countries when I was responsible for the Bank of America's overseas lawsuits.

My job was to try to make sense, control, and bring to a conclusion lawsuits against the bank around the world. That led me to the logic of mediation and ultimately, to embrace it, first as a lawyer and later as a commercial mediator, in London and San Francisco.

The charms of mediation are many. Unlike an arbitrator, the mediator decides nothing. All the mediator can do is try to facilitate a resolution of the dispute among the parties, but whether they resolve the dispute and on what terms is up to them. It seems to me that people and institutions should settle their own disputes. They do not need to spend enormous money and tremendous travail in a courtroom to get to the psychological satisfaction and economy of resolution. At the bank, I thought it was good for both the bank and the people or companies suing or being sued by the bank. Although I did not intuit that it would, it turned out that reporting helped make me an effective mediator—even in different cultures and languages.

While I did not get to live my dream of being a widely wandering foreign correspondent, my travels for the bank took me to many places to oversee the lawsuits. But, more importantly, it exposed me to the possibilities of mediation.

Mediation was in its beginnings in California and in the United States, and I saw it as a cheaper, kinder future. Later still, I became a Registered Mediator in the UK.

After I had left the bank, I practiced trial law. My first bank president client promised to give me enough work so that I could hire a secretary. He saw me as a step up. He had been using a lawyer who drove around in a truck, with his dog in the bed.

Courtroom work became part of my toolkit. There are few things as sobering and instructive as representing a bank facing charges of fraud for allegedly promising to lend to a family business in the San Francisco area, and then not making the loan. I knew that if I lost the trial, the bank would sink into receivership.

Happily, as my firm began to get business and grow, I stopped worrying about slipping and falling.

CHAPTER FORTY-FOUR

The Indecipherable East End; The Story Business; The Mystery of the Iraqi Harp

'Allo me old china (mate)—wot say we pop round the Jack (bar). I'll stand you a pig (beer) and you can rabbit on about your teapots (kids). We can 'ave some loop (soup) and tommy (supper) and be off before the dickory (clock) hits twelve.
   —A COCKNEY RHYMING SLANG DICTIONARY[124]

Understand and judge not.
   —COMMISSAIRE JULES MAIGRET AND HIS CREATOR,
   GEORGES JOSEPH CHRISTIAN SIMENON

Sometimes . . . it's better to hear answers to the questions you wouldn't ever have thought of asking.
   —BERNIE GUNTHER IN *PRUSSIAN BLUE* BY PHILIP KERR

LONDON, 2005–2006

It must have been somebody's idea of a Rum and Coke, as the Cockneys say.[125] Test this new guy from San Francisco on his first day of work: Send him to London's East End to resolve a small dispute, between a youngster and his yuppie neighbors. The youngster fancied himself a disc jockey. Need I say more? The joke: The youngster was a Cockney, and spoke Cockney.

I was the new guy. I had been hired to manage mediation at CEDR— the Centre for Effective Dispute Resolution in London. I was supposed to know what I was doing, in all mediation contexts. But I found I could not understand Cockney—at all.

The East End is a part of inner London that stretches from the city's edge to the River Lea. It is an area that became historically synonymous with poverty, overcrowding, disease, and criminality. In the late nineteenth century, it was Jack the Ripper's killing ground and in the early twentieth, the Siege of Sidney Street. In that siege, anarchists took on Home Secretary Winston Churchill and the Army.

As for language in England, there is Received Pronunciation (also called BBC English, Standard English, Queen's English, or Oxford English). Then among other variants, there is Cockney. This produces, for example, the Cockney phrase: "A li'le bi' of breab wiv a bi' of bu'er on i'." Kindly say this aloud five times quickly—preferably to your dog or cat, so as not to invite a diagnosis of madness—and you will understand the dilemma of a Yank mediator who knew French, German, Spanish, and university Russian, but no cockney. Cockney speakers also occasionally use rhyming slang.[126] But it is unnecessary—'eaven be thanked—for me to go into that (as if I could).

I'd been mediating for a dozen years by the time I arrived at the mediation in the East End in 2005. The argument was about bass. Loud bass. The young complaining couple lived in the apartment above an amateur disc jockey in his early twenties. We, and the Brits, would call the couple yuppies. I was accompanied by an examiner to make sure I really could mediate. She lurked nearby, taking notes. With the help of a visiting Irish aunt—or aintín—I explained the process to the couple and the DJ and got a conversation started.

They were going at it. I got that—but little else. Several times I heard the word bass. Also the word loud. I understood the couple worked long and hard and valued their sleep. The participants in the mediation were, happily for me, chugging along. I wouldn't say amiably, but—as the diplomats say—in a frank discussion.

I quietly stood up. Gently and slowly, I moved my plain wooden chair to a corner of the room. I sat silently. I watched—just watched. The participants were lowering their volume. And they seemed to be slowing down.

I looked at the aintín.

"They're agreed," she said.

I moved my chair back to the table, and—by example—encouraged the shaking of hands.

And I thought: Sometimes he mediates best who mediates least.

The next day, I became director of mediation at the Centre for Effective Dispute Resolution. And I thanked those reporters and editors who had taught me to listen, just listen—when you don't understand a damn thing, and when you do.

I knew something about mediation, and I knew something about trial law—not because of Yale Law School, but mainly because of journalism and the *Times*. Reporters are trained to listen carefully. They are used to interviewing everyone from the elevator operator to the CEO. They are also used to putting themselves in the shoes of the people they are interviewing, and then stepping out of those shoes. They have to earn trust and gain rapport.

Like journalists, mediators deal with stories all the time. They have to try to find out the real (often unspoken) story and use it to persuade to fashion a compromise. That's why Peter Kihss, Homer Bigart, and Long John Phillips would be right at home as mediators (if they knew the other—the less important—legal stuff involved). They were all beguiling storytellers.

In mediation, the stories can also, importantly, bring catharsis. This is the only time for the people in conflict to tell the story that may be haunting them. They get to tell it in that upscale conference room instead of to a jury in a courtroom.

Journalism, trial law, and mediation have another important element in common: Imagination. The stories that follow involve the value in mediation of imagination, catharsis, and even language.

Suppose you are in these situations:

Catharsis—Defining "Art" for Cash

In a conference room in San Francisco's Mission District, three dozen people faced me. Some of them didn't speak English. Some didn't have money for the parking meters. Some were wealthy property owners and developers. Some were passionate artists. Some were lawyers.

The argument concerned a building that had been redeveloped. It had had a mural on one exterior wall, but the mural was no more. The destruction of the work, the artists argued, had trampled on their rights.

Emotions ran to a boil over issues like "Was it art?" The developers and real estate folks complained loudly that whatever it was, it wasn't art, pointing to the "before" photos.

"*Maravilloso!*" the artists and their supporters chanted, furious with the crass merchants.

Both groups looked at me, seeking support for their respective positions. I inspected the photos with care, paused, then politely invited the artists to join me down the hall. Separate caucuses ensued. Statutes were consulted, photos viewed and reviewed. Parking meters fed. The conference rooms sounded like the Tower of Babel.

The one clear point was that the art—if those who thought it was art were right—was gone, never to be brought back. Perhaps artists could create a replacement mural? Not to be. What was to be was a monetary resolution. Sometimes, even art will accept mammon in order to avoid litigation.

Imagination—The Greek Islands

I was mediating a personal injury case involving a pilot and an airline. The case was resolved except for that most necessary component—the plaintiff lawyer's compensation. Parties and counsel were stumped.

I met privately with plaintiff's counsel and learned that he was about to get married. I asked where he was taking his bride on their honeymoon. He told me they had not yet decided.

"If you could go anywhere in the world, where would it be?" I asked him. He leaned back, rested his cowboy boots on the table, studied the ceiling and finally said, "The Greek Islands."

I hurried down the hall to the airline executives and told them they could settle the case for round-trip tickets for two, first-class of course, to Athens. Since this was a relatively low-cost solution for them, they said no problem, and the lawsuit was resolved.

No court could have ordered that resolution, and no jury could have awarded it. Mediation had brought imagination to the table.

Language—Giving Away Too Much

There was a squabble royal between a Quebec outfit that had sold equipment and a Chinese company that had bought it. The mediation took place on two days. I tried to strike up rapport with the lead Quebecker by speaking French and was even able to pry him off one of his cellphone calls to a girlfriend in Australia. That was no small feat. Well, perhaps it was mean. So I was astonished when the second session came and the Quebecker refused to speak French.

My stomach sank a great many floors through the high-rise building. "*Pourquoi pas?*" I gasped, thinking my French must have been incomprehensible the last time. "We gave away too much," he said in English. He went on to explain that he'd felt too comfortable in his native tongue and believed he had been too flexible with the Chinese.

Imagination, catharsis, and language frame the "story business." But the business rests on getting information—which often means interviewing and listening.

Carl Bernstein shares my view about just listening. He said this in a talk:

> *Many if not most journalists are lousy listeners. Really where you get the most information is listening to what people have to say. Invariably, you're going to learn something if you give them a chance to get it out. They'll tell you some real surprising things.*[127]

In 1947, Peter Kihss wrote about how to interview:

> *Every source is a different problem. Some men will be glad to sit down and explain a problem from the beginning. Most men like to consider themselves authorities on a subject, with the inquirer a learner at their feet. . . .*

There are various tricks for priming the interview pump. Sometimes a man will get started on a significant line simply by a question about what he considers the most pleasant thing that ever happened to him.[128]

The Zero-Sum Harp

I thought of Peter when I visited a town near Nottingham, England, for a dispute that promised challenge. I knew I would need some of his Scent.

The mediation concerned a harp. An Iraqi harp. A wonderfully wrought harp. A work of art, with value—cultural, historic, sentimental, monetary. One of the parties was Iraqi, the other English. They were arguing about who owned the harp.

The question on my mind was: Could I keep the rival owners in the room? The harp sat on a cloth on the carpet in front of me. I was afraid to touch it. I resolved to proceed very slowly; care and circumspection were on the menu.

"That's a remarkable instrument," I began, trying to set a tone and induce flexibility through reverence.

"Don't you think so?"

They both agreed; at least it was a beginning.

"A great treasure—forgetting the monetary value. Don't you agree?"

They both agreed, again.

"Something to be cherished," I ventured softly.

They nodded.

"And there is only one of it—so, unfortunately, only one of you can have it."

I continued gently.

"May I ask, what you'll do with it if you are the one who leaves with it today?"

I was on dangerous ground. It was none of my business, and not something either, or both, might like to disclose. I was beginning to feel both the delicacy and the heat of the situation. The pressure on mediators is sometimes so extreme that, on rare occasion, one of my colleagues occasionally departs from this life—literally *dies*—during the mediation.

The Scent better work, I thought, or this mediation isn't going to provide a home for the harp. You can mediate hundreds of times and still be in search of both a moderate heart rate and a civilized, constructive conversation.

The Brit became a bit assertive, cranking up the temperature in the room. I knew the Iraqi would respond by adding to the heat. I took off my suit coat.

I continued to focus on the harp, with its elegant angles and long strings. I hoped they would follow my lead, before we got to the bargaining. But mammon seemed to be outrunning history and sentiment.

The argument did involve artistic appreciation, respect for tradition—and cash. I found out later that harps have been found in Sumer and in Ur, early civilizations in Mesopotamia.

What would Peter do? I couldn't very well sit on the floor. But I could be silent, or speak little. The argument turned on a mystery—the provenance of the harp. That mystery was not likely to be solved, at least not that day and maybe not ever. Each side presented its own view of the mystery. As a mediator, I am not allowed to tell you what their views were. Obviously, they were decidedly different.

I listened, and stared at the harp. Besides the angular shape and long strings, it had what I thought was a stained or painted sound box. I asked everyone again to take a moment to look, just look at the harp. I kept myself from asking anyone to play it, though I was absurdly curious what it would sound like.

Pounds sterling began to dominate—in what we call positional bargaining. This is an adversarial kind of bargaining, in which everyone has a position and clings to it. It is zero-sum, in the sense that it assumes that someone will win, and the other side will lose. It shuns imaginative solutions that might produce a win-win. Despite my consistent refrain as to its astounding non-monetary qualities, neither I nor the wondrous harp was encouraging win-win sentiments. I loosened my tie.

Sharing, it quickly became clear, was not within reach. Nor was presenting the harp to a museum. Nor, as I loosened my tie further, was selling it to a worthy, appreciative buyer and sharing the proceeds—in some, in any, proportion.

Would these rivals reach a resolution? Could I induce them even to stay and continue?

I was walking, ever-so-charily, on heavily mined ground. I didn't fear for the safety of the instrument before me on that carpet in that room in Nottingham on that gray day. I did worry about its uncertain, contentious future. The participants gave a prompt and unsympathetic dismissal to proposals I made that did not put money front and center. This,

I thought, is what a Christie's auctioneer must feel like when trying to flog a masterpiece.

But, as always, this was their mediation, not mine. My work was to facilitate a resolution, however energetic the negotiations. I knew that, as almost always, someone was going to be less happy, someone more. And I knew the harp would leave, likely at day's end, with its new owner—with its grace and sound intact. But the conversation was remaining contentious. The harp could not be asked its wishes.

Still, I encouraged dialogue and remained as silent as I could. Then I rolled my sleeves up. I was slipping back into my comfort zone, watching a quite normal blend of the sincere and insincere in offer and counter. Would the continued parlay bring a result? I stared at the harp and listened.

Eventually, offer and counter did meet, and they reached an agreement. I am no more allowed to discuss the result than I was the negotiations that led to it. I congratulated both Brit and Iraqi on the resolution. I hope Peter would have been proud. But then Peter was an extraordinarily humble fellow.

The resolution of who would ever-so-carefully take the harp away from that mediation did make me proud, and it reminded me of the value of my craft. The harp had found a home (at least temporarily) without violence, without more bitterness, without the dictate, trappings, emotional burdens, and expense of a British court.

It was late in the day. I rolled my sleeves down, pulled my tie vaguely to my collar, put my gray suit coat back on, and called for a car. I returned to my home in the Jericho district of Oxford, worn out, disheveled, and—as usual—wondering whether I had neglected a more productive approach toward resolution. When I was a trial lawyer, my colleagues told me we made three arguments in court: the one we planned to make, the one we actually did make, and the one we wished we had made. Whatever I had done, it was time for a Pilsner at the Middle Eastern restaurant a few blocks from my home.

I promised myself to do something relaxing the next morning. Jericho is a quiet, historic part of Oxford. My house was near the Oxford University Press and the Oxford Canal with its towpath along the river. I liked to run on that towpath, and I felt I'd earned a run. The morning weather might be wretched, but at least I'd enjoy some unburdened, quiet peace. Unless the fearless, unpredictable swans—flapping insanely and hissing clamorously—turned out to be on the towpath. I had learned those swans did not respond to the Scent—or anything other than a reversal of my direction.

CHAPTER FORTY-FIVE

Fontainebleau: Just Keep Those Euros Coming!

Freedom of the press is guaranteed only to those who own one.
—ABBOTT JOSEPH (A. J.) LIEBLING, WRITER FOR
THE *NEW YORKER* AND PRESS CRITIC

FONTAINEBLEAU, 2007

Reporters and editors used to be regular guys and gals. Now, the industry reminds me of my short stay as an academic visitor at INSEAD in Fontainebleau, France. The *Financial Times* rated INSEAD the number one business school in the world (tied with Stanford).[129]

I sat at a table in the cafeteria with half a dozen students. The students came from sixty countries, and all were bright. But at that table I realized how far behind I had left Oxford and any kind of philosophical inquiry. In their lunchtime discussion, the students held like Super Glue to the notion that companies exist to make money for their officers and management. They don't exist for their stockholders, certainly not for their workers, most certainly not for consumers, and decidedly not for society at large. I just listened, eating an apple.

One Israeli woman attacked with energy the view of the other students, but no one budged before what they saw as her naïve arguments. Euros danced until my apple became a core. I hoped these future titans would keep their mitts off the media.

Reporters don't have such concerns. They are not rich. They are lucky to be middle-class.

Their slim purses may begin in their training. At the Columbia Graduate School of Journalism—thought by some to be the best—tuition, fees, and living expenses for a full-time master's degree student are more than $100,000.

An average Washington correspondent earned $86,270 in 2016. A government bureaucrat in Washington earned $112,601, according to the United States Office of Personnel Management. The average plumber (the real kind of plumber, I mean) in Washington earned $71,120. The average lawyer in Washington earned $182,810.

If $86,000 doesn't seem slim, outside of Washington, US reporters earned a median annual income of $36,360 in 2015. They were paid $43,830 in 2004. In my day, reporters were also poor, or at least middle-middle-class.

According to the Bureau of Labor Statistics, public relations people earn more. In 2013, they earned $54,940.[130]

"With diminishing salaries and job security, some warn aspiring journalists that journalism can't provide a 'decent' or 'modest' salary," Alex T. Williams, a doctoral student, wrote in *Poynter*.[131]

In 2015 *CareerCast* ranked newspaper reporter as the *worst job* in America.[132]

Why?

The Bureau of Labor Statistics reported that thirty-nine thousand people worked as reporters, editors, or photographers for newspapers in 2017—down 15 percent from 2014, and 45 percent from 2004. Wages for newspaper editors in 2017 were about $50,000, while the salary for reporters was $34,000.[133]

At least a third of the largest newspapers—together with nearly a quarter of the highest-traffic digital news outlets—had layoffs between January 2017 and April 2018, according to Pew Research Center.[134]

Pew reported that major staff cuts took place between 2015 and 2016 at the *Philadelphia Inquirer* and *Daily News*, *Tribune Publishing* (including the *Los Angeles Times* and the *Chicago Tribune*), the *Wall Street Journal*, the *New York Daily News*, and the *Boston Globe*, among many others. (*Globe* editorial employees even spent one Sunday helping to deliver the paper.) The *Los Angeles Times* had the misfortune to undergo a change in ownership, a bankruptcy, reduction in staff, a change of editors, and a decline in circulation.[135]

The staff cuts have resulted in less regional coverage, the disappearance of certain kinds of news, and less investigative reporting.[136] Newsrooms today are swapping experienced, high-salary reporters for less experienced journalists with great multimedia chops but less institutional knowledge or experience in any particular field, according to Joe Skeel, the executive director of the Society of Professional Journalists.

The *New* York *Times* reported in August 2019:

> *As print advertising and print circulation have significantly declined, up to 1,500 papers—or close to a quarter of all newspapers—have drastically cut their staffs and pared back their coverage.*
>
> *Many metro regional daily newsrooms that once employed hundreds of journalists* now operate with only a few dozen reporters and editors, *and have become ghosts of their former selves.*[137] *[Emphasis supplied.]*

The *Times* continued:

> *Smaller staffs mean* less focus *on investigative reporting. The Daily News in New York has won the Pulitzer Prize . . . 15 times. . . [It was bought by Tribune Publishing.]* A year later, the staff at the News was slashed in half.[138] *[Emphasis supplied.]*

The *Times* also reported that, over the last fifteen years, a quarter of all local newsrooms have either merged or stopped printing. It said that more than two hundred counties have no newspaper. It added that this has resulted in "a news vacuum that affects an estimated 3.2 million residents and public officials."[139]

In terms of public respect for the press, The Pew Research Center said in 2013: Compared with other professions, journalists have dropped the most [ten percentage points] in public esteem since 2009. *Only 28 percent* of Americans believed journalists contributed "a lot" to society in 2013.[140]

Perhaps this explains the disconnect: The media thinks it is important. The public doesn't. If the media—or at least the top end of it—is so important, how was the top end of it so out of touch with the Trump phenomenon?[141]

Because there are those in the media who believe themselves to be important. These include an often vapid and vacuous gaggle of pundits who seem to spend their leisure time selecting red neckties and colorful scarves for their next television appearances.

The vapidity results, in part, because reporters are paid to analyze the news rather than uncover it. I once did a piece on this for *MORE*, a short-lived, feisty journalism review.[142] In *MORE* I argued, among other things, that investigative reporting, done well, requires skill, sophistication, and time. I tried to differentiate investigative reporting from "getting the story [from a friendly source] one day ahead of its release."

The *Times* continues to offer both analysis and investigation. Trump continues to say both are "fake." He has also repeatedly said that the *Times* is "failing" financially. He is wrong—in part, *because of his own attacks*. (Ironically, the attacks have driven the *Times's* profits up.)[143]

Despite those profits, and the modest wages of reporters, the paper has had some financial problems. At one point, it even had to ask a Mexican billionaire—Carlos Slim—to supply the reduced rations of hardtack and grog for the crew to continue its journalistic voyage.[144]

CHAPTER FORTY-SIX

Climbing into the Jury Box

[T]he honesty of floral signals can play a key role in . . . attractiveness to pollinators. In plants, a genetic constraint . . . and sanctions against cheaters may contribute to the evolution and maintenance of honest signaling. [Emphasis supplied.]
—A. C. KNAUER, F. P. SCHIESTL, ECOLOGY LETTERS

SAN FRANCISCO, 2019

I had won the prize. At twenty-seven I had become a correspondent in the Washington Bureau of the *New York Times.* A year later I found myself covering the White House. But I left. Peaked too early? Needed to be the businessperson my family had not yet produced? Wanted to be a participant, not an observer? Too fearful of what would happen to me as a *Times* reporter in later life in the back rows of a cavernous newsroom?

Law in San Francisco at a big commercial firm was boring. I would look at the attorney list I had stuck to the wall by my phone and scan through it to see if there was someone I might want to have lunch with. Some nice people, but not *interesting* people. After the *Times* Washington Bureau, whom would I find interesting? A blessing with a lifelong curse. When I told him I was going to San Francisco, Gene Roberts, the national editor, warned me: "You're too young to retire."

I thought the Carter Administration would show me the other side—what was behind the curtain I had been trying to peek around as a reporter. It did show me a few things—the sad pettiness of bureaucracy, and the thrill of the World Court. On the other hand, I was tied, as Justice spokesperson for the administration, to a shrewd, but exceedingly careful, nearly silent man. It turned out to be a poor investment of time and a lot of energy: In the end, I learned little.

Being a prosecutor showed me how to make my way around a courtroom and gave me skills to use in a firm—this time, my own. That was a challenge, but at last I was an entrepreneur. Legal disputes propelled me to corral three dozen banks and other financial institutions as clients—and showed me how silly it all could be. Some of it was fun; I especially loved talking to jurors. (Despite the common assumption, juries do get it right.)

I came to realize that a new approach, another method was on the horizon, and I grabbed it: mediation. I went on to practice mediation in several countries—and in disputes small (tree interfering with sun on swimming pool), spiritual (who gets to use this church building), to grand (billion-dollar transnational merger in London). I even got to teach mediation to the UN and at Oxford.

And it was no small thrill when I actually became a real British barrister in November 2002.

Consider all the times that suicidal tomfoolery insinuated itself in the restless march that led me to mediation:

- Reporting Chinese subs in the East River;
- Wearing Italian racing jackets;
- Drinking the FBI's Coca-Cola;
- Approaching FBI agents who were pretending to be reporters;
- Telling the executive editor to chill out about less-than-polite words in the story;
- Refusing to give Scotty Reston the name of my source;
- Sporting cowboy boots in the Oval Office; and
- Posting reporters' salaries on a Washington bulletin board.

In mediation there is occasional humor but little tomfoolery.

Mediation combines the interviewing, the empathy—the *scent*—of reporting with the experience and expertise of trials. My trial experience lets me credibly say, "Here is how this may proceed and turn out in court, if you can't work things out." It also lets me try to help the woman locked in a bank and a distraught Harlem photographer without inflicting on them the expense and tribulations of a courtroom.

Negotiation is at the heart of both mediation, my current billet, and investigative reporting, my former billet. Whenever I am mediating, I am trying to help others negotiate, and I am negotiating with them—all of them—to get to a result.

Only now—much nearer the end of work than the beginning—I see why Nicole, my assistant, asked how I had managed to get my index finger into so many different pots of professional jam.

"How did you do it?" she asked.

"Do what?"

"Change from field to field with seeming ease?"

She actually said, "seeming ease." She had been my assistant too long. There wasn't any ease about it. It was something else.

Back to Gene Roberts, the seventeen-Pulitzer-Prize guy. Gene has intuition, in an almost primal way. His mind raced so fast when he was an editor that there would be long empty spaces on the phone line because he was so far ahead of you.

"You give off a scent," he told me once. "There are only a couple of reporters in the country that do."

"A scent?" It's Salvador Dali cologne, a Surrealist scent for men.

"No, a scent that you can be trusted. People can smell it."[145]

Maybe Gene was right. Perhaps I emitted some sort of scent that made people trust, relate, and reveal. Gene said you couldn't fake The Scent—the convincing mien of honesty, or perhaps in my case, naïveté. Certainly, Peter Kihss had it. I can still see that large circle of students leaning intently in concert toward Peter.

Peter was sitting like a lanky, ungainly guru, in the middle of the circle, notebook out, pen flying, battered hat tilted on his head, dark overcoat open like tent flaps. Everyone had forgotten the noisy mayhem surrounding the circle. The serious business of intimate truth-telling was at hand.

When I later tried cases in federal court as an assistant US attorney, sometimes I would go to the judge afterwards and ask for suggestions as to how I might improve my advocacy skills. I once asked Judge Robert H.

Schnacke. He replied, "You know, you have the ability to climb into the jury box with the jurors."

Climb into the jury box?

Judge Schnacke evidently thought the Scent had carried over to trial law.

CHAPTER FORTY-SEVEN

The Church Rejects an Offering: The Go-to-Hell Fund Is Damned

One of the greatest qualities of those who are humble is that they accept gifts no matter what their value. . . . . [O]ne should accept it and appreciate it and feel that the true gift is the love that motivated them to give, not the value of the gift.
—JURISPRUDENCE AND ISLAMIC RULINGS

Go with what you've got.
—JOHN HOHENBERG, PROFESSOR AT COLUMBIA
GRADUATE SCHOOL OF JOURNALISM

PARIS, 2007

Columbia Graduate School of Journalism awards the Pulitzer Prizes. Note, please, the prizes are named for a publisher, not a journalist. Joseph Pulitzer was publisher of the *St. Louis Post Dispatch* and the *New York World*. He introduced yellow journalism to those papers in the 1880s and 1890s. Yellow journalism brandished big headlines and showed not much interest in accuracy.

I must confess that Pulitzer was not on my mind when I met with Nicholas Lemann, the dean of the Columbia J-School in 2007. The meeting was in Paris, near where I was living. Nick, as he is called, was accompanied by a pleasant development officer. The subject was the usual one: a contribution for the School. I offered Lemann more than a contribution. I offered an endowment.

Reporters and editors are sometimes told to do something they think is unethical by business people with different standards. If they feel they have to quit, who will feed them and their families and pay their mortgages? The answer is no one, unless they get a job fast, in an ever-more-difficult job market.

So I proposed to Lemann the Go-to-Hell Fund. Suppose I give an endowment to the J-School of enough money to tide over one or two journalists a year who have said "Go to Hell" and obeyed their journalistic consciences instead of their corporate bosses? The earnings on the endowment could fund the journalists living for a couple of months in New York. They could be some sort of short-term fellow at the School. They might even teach the naïve. Lemann was not thrilled by the Go-to-Hell idea, but he said he would consider it. Ultimately, he said no. His reason was that it was "too difficult administratively."[146]

The J-School does manage to administer the Pulitzer Prizes. Here's how it does that:

> *In late February or early March, 77 editors, publishers, writers, and educators gather in the School of Journalism to judge the entries in the 14 journalism categories. More than 2,400 entries are submitted each year in the Pulitzer Prize competitions, and only 21 awards are normally made. The awards are the culmination of a year-long process that begins early in the year with the appointment of 102 distinguished judges who serve on 20 separate juries and are asked to make three nominations in each of the 21 categories.*
>
> *. . . [I]n early April . . . the Board assembles for two days . . . In prior weeks, the Board had read the texts of the journalism entries and the 15 nominated books, listened to music recordings, read the scripts of the nominated plays, and attended the performances or seen videos where possible. . . .*

The J-School does not seem to trip over its shoelaces in administering the Pulitzer.

The story of rejection shows that realism is in residence at Morningside Heights. After my meeting with Lemann and his rejection of my offer, I mentioned on a J-School listserv for my classmates that I had offered the money. My classmates—many of them working journalists—allowed as how it was a great idea and told me they couldn't understand why the School wouldn't jump at the endowment.

My classmate, Howard Weinberg, a longtime television news producer, told me he would approach the dean again about the idea. Howard was founding producer of *The Robert MacNeil Report*, executive producer for *Listening to America with Bill Moyers*, and a producer for *60 Minutes*.

Howard did speak with Dean Lemann and afterwards reported to the listserv: No. Too hard to administer. I had to wonder, though I didn't say it to Howard, if *60 Minutes* would have believed that. The school administers not only the Pulitzer but the Cabot Prizes, the John Chancellor Award, the Mike Berger Award, the duPont Awards, and the John B. Oakes Award for Distinguished Environmental Journalism. If the J-School people can administer all of those, couldn't they administer a paltry Go-to-Hell Fund without exhausting themselves?

But there's an important difference: Publishers like the Pulitzers. Publishers whose miscreant reporters and editors said "Go to Hell" and sought the shelter of the J-School might have a different reaction. They might not like the notoriety and might not like the J-School for its role in the fund.

Please consider this irony:

The J-School is teaching young reporters to do just what I was trying to promote here: Have the truth see the light of day, not pass over it so that their paper can prosper. But those who run the school have had to consider the Slippery Slope and the flexible ethics of survival. And why shouldn't they?

The alumni chant, and in unison: This is a good idea. The people who ran the School demurred: "Administratively difficult."

I thought of the J-School as a craft shop in the basement of a church, with experienced pros teaching youngsters how to find out about things and write about them, seasoned with a heavy dose of ethics. A. J. Liebling, the *New Yorker* writer and press critic, who attended the J-School, had a different view. He wrote in the *Wayward Pressman* that it had "all the intellectual status of a training school for future employees of the A & P."[147]

This brings us to circumstances where the *Times*—earlier and recently—has had to confront the administrative, ethical, and economic difficulties of blending innocence with realism. I'm not talking about how to keep the police from interfering with rows of *Times* trucks queuing to pick up the paper in the evening when the paper was printed in Times Square. How do you suppose the *Times* managed that bit of bureaucratic survival? I'm not referring to the *Times Magazine*'s practice of putting its table of contents *after* heftily priced ads.

I'm talking about whether to leave information—news—out. Whether to censor itself.

Shades of Reston and Harvard's President Pusey.

Shades of its Pentagon correspondent and the My Lai Massacre.

Shades of business reporters and problem banks.

Shades of rejecting a powerful Watergate offering from the head of the FBI?

CHAPTER FORTY-EIGHT

Getting the Director's Trust

If you want to keep a secret, you must also hide it from yourself.
—GEORGE ORWELL, *1984*

If I maintain my silence about my secret, it is my prisoner . . . if I let it slip from my tongue, I am its prisoner.
—ARTHUR SCHOPENHAUER

There are no secrets that time does not reveal.
—JEAN RACINE

WASHINGTON, AUGUST 1972

Why did the acting director of the FBI choose me to leak Watergate to? Remember, please, that he had no idea I was leaving the *Times*. And at that disclosure he displayed great surprise. I was dealing with a naïve fellow. To sit with me in a French restaurant, in the open, and to tell me what he did betrayed great naïveté, great carelessness, or a reckless desire to get caught.

Gray was born in St. Louis, the son of a railroad worker. He attended Rice University in Houston. He left Rice in his last year to enter the Naval Academy, where he played football. He graduated in 1940 and served aboard the battleship *Idaho*. Two years later, he joined the submarine corps. He participated in five submarine combat patrols against the Japanese. He graduated from George Washington University's law school in 1949. Back in the Navy, he commanded a submarine during the Korean War. In 1958, he became military assistant to the chairman of the

Joint Chiefs of Staff and special assistant to the secretary of defense. He retired from the Navy in 1960.

Twelve years later, after he had served as the assistant attorney general for the Civil Division in the Department of Justice, President Nixon appointed Gray to the position of acting FBI director. Within weeks at the FBI, Gray had relaxed the formal dress codes and weight limits, welcomed women, visited nearly all of the field offices, and forced out some of Hoover's trusted lieutenants.

But he also did at least two less laudable things: He burned secret files at Nixon's insistence and updated Nixon's lawyer, John Dean III, on the FBI's Watergate investigation.

One of Mr. Gray's sons confirmed that Gray's diary reveals a lunch he had with me on that warm Washington day—August 16, 1972—but he insisted his father never would have made such disclosures to me.

Here is what Pat Gray wrote about burning the files in the book he co-authored with his son:

> *So the three of us, [Dick Kleindienst, Assistant Attorney General Henry Petersen, and I] went into the attorney general's small private office where Dick and I took seats while Henry went to the cabinet and fixed drinks. I declined.*
>
> *I explained to them what I knew about the two files, which had come from the safe of E. Howard Hunt, one of the Watergate conspirators.*
>
> *Though I hadn't studied them in detail, it had been clear to me that they were copies of some sort of top-secret State Department cables, as well as some flimsy copies of muckraking correspondence about Senator Ted Kennedy's car accident at Chappaquiddick in 1969.*
>
> *I told them both, again, that when White House counsel John Dean had given me the files in the presence of John Ehrlichman, the assistant to the president for domestic affairs, both men had assured me the files were in no way connected with Watergate and that they had national security overtones.*
>
> *When I asked Ehrlichman and Dean if these files should be placed in the FBI files Dean responded, "These should never see the light of day."*

I took their statements at face value, so that when I actually went to burn the files I casually flipped through them and noted for myself that these indeed were not related in any way to our investigation of the break-in.[148]

The *New York Times* wrote in Gray's obituary:

[H]e said he believed he had direct orders from presidential aides and no inkling "that these guys are trying to sandbag me," adding, "I know it's hard for people to think somebody could be so stupid, but I believed them."[149]

A submarine commander. A lawyer. Acting director of the world's leading investigative agency burning secret documents in his backyard in Connecticut. But before he tossed the documents unto the fire, he "casually" flipped through them to make sure they weren't related to Watergate? And his son Ed seriously believes he didn't leak to me at a French restaurant in Washington?

I think Pat Gray was a decent guy who understood what the administration was trying to do with Watergate and wouldn't go along. He decided to do the only thing he could, short of resigning. (And if he resigned, what would have happened? Wouldn't the president have appointed a loyalist?) He would leak to the press. But put yourself in his shoes. To whom? I had done a piece on the FBI when he took office. Here's the article Gray referred to:

WASHINGTON, MAY 11 [1972]—L. Patrick Gray 3d, acting director of the Federal Bureau of Investigation, disclosed today a series of steps that may radically change both the appearance and substance of an agency held rigidly to a single pattern by J. Edgar Hoover for nearly 50 years.

In an interview, Mr. Gray said that he would immediately begin discussion with his subordinates about a wide range of topics that deal with basic policies and practices, including some that have recently drawn heavy fire from liberal critics of the bureau . . .

> *Mr. Gray stressed that the agenda constituted only topics for discussion and included "questions raised by some critics." However, he promised at a minimum the following changes in the bureau:*
>
> *. . . More exposure of the bureau's operations to public exposure and scrutiny. "I want to open the window a little," he said.[150]*

Open the windows of the FBI? I honestly thought he just didn't know how tightly sealed—no, riveted shut—they were after forty-eight years of John Edgar Hoover.

The backstory: I had just been chatting on the phone with Gray when he—innocently—mentioned that a *Washington Post* reporter had just come in to interview him at length.

"He did?" I nearly screamed. The man obviously had no idea of what he was telling me. My chief competitor was about to scoop me with a lengthy exclusive interview—*with him.*

I proceeded to beg for ten minutes of time to ask him questions on the phone. *Did the* Post *reporter have a photographer?* I asked. "No," he said. I immediately dispatched one of our Washington Bureau photographers, Mike Lien, to Gray's office. I told Gray he was on the way. Until he gets there, I suggested we might chat a bit. I then interviewed the poor guy up, down, and sideways. My story—with Mike's photo—appeared the next day on the front page of the *Times* with a long rendition of the interview. Surprise! The *Post* fronted its story with a shorter interview and no photos. Attack repelled.[151]

Gray called and said he thought the piece was good, and the *photo* was great. Could he get a copy?

So Pat—if I may call him that—knew me.

Gray's innocence supposedly also extended to his assessment of his close associate, Mark Felt. According to the *Washington Post*, Gray said he resisted five separate demands from the White House to fire Felt.

"This was a tremendous surprise to me," Gray told George Stephanopoulos on June 26, 2005 on ABC's *This Week* program. "I could not have been more shocked and more disappointed in a man whom I had trusted. . . . It was like I was hit with a tremendous sledgehammer. . . . "He told me time and time again that he was not Deep Throat."

According to his obituary in the *Washington Post*, Gray trusted Felt so much that he put him in charge of tracking down the leaks of information that were showing up in the media. In his book, *In Nixon's Web*, Gray said flatly that he would not leak. But he also writes about our relationship and lunch:

> *I had resolved not to tangle with the Washington press corps regarding the contents of a story. Despite their protests to the contrary, my early experience in Washington led me easily to the conclusion that the press is always right and the facts are what they say they are. I did not even consider showing John Mohr's memorandum to Scripps-Howard or the Washington Daily News. Though both had written highly inaccurate stories that now repose uncorrected in their archives I knew that there was little or nothing I could do about it without becoming a leaker myself. That I would not do.*
>
> *What I would do was talk to reporters on the record. Less than a week after I took office, even before I moved to the FBI spaces, I started giving one-on-one interviews. Among the first was to Robert Smith, a young reporter for the New York* Times. *His article ran on May 12 and its lead sentence encapsulated almost perfectly what I had set about doing at the FBI.*
>
> *Bob would leave the newspaper later that fall to go to law school. By that time we had become quite friendly and he and I had lunch together at Sans Souci just before he left.[152]*

Pat Gray contradicts me in two ways. He says that he did not leak to reporters. And he says that he never told Mark Felt to leak. As to Felt, maybe Gray was being honest. I doubt it, but I leave that for you to judge. We know he did lie about leaking to me. Even if I were inclined to fib, there is too much evidence for me to be making the story up. I have a theory.

My theory: What seemed puzzling to me at the time—but important to me now—is that when we were at the restaurant, Gray still did not know I was leaving the paper. I told him that on the sidewalk. He had a pronounced reaction of surprise—almost incredulity—and disappointment. At the time, I did not understand why. He had just confided in—and bet on—the wrong reporter. Please put yourself, again, in Gray's shoes. Wrong colt. What now? More French lunches? Whom could he trust?

Why not give the task of being the pipeline to one of his deputies . . . say Mark Felt? An old Washington hand who might prefer a dark garage to a candle-lit restaurant? Especially if the deputy volunteered.

That's my theory. And since Pat Gray died after keeping his secret for thirty-three years, a theory it will likely remain. His son Ed disagrees with that theory:

> *In not one of any of those other interviews did L. Patrick Gray pass along anything like what Phelps and Smith now claim he passed along to Smith.*
>
> *Readers of Phelps's new book will have to judge for themselves why . . . neither the young reporter nor the then-editor can explain why no story was ever written based on the "explosive aspects" supposedly passed along by Gray on this one occasion.*
>
> *Had my father intended to leak anything at all about Watergate or any other subject of interest to the FBI, rest assured that he would have made sure that the story got published.[153]*

Ed wrote in *American Journalism Review*:

> *He [Gray] looked me in the eye without denial—or any comment. In other words, confirmation."*
>
> *Wrong. That was not "confirmation." That was "no comment," the same answer my father gave to every reporter who asked him anything at all about Watergate.*
>
> *Since I was not present at that August 1972 luncheon, I cannot categorically deny all of Smith's account. But little of it rings true to me. Yes, my father may have mentioned Segretti, who really was a bit player not involved in the break-in, but did he accuse the president and the attorney general of complicity? No, he did not. That much I can categorically deny.*
>
> *During the many months before that moment of shock, my father gave dozens of on-the-record interviews to many reporters, including*

Bob Woodward. He talked at length and on the record with other New York Times and Washington Post reporters. He gave interviews to nearly every important Washington bureau reporter, many of whom are still reporting today. In not one of any of those other interviews did L. Patrick Gray pass along anything like what Robert Smith and his then-editor Robert Phelps now claim he passed along to Smith.

Readers will have to judge for themselves why neither the young reporter nor the then-editor can explain why no story was ever written based on the "explosive information" supposedly passed along by Gray on this occasion and why no record of the supposed revelations exists, either in the files of the Washington bureau of the Times or in the possession of either claimant.[154]

The son believes his father would not betray secrets. That would make him bad. Wrong! That makes him good. No one could seriously believe, except Ed Gray, that exposing Nixon was a bad thing. In fact, it was patriotic.

What can I say? Pat Gray told me these things. I say so, Bob Phelps said so, and—somewhere—there is a tape contemporaneously saying so.

You may ask: Why me? Why did Gray choose me to confide in? Well, we got along well. I had treated him fairly in print. I flatter myself to think I had a good reputation.

Running the FBI, he had access to my file. It exuded innocence. I found this out later when I got a copy: except for an angry landlady in San Francisco who thought mice were fine co-tenants and it was not her problem that I had grown up in Roxbury and feared the vile gray beasts.

So why did Gray trust me? Why did any of my sources—all at risk, in various ways, to themselves? Why did they decide to speak? I don't mean what selfishness, what altruism prompted or compelled them? I mean why *me?*

I wore an ill-fitting jacket that I had worn in college, chino pants, a blue Brooks Brothers button-down shirt, and a striped tie. My hair was a kinky mop, and my spectacles not modish. I used a ball-point pen and a cut-down reporter's spiral-bound notebook. Someone once described me—I cannot judge the accuracy—as looking like Henry Kissinger and talking like Woody Allen.

Throughout the years, I never said a word to anyone about Patrick Gray's having been my source on the Watergate story. From my point of view, I'd promised to keep that secret. Years passed—I became a lawyer, a barrister . . . and I was working in London, on Fleet Street (where there used to be newspaper offices). I was in a leafy red-brick area called Temple, the legal area of London, home to the Inns of Court, which oversee barristers. I had gone to London after the death of my second wife, Clarissa. Clarissa was the world's most beloved third-grade teacher. After her death, her little students made this clear in the elaborate book of carefully scrawled reminisces they collected and gave to me. It is my habit to find solid ground and freedom, after personal tragedy.

It was on a busy day in London in 2006 that I got an unusual phone call from California. I was at the Centre for Effective Dispute Resolution. The switchboard operator put through a producer from Hollywood. The fellow, I've lost his name, had an inkling of my involvement with the Watergate disclosures and wanted to hire me to participate in the making of a movie that would, he explained, rival *All the President's Men.*

I was not to star or even have a Hitchcockian cameo. He asked me to be an adviser, to *spill the beans.* But the beans were in a still-sealed can. The producer did not tell me how he knew about my connection, and I wasn't able to ask him how he knew without breaking confidentiality. That would have confirmed what he was asking about. Gray had died a year earlier, and I wondered whether I could disclose what I had learned from him—and what I had done with that information and what the *Times* had not done. On the one hand, some would see Gray as a traitor, a leaker of secret information. On the other hand, some would see him as a hero, serving a corrupt president and doing the only honest thing he could think to do: Turn to someone he trusted in the press to get the story out.

I didn't know whether I could share the secret. At that point, I called the best man I could think of to call to advise me: the general counsel of the *New York Times,* Ken Richieri. I called Richieri. He took the call and I laid out the situation. I didn't ask whether he knew about what had happened.

"No," he said. I was still bound. And—amazingly enough—he didn't tell anyone at the paper about the call. The promise of confidentiality to Gray still bound me.

In retrospect, perhaps I had chosen badly for a second opinion. After all, Richieri worked for the *Times*. I had access to the law faculty of Oxford. I was an academic visitor and fellow of Lincoln College, teaching an informal seminar on international commercial mediation. But I trusted Richieri, and I turned Hollywood down. All those starlets (beguiling, I confess, in my widowed state), colorful celluloid, and hefty residuals went down the drain. While Gray had died, his family and friends had not. I believed the man had done something laudable, but if others disagreed, they deserved to have his memory protected.

Bob Phelps kept the secret for many years. Then, Phelps betrayed both Gray and me. I kept the secret, because I had pledged to and because Richieri had advised me to. So, secret it remained.

CHAPTER FORTY-NINE

Suppression, or the Fix Is In

It can be held certain that information that is withheld or suppressed contains truths that are detrimental to the persons involved in their suppression.

—J. EDGAR HOOVER

Everybody knows there is no fineness or accuracy of suppression; if you hold down one thing, you hold down the adjoining.

—SAUL BELLOW

The media want to maintain their intimate relation to state power. They want to get leaks…[T]hey want to rub shoulders with the Secretary of State.…To do that, you've got to play the game…and [that] means …serving as their disinformation apparatus.

—NOAM CHOMSKY

SAN FRANCISCO, 2008

It wasn't the government (against whom the media so often rails) that suppressed what the acting FBI director gave the *Times* about Watergate. Or the courts. Or the Mafia. Or the unions. Or extraterrestrials. In my view, it was an editor or editors of the *Times* who suppressed Watergate. And it was likely for reasons built into the Old Gray Lady.

A week or so after I had brought the material to Bob Phelps, he left for a long vacation. He never said a word to any of the three dozen reporters in the large newsroom of the *Times* Washington Bureau. Later on, he told me he couldn't remember where he had put the tape of my briefing him or even if I had given it to him. Seymour Hersh, who worked on Watergate for the *Times*, told me he was never told about the tape or my lunch with the FBI director. How could the paper of record drop this information into an abyss, never even retrieving it when the *Times* was being lambasted by Woodward and Bernstein in their coverage of Watergate? Wouldn't that seem like a lot to blame on negligence? Especially, when the *Times* is by temperament compulsive—far from haphazard? The *Times* is not the kind of place that loses news.

After publication of his book by a university press, I called Phelps. I asked him what had happened.

"You remember my briefing you in your office for a half-hour?" I asked.

"Yes."

"You remember you sat on your little sofa and took notes in a notebook I handed you?"

"Yes."

"You remember I paced back and forth while I was briefing you—I couldn't sit down?"

"Yes."

"You remember I had a small tape recorder going and at the end gave you the tape?"

"Yes."

"So . . . why didn't you pursue the story—the story of the century?"

"I went on a cruise to Alaska."

"Bob, you didn't go on that cruise for a week. Let's not fool around. You walked back into the newsroom. I went to my desk to pack it up. You had the tape and the notebook in your hand. You had three dozen first-rate reporters in that room. Why didn't you just give the information I gave you to any one of them, or a couple of them, to chase?"

"I don't know."

"You don't know? That's impossible."

"I don't remember . . . What do you want me to do . . . Take truth serum?"

"If that would help, yes."

No matter how I pressed, Phelps continued to tell me he didn't remember. Phelps had always been a guy who acted on quick deadlines—minutes, if not seconds. Never weeks. And why was the location of the tape "the crucial point"? That had all the smoked rosiness of a dried red herring. Does that sort of journalist forget to use, or to follow up on, the story of the century?

In my opinion, that is not—*cannot be*—the story. The *Times* is a bureaucracy. Unless he utterly didn't believe me, Phelps would have had to tell Max Frankel about my reporting. But he had every reason to believe me: I was giving him details, like Donald Segretti's name. And he had my track record—I had won many Publisher's awards at the paper and had never been accused of being wrong, or fabricating a story. He also knew I had a good relationship with Gray. So, *why?* Why bury the information, keep it secret from his reporters? From New York? Apparently never tell *anyone* about it until he wrote his book?

I have asked myself that many times. I have asked *Times* people past and present. And I have asked reporters and editors outside the paper. They all have one theory: Phelps reported to Frankel. He told him—of course, he would—about my reporting. And Frankel told him not to use it. Frankel denies this, saying he knew nothing at all about it. I find that hard to accept: Would Phelps, the Washington news editor, not tell the Washington bureau chief? No one would describe Bob Phelps as a cowboy.

Phelps *knew* what he had just been told. It could not have been a cruise the following week. The fact that Phelps even used the cruise as an excuse undercuts his story. He was an experienced editor, one of the top editors in the nation: news editor of the Washington Bureau of the *New York Times*. Would a trained editor forget the information in his hand?

In my mind, this could only have been deliberate. But why? Conspiracy theories always abound. But, in the context of the *Times* in Washington, with a bureau chief eating out of Kissinger's hand, and—from at least one point of view—dependent on Kissinger (and others in government), isn't the likeliest scenario that Frankel told Phelps at least to hold the information (until he couldn't)? Especially if Kissinger warned him off the information (while Watergate was still at a stage where he could do that)? Phelps denies this too. Frankel says, essentially, he relied on Phelps.

Sy Hersh shares my view on this. According to Miraldi,

Hersh was sure that Frankel had talked to Secretary of State Henry Kissinger, who assured him the break-in did not reach the Oval Office.

But Phelps said if Frankel was told the story had no merit, he never passed it on nor did anything to call off the staff. "From the top editors on down we all shared in the blame," Phelps said. Which didn't convince an angry Smith and a dubious Hersh.[155]

Here is more of Miraldi's view:

Phelps simply did not think the scandal could possibly reach into the White House. He and Frankel both asked their reporters to check out the early reporting of Yale graduate Woodward, twenty-nine, and the long-haired, twenty-eight-year-old Bernstein—"snot-nosed" kids, he called them—to see if anyone trusted their findings.

The Times concluded that the Post was "headed down the wrong path," said Frankel . . .

Unfortunately, Frankel bemoaned later, the Times relied on reporters with "vested interest in bureaucracies, not rookies" with no predispositions.

. . . Frankel was a career Times man, rising from the metro desk to foreign correspondent. [H]e accompanied Richard Nixon and became friends with Kissinger on their historic trip to China. . . .

Frankel was getting ready to leave Washington to become the paper's Sunday editor in New York.

"My involvement with any of the Watergate stuff was so marginal," he said. If anything, Phelps noted, Frankel "wished he had taken a more active role."

But Frankel might have ignored the story because he simply could not believe it had sinister implications. "Not even my most cynical view of Nixon had allowed for his stupid behavior," he wrote.

There he sat at the peak of his power; why would he personally get involved in tapping the phone not even of his opponents but only a Democratic Party functionary?

Think about it: the Washington bureau chief of the *New York Times* said of the biggest story of his stewardship: *My involvement with any of the Watergate stuff was so marginal.* Is this credible?

Charles Kaiser, a Washington reporter, wrote in "How the *New York Times* Let a Watergate Lead Slip through Its Fingers" in 2009:

Max Frankel was the Washington Bureau chief in 1972. . . .

So you might expect Frankel to be the most shocked of all by Phelps's account. But Frankel told [Kaiser] that he wasn't shocked at all.

"I wasn't around then," said Frankel, explaining why Phelps might not have told him immediately about the leak from the FBI Director. "I was at the Republican Convention in the period they were writing about."

However, Patrick Gray's diary says the lunch [with Smith] took place on Wednesday, August 16, and the Republican Convention did not begin until the following Monday, on August 21.

"If he had been at the convention, I would have been at the convention, too," Phelps said. . . .

However, Phelps added that he had no recollection of sharing the leak with his boss at the time.

In any case, Frankel said he did not believe that the FBI Director "was leaking."

"I don't know what happened," Frankel said. "I'm skeptical about the whole thing. I think he was schmoozing."

But didn't Frankel wish that Phelps had told him what Gray had told Robert Smith over lunch?

"No," said Frankel. "I think Bob had good news judgment and whatever it was, I doubt that it was very important."[156]

In 2008, just before Phelps published his book, he sent me a copy of the galleys to look over and correct. When I read the section about Gray and me and the briefing I had given Phelps, I was startled to read his version:

We never developed Gray's tips into publishable stories. Why we failed is a mystery to me. In fact, while I can still picture the debriefing, my

memory is fuzzy on the crucial point of what I did with the tape.
Betty and I flew to Alaska the next week and vacationed there for a
month.[157]

After I read the galleys, I didn't respond to Phelps. When he called before the book came out, I explained that he ought not to be publishing the material. I told him I was angry that he was violating my pledge of confidentiality to Gray. I was still honoring that pledge. I had given him the information with the promise of not attributing it to Gray. I let my anger show. He told me that under the Wicker Rule, when the source is dead, others are free to name him. I told him I didn't agree. Though I agreed with some of Tom's rules, this one seemed wrong. I had promised, and there was his legacy and family to consider. After all, he had chosen never to say anything.

I guessed that he had a problem: Getting his book—something to do with religion and the *Times*—published, and the newsworthy bit about Gray apparently solved his problem. He needed the tantalizing facts he'd chosen all those years ago not to use.

Phelps didn't take the truth serum that I suggested, but he did publish the book. And the stars fell on me. I became the object of journalism. And, as you have seen, a lot of that journalism was wrong.

Even though it had been thirty-seven years since the Watergate story first broke, it had lost none of its magnetism, and the *New York Times* manqué was a source of piquant relish for journalists. What caused the outlandish, howling thwack? Phelps's admission that I had given him the information leaked to me by Gray and the fact that the *Times* had done nothing at all with it.

Never mind that I had forced a lengthy, detailed, tape-recorded briefing on Phelps. Never mind that all this happened on my last day at the paper. Never mind that someone would have to take a whack at further reporting and write the story. Never mind that there was no information left in my pockets, or notebook. Never mind that I had obviously given Phelps the name of my source, the acting director of the FBI, or he couldn't have put it in his book years later. Never mind that, as he walked the twenty steps from his private office to the Washington news desk, Phelps could have turned his notes and the tape over to any one of three dozen excellent reporters. He didn't do that. Please ask yourself: Why?

The *Times* is a hierarchical place. Editors manage reporters and make decisions every day, every hour. Bureau chiefs have responsibility and power. No *Times* person I have talked to believes it credible that Phelps buried the notes and tape in his lowest, darkest desk drawer without instructions.

When Phelps's book came out, Charles Kaiser quoted Arthur Gelb, former managing editor of the *Times* and one of Rosenthal's closest friends as saying, "I can picture Abe Rosenthal howling in his grave, and howling loudly. Rosenthal desperately wanted to get the Watergate story. He always believed that management of the Washington Bureau at that time left an awful lot to be desired, but never to the extent that we are learning now. The new facts are truly shocking."[158]

Ironically, the paper's Watergate failure gave Rosenthal his wish to bring Washington into his domain. The Bureau's performance allowed him to make a convincing argument that it was incompetent. Reston had managed to enforce the hands-off Washington policy until Watergate.

CHAPTER FIFTY

I Tell the *Times* Not to Hire Robert Upshur Woodward, But Don't Worry: He Gets a Job

It's called "shoe leather" reporting because . . . the journalist is literally on foot, walking from . . . source to source, conducting interviews . . . hunting down facts. . . .
—JAY ROSEN, PRESSTHINK, APRIL 16, 2015

How often have I said to you that once you eliminate the impossible, whatever remains, no matter how improbable, must be the truth.
— ARTHUR CONAN DOYLE

SAN FRANCISCO, 2008

One day in the early 1970s, while still a reporter at the *Times* and even before I considered law school, Bob Phelps asked me to let him know what I thought of a job candidate from the *Montgomery Sentinel* in Maryland. I looked at the résumé and shook the applicant's hand. It was Bob Woodward. I talked with him. Then Phelps asked me whether the Washington Bureau should hire him. I ventured that he seemed a little light on experience. Woodward was working as a reporter for the *Sentinel*. He was hired there after he had failed a two-week trial hiring at the *Washington Post* (though I didn't know that at the time).[159]

It could have been the team of Robert Upshur Woodward and Deep Throat making their revelations in the *Times*, instead of the *Post*—if only

Woodward had been hired when he applied to the *Times* Washington Bureau. But that fellow Smith. . . .

Well, maybe. But I just did the interview and made the recommendation. Hiring decisions were made by Phelps and Frankel, likely in concert with executives in New York. I do wonder whether rejection by the *Times* added a special energy to Woodward's efforts for the *Post*.

There may have been other reasons for able and energetic *Times* reporters not to be able to match the *Post*. After I left for Yale, Sy Hersh joined the intense group of *Times* Washington reporters chasing the Watergate story. Sy soon found out that at seven each evening the *Times* guys—they were *all* guys—met at a bar across the street from the Bureau, and drank. He told me he did not think the nightly *soirée bien arrosée*, as the French say (well-watered evening), got the group anywhere, and he stopped going.

People who have jobs with reasonable hours may find chiding reporters chasing Watergate for drinking after work as unkind, even unfair. But reporters will know what I'm talking about. Sometimes stories require extra hours, odd hours, systematic pursuit, or spontaneous pursuit.[160]

To Woodward and Bernstein, reporting involved getting off the couch and working until the job was done. They would knock on doors at 11:00 p.m., often with no appointment. They described the nighttime visits as "fishing expeditions."[161] On one of these forays Judy Miller, a bookkeeper for the Committee for the Re-Election of the President, or CREEP, let Bernstein in and gave him the initials of people involved in the scandal.[162] This became a crucial step for the reporters in following the money.

Imagine: Woodward and Bernstein find out significant information about Watergate, bring it to their news editor, and he doesn't touch the material until the *New York Times* begins to hammer the *Post* with the story three months later.

Also imagine that W & B had gotten their information not in an underground garage but from the acting director of the FBI himself.

Also imagine that W & B had thoroughly briefed their editor on what the FBI director had told them, had given him a notebook, and made him take notes.

Imagine that they had even recorded the briefing and given him the tape.

Imagine that the director's information included names—and that the director had even told W & B that the plot ran right up to the president.

Imagine that *none* of it appeared in the *Post*. Because the editor did nothing with any of it. Imagine that, when pressed, the editor explained he had gone on an Alaska cruise.

Would Holmes conclude—could he conclude—anything other than that the editor had suppressed the information? Especially if the editor admits he made a terrible lapse and says he can offer no explanation for the lapse?

Forty-five years later—in March 2017—the *Times* continued to miss the story. Here is reporter David Dunlap's innocent perspective of what happened:

> *If there is a first runner-up to Mr. Trump in adversarial relations with the press, it was almost surely Richard M. Nixon. During Max Frankel's years as chief, from 1968 to 1973, his bureau was busily competing with the Washington Post for details of President Nixon's abuses of power.*
>
> *The Times, Mr. Frankel recalled, was looking closely into the sources of the Watergate burglars' money and into the question of who had erased critical conversations taped at the White House.*[163]

Many years earlier, Dunlap had begun at the *Times* as Scotty Reston's clerk. And now he presents that as the *Times*'s take on Watergate?

So it's my word. I clearly remember Segretti-spaghetti. What does it mean that Gray's deputy Mark Felt, who later acknowledged he was Deep Throat, began talking to the *Washington Post*? Could Felt have really been doing that without Gray's knowledge? Or perhaps Gray was that naïve and hopelessly inept at media manipulation and covert disclosures. Or maybe after being foiled at the *Times*, he decided to move on to the *Post*.

Or perhaps—in a town where deniability is emperor—having a Washington-savvy deputy stand in for an honestly maladroit boss was a wise choice.

Maybe Gray had a conversation with a deputy, wiser in the ways of Washington, who excoriated him for his innocence in using a public restaurant and ended up handling the leak himself (in underground garages)?

But the story stayed with me for decades, and in 2009 I decided to detail it all in a piece I gave to the *New York Times*. The *Times* editors chose not to run it—until they were forced to by my offering it elsewhere.[164] Then they denied they had received my pitch and scrambled to interview me to avoid being scooped on the story.

CHAPTER FIFTY-ONE

Who Has Thinner Skin—Trump or the Reporters? Scribes Seek Revenge; The Piñata President

Journalists don't have thin skin—they have no skin.

—EDWARD R. MURROW

In America the President reigns for four years, and Journalism governs forever and ever.

—OSCAR WILDE

I have only two rules. . . . The first is: Have no rules. The second is: Be independent of the opinion of others.

—ALBERT EINSTEIN

SAN FRANCISCO, 2017–2019

Isn't the ongoing, appalling caterwauling by President against Press, and the reverse, giving you a headache—and making you think less of both? As a mediator, I am used to seeing people and companies fight it out. I know when people climb into the ring. But it doesn't take a mediator, a medic, or a referee to see Trump and the *Times* smash and thwack each other, over and over.[165]

I sit watching from a neutral corner—and wish the *Times* would too, or, better, get out of the ring. This is a persistent, obdurate part of Trump and *Times*, lamentable and ironic. It makes both of the fighters right: Trump says the *Times* is in the ring with him, the *Times* says Trump is attacking it. The odd thing is that both are profiting from the pugilism—Trump politically, the *Times* economically. And—without negotiation, reconciliation, or even truce—their fight continues to inflict itself on the rest of us.

The liberal bias of the *Times* has reached an all-time high in its coverage of Donald Trump. My argument applies *however you feel about Mr. Trump*—whether you think him a worthy fellow with a few flaws or an irrational, lying, criminal fascist out of touch with reality.

Carl Bernstein has contended that Trump's attacks on the press as "enemies of the American people" are more treacherous than the views of his old nemesis, President Nixon.[166] But according to an article in the *Washington Post* on February 19, 2017, Nixon said privately to Henry Kissinger in 1972:

> *The press is your enemy. Enemies. Understand that? . . . Now, never act that way . . . give them a drink, you know, treat them nice, you just love it, you're trying to be helpful. But don't help the bastards. Ever. Because they're trying to stick the knife right in our groin.*[167]

Kissinger replied, "I'm in agreement with you."

What's unusual about Trump's *The press is your enemy* is not the sentiment. It is the fact that it is being said, loudly and in public, and the fact that it is being supported by the public.[168]

Nixon had millions of supporters who believed their president no matter what disclosures appeared. When Nixon swore that White House staff were not involved in the Watergate break-in, supporters believed him. In 1972, he was re-elected in a landslide. Millions of people also believe Trump rather than the media, despite evidence of his lies.

The Trump victory was not a landslide, but it was a win, and it may have resulted in part from his conflict with the press. The press, perhaps particularly the *Times,* seemed not to know it was being used.

In an article on March 20, 2017, Andrew Marantz noted correctly in the *New Yorker* that Trump seemed to assume that he "would benefit from setting up the mainstream media, one of the most disliked institutions in the country, as a foil; that he could lie more effectively if he continued to assault the very notion of facticity; and perhaps most important, that conflict boosts ratings."[169] Trump proved not just that he didn't need the Washington poohbahs or the most powerful parts of the country's media. He showed that the public agreed with him when he attacked them. He was elected, in part, *because of his statements about the media.*

The nerve of the public! It believed Donald Trump instead of the Washington Bureau—or any bureau—of the *New York Times.* This gave rise to a wailing and gnashing of teeth in a press gang of group therapy sessions never before seen. When you have some power and are treated as if you do—the way Washington correspondents of the *Times* are, for example—a sudden, enforced diminution in your power does more than sting. It instigates a cry for revenge. Reporters at the *Times* began to feel the way the educated but unemployed intellectual feels. Their rage against Donald J. Trump became more than obvious—during the campaign, on election day, and during the first days of the administration.

Oddly, Trump's "fake-news" campaign and the *Times*'s counter-campaign remained good for both sides. Trump continued to say that the *Times* lies. This continued to garner him attention and political advantage. For its part, the *Times* said: "The truth is hard [but don't panic]. The truth has a voice." The voice of truth is, of course, (exclusively?) that of the *Times.* You had better buy the *Times,* if you want the truth—or even, I suppose, if you want to keep up with "fake news."

Rage is the only word for what the media displayed, and the more powerful the journalistic institution, the more powerful the rage seemed to be. Even the *Columbia Journalism Review* took a whack at President Trump, criticizing his age, cosmetics, clothes, size, and "sharp elbows." Without apparent hindrance from the Journalism School, Patrick J. Sloyan, a Pulitzer Prize–winning journalist, wrote in *CJR*:

> *Trump's bungling is amplified by his persona. At 70, he is the oldest person ever elected president. To compensate, he appears with dyed blond hair and a face frequently pasted with bronzer. The potbelly is hidden by a long tie and an unbuttoned suit coat. His size, demeanor, and invective projects Big Bully, a New York real estate hustler with sharp elbows.*[170]

Why do reporters write these things? They say they are trying to cover a genuine fascist—a knave and a madman. But we have had fascists, knaves, and madmen before. *Remember Watergate?* What's the difference, I kept asking myself, and all I could see was that the "fascist" Trump was attacking journalists. He was going around them and treating them with disrespect. And he did it with purpose.

The *Times* and its correspondents are used to deceit—that's commonplace in Washington, always was and likely always will be. But they pretend to horror at catching this president out as a serial liar and take his dislike for the mainstream, or at least "progressive" media as a full-bore assault on the First Amendment. The *Times* was even driven on February 27, 2017—a mere month after inauguration day—to devote a full page of its own paper to reassure everybody that it was sticking to the truth:

The truth is hard.

The truth is hidden.

The truth must be pursued. . . .

The truth is under attack. . . .

The truth is more important now than ever.

Why did the *Times* feel compelled to say this? Why couldn't it brush off the criticism? As one tweeter responded to the ad: "Hahahahaha, Trump is destroying you so badly that you have to buy ad space to defend your legitimacy. This is beautiful to watch."

It's clear to me as I read the *Times* that the paper detests Donald John Trump.[171] I see evidence of that every day in the paper, and I'm ashamed, because I retain great affection for the paper. It is supposed to be a mature, adult institution, even if those who attack it are not. The *Times* has a duty to rise above criticism and not engage in spasms of adolescent pouting and lashing out, at least not in its news columns. This reaction reveals a sensitivity to loss of power—an arrogance and self-absorption.[172]

The *Times* routinely calls the White House a large, institutional vendor of lies but seems not to recall an operation of the Obama White House that targeted at least one part of the media. Anita Dunn, the

White House communications director, led the operation that attacked Fox News with vigor, lambasting it as "opinion journalism masquerading as news."[173] Indeed, in a White House blog post from 2009, the White House pointed readers to *PolitiFact* "for even more Fox lies."

It was President Obama who praised a free press, and President Trump who identified the press as the nation's enemy. Yet it was the Obama Administration that brought criminal charges against more people for alleged news leaks than all previous administrations combined.

Some journos (as UK reporters call themselves in modish shorthand) will say I am an old-fashioned reporter. I confess: My mediation clients never tire of saying, "He wears a pocket watch!" I guess, in some way, that does describe not just my sartorial style but my approach. But—even when my phone is out of reach—the watch lets me keep time. And the watch doesn't get in the way of my recognizing biased journalism.

There have been many changes since my days in the Washington Bureau. The *Times* has also changed—and not just since my days. On page two of its very first issue on September 18, 1851, the *Times* explained:

> *[We] shall... seek to be temperate and measured in all our language. We do not mean to write as if we were in a passion,—unless that shall really be the case; and we shall make it a point to get into a passion as rarely as possible. There are very few things in this world which it is worthwhile to get angry about.*

Some basic principles should persist. The paper should at least be neutral, and appear to be neutral. The *Times* should not have items like these, randomly collected since Trump's inauguration:

[About the president's address to Congress]:

> *That the proposal did not ultimately make it into the speech may speak to the influence of Mr. Bannon's wing.* But the town was confused and off balance, just the way Mr. Trump likes it.—*Peter Baker (Chief White House correspondent) and Maggie Haberman (White House correspondent), March 1, 2017. [Emphasis supplied.]*[174]

The *Times*, on Sunday, March 19, 2017, on page 19:

In One Rocky Week, Trump's Self-Inflicted Chaos on Vivid Display

Once again, Mr. Trump's agenda was subsumed by problems of his own making, his message undercut by a seemingly endless stream of controversy he cannot seem to stop himself from feeding. . . .

But it has also become clear that Mr. Trump, an agitator incapable of responding proportionately to any slight, appears hellbent on squandering his honeymoon. . . .

Instead, he has sowed chaos in his own West Wing, and talked or tweeted his way into trouble, over and over again. . . .

Even more self-lacerating: his insistence that President Barack Obama had authorized surveillance on his 2016 campaign. . . .

The public outbursts are mirrored by internal tensions. . . . [175] *[Emphasis supplied.]*

And from the front page on February 17, 2017:

WASHINGTON—President Trump, smarting from a series of crises, moved his surrogates aside on Thursday and assigned the rescue of his month-old presidency to the only spokesman he's ever really trusted—himself." *[Emphasis supplied.]*[176]

This article led the paper (that is, it was in the far right-hand column of page one):

President Trump on Thursday dismissed reports . . . in a contentious news conference that showcased his . . . unconstrained *presidency."* *[Emphasis supplied.]*[177]

Unconstrained? A federal court had struck down his immigration policy. That was an international embarrassment for the president. He had not yet made inroads on Obamacare. He had signed an executive order to begin building "The Wall," but funding for it was not clear. He didn't get to keep his national security adviser. Congress turned down his nominee for labor secretary. Finally, at the time Baker was writing, Trump's approval rating was 40 percent or so. Does this seem "unconstrained"?

A headline from the front page of the paper on April 26 referred to President Trump's tax plan this way: "A 15% Rate Extends to Companies Like Trump's Own."[178]

In fact, the article explained that the plan would cut taxes for "not only . . . corporations but also . . . companies that now pay taxes through the personal income tax code—from mom-and-pop businesses to his own real estate empire, according to several people briefed on the proposal."[179]

Then there is the treatment of Trump vs. Comey. The *Times* reported that Trump had appealed to James Comey, acting director of the FBI, to stop an inquiry into a national security advisor.[180] Who said Trump had appealed to Comey? Comey said so in a memo. Had the *Times* seen the memo? It had not. The article explained: "One of Mr. Comey's associates read parts of it to a *Times* reporter."

A sitting president says one thing, a former FBI acting director another. How could the *Times* call what the FBI director says a fact?

Apparently aware of this problem, the *Times* argued: "An F.B.I. agent's contemporaneous notes are widely held up in court as credible evidence of conversations." Credible, but not incontrovertible.

It doesn't matter who is right or wrong. It may be true that Trump is a crazy, lying fascist who has lost touch with reality, but even a crazy, lying fascist out of touch with reality deserves accuracy and fairness from the journalists covering him.

Another headline troubled me: Special Counsel Will Investigate Russia Influence . . . Legal Risk Rises for President.

Legal Risk Rises for President? Maybe. But maybe not. You may see the Potomac flooding its banks and roaring toward the White House. But you may also see a dry bed or a contorted stream. Editors review those headlines, before and after publication.

When I read these stories, I feel as if I have been catapulted back to *Time* magazine of the 1970s. Some of the *Times* has come to resemble *Time*—an undifferentiated mixture of news and opinion—the *Time* I fled as a youngster. Even the results of the November 2016 election do not appear to have led *Times* reporters to understand the changes the election brought. One result of Trump's victory was that the *Times* doubled its White House team of correspondents from three to six. The message was crystalline: This joker fooled the people; he is not going to slip anything past us.

David Folkenflik of NPR was biting:

The nation's journalists like to think of themselves as people who hold the powerful accountable, who are skeptical rather than cynical, constructive rather than carping, institutionally adversarial but not personally opposed. I don't think that's how the public thinks about the media. Not at all. The media have come off as petty, grasping and out of touch, all part of the great establishment party from which many Trump voters felt excluded.[181]

Michael Massing suggested in *The Nation* that the *Times* might ignore advertising demographics and create a blue-collar beat. He also recommended taking a reporter from each of the high-end *Times* sections—like Styles, Travel, Food, and the magazine—and assign them to cover uncovered parts of America, like the Bible Belt. That might get the *Times* in touch with the anger of blue-collar America. A problem would be making those beats prestigious rather than training assignments or pre-retirement cushions.

The disdain of some of the members of the press for the less-than-wealthy has a history. In his 1947 article, *Horsefeathers Swathed in Mink*, Joe Liebling wrote: "There is no concept more generally cherished by publishers than that of the Undeserving Poor."[182]

James Hohmann wrote a brief postmortem in the *Washington Post* in November 2016:

The big idea: President-elect Donald Trump was right all along. He had a silent majority. The media, the pollsters and Republican elites never saw it—even though it was right in front of them the whole time.

"Confirmation bias" is the tendency to interpret new evidence as confirmation of one's existing theories. Since he came down that escalator at Trump Tower 17 months ago, many elites could never fully visualize Trump as the president of the United States. That made it very hard to see him winning the nomination—until he did—or

winning the White House—until he did. Confirmation bias does not mean one preferred a particular outcome. Rather, it is a condition of psychology: All human beings tend to put a premium on information that validates their existing expectations and downplay new data points that undermine them.[183]

The *Times* talks to the *Times*. In this hothouse, attacks—*attacks on the Times?*—are seen as attacks on the Constitution and the beginning of fascism. We, the paper proclaims, are in *the resistance*. And it would seem that much of the media is following along. Pack journalism?[184]

Psychologists give attention to some types of consensus.

The *Encyclopedia of Social Psychology* describes false consensus as:

[An] effect [that] occurs when we overestimate the number of other people (or extent to which other people) share our opinions, beliefs, and behaviors. Thus, sometimes individuals tend to believe that others are more similar to them than is actually the case. For example, if I enjoy eating chocolate ice cream cones, I will tend to overestimate the percentage of other people like me who also enjoy eating chocolate ice cream cones relative to the percentage that do not.

Another study, by Ohio State University, concluded:

The false consensus effect may also be a result of motivations such as self-esteem maintenance. . . . One's self-esteem may hinge partly on the belief that one holds correct attitudes, and perceived agreement of others may help to validate those attitudes.

You don't have to engage in social-science research to know that when people work in an environment in which their coworkers share their views, they tend to adopt the same values and perceptions. If a whole industry more or less feels that way, you have . . . the complete misreading by the media of the 2016 elections. The difficulty is: The election showed the American people sided more with Trump than it did with the *Times*.

Trump is what he is. He may be all bad. He may even be pure evil. But the industry-wide reaction he produced was not without emotion. It was the impotent anger of the little boy or girl whose weekly hot fudge sundae is denied, whose "Champion Speller" button gets lost, or whose cherished doll has been taken away. Suddenly, the auto mechanic, the TV repair person, and the schoolteacher all changed their attitude towards reporters to, "So you're a reporter?" instead of, "Let me adjust those brakes now," "Let's see if we can get you a few more channels," or "Johnny's taking right after his father and mother in spelling."

Reporters aren't motivated by money. They don't make enough of it to be. Maybe, like Bruce Wayne, all that some of them want is to keep Gotham safe. Maybe they are would-be poets. Just as I did, they may get a kick out of seeing their stories on page one, with a byline. They enjoy having the barber or bartender or politician say, "Saw your article. Real good!" But there is not so much joy when the barber cranks the chair up a notch, reaches for scissors, and says with a grin, "See what Trump said about the *Times* yesterday?" This provides a startling contrast to the paper's earlier journalists.[185]

If the *Times* is bent on undercutting Trump, the paper would be *more effective* if it stayed out of the ring and appeared neutral. Being brazenly biased undercuts its own apparent efforts.[186] But the *Times* continues to climb through the ropes and into the ring. For example, when Trump said the paper was wrong, the *Times* issued a Twitter statement: "We are confident in our reporting, and as with so many occasions, our stories stand up over time and the president's denials of them do not."[187]

The irony of the *Times* being where it shouldn't be—in the ring with the president—is that it has profited. Trump profited in votes, apparently. The *Times* profited in money. Its paid circulation—print and digital—rose from about 2.5 million in 2016 to about 4 million in the third quarter of 2018.[188] It is like an impressive win-win real-estate deal.

If readers were doing the reverse—deserting the *Times* in large numbers because of its coverage of Trump—would the paper's editorial policies change?

It would help everyone, including its readers, if the *Times* retrieved its sense of humor and informed candor. If it dialed down its self-importance. The Gray Lady is mighty earnest. Mighty proud. Mighty sensitive. And mighty resentful. The president may have a bully pulpit. (When Theodore Roosevelt said that, he meant a loud platform.[189]) But it's hard to bully the press. It owns not just the pulpit. It owns the church. It is entitled to lash out during the Sunday sermons. But it's not supposed to do that in the daily, or even Sunday, news columns.

The *Times* lashes out because it questions Trump's sanity, and it may be right. But as a mediator I have seen Trump's type of behavior many times. Rather than a loss of mind, it betokens a present and purposeful mind. It is an approach to negotiation.

CHAPTER FIFTY-TWO

Trump—Daft or Dealing?
The Ali Khamenei Gambit

Your goal is to create a sense in others that you are an unpredictable soul, not out of calculation, but out of foolishness and carelessness. Each month there is going to be one magnificent [poker] hand, and . . . when the hand is dealt, no one knows what you are doing, and you clean the table's clock.
—GEORGE FRIEDMAN, "THE USE OF IRRATIONALITY
IN FOREIGN AFFAIRS"

They might have been successful in forcing people into unreasonable business deals before. Whatever you do, don't give in to their demands. . . . They will only become more demanding. . . . [P]retending to walk away may sometimes make them suddenly reasonable.
—"DEALING WITH AN IRRATIONAL NEGOTIATOR,"
STITT FELD HANDY GROUP

2020

The wealthy fellow who had flown to San Francisco from Florida in his private jet altered the course of the negotiations yet again. The lawyers on the other side in the mediation were furious—and confounded.

"He is crazy, just crazy," they said in fatigued and angry unison.

"And unbearable," one of them added.

The East Coast multimillionaire would take them down one road in the negotiations, make them think about that road, and encourage them to make an offer. When they responded, he would exasperate them by saying, "No, on second thought, I don't think that's the right approach. Let's try this one instead." Then he would absent himself to continue negotiations on his cellphone with businesspeople in China, while his adversaries across the hall in San Francisco tried to reorient themselves and construct another offer.

By the time I was mediating this case, I had seen the technique used several times by some business negotiators. They pretend to be irrational, fickle, headstrong, unreasonable, but always portray themselves as *really* wanting to settle this dispute. They are careful to reassure everyone that they do want to settle in order to give the other side some hope and encouragement not to walk away.

This negotiating approach—the gambit of irrationality—was sometimes attributed to Iran's Supreme Leader, Ayatollah Ali Khamenei. It may also be the approach Donald John Trump uses, causing people to say, "The guy's crazy. Wait, he's shifted again . . . He has another goal, another demand, another proposal. . . ." How can you negotiate with someone who is irrational, even if you want to?

I have never seen President Trump in action in a commercial negotiation or mediation, but I have watched his public negotiations, electoral shape-shifting, and diplomatic démarches. They are done with the same style: the mask of irrationality. It's a commercial deception in the service of a cause, or at least, a desire. Mr. Trump has exported a commercial negotiating style—"pretend" positional bargaining—into the realms of politics and diplomacy. One of the main risks of that strategy is this: The other side might just get up and walk away.

The electorate didn't walk away. But whenever pressed hard, Mr. Trump has been careful to show his more rational, reasonable side. If I'm right, he is using the Ali Khamenei approach, or a variant of it.

But this isn't a new style. We've seen it before. As Patrick J. Sloyan noted in 2017 in the *Columbia Journalism Review*:

> *Nixon once boasted that his demeanor was effective in keeping foreign enemies off balance. "I call it the Madman Theory," Nixon said in a tape-recorded session with his staff. "I want the North Vietnamese to*

believe I've reached the point where I might do anything. We'll just let slip: "We can't restrain him when he's angry and he has his hand on the nuclear button."[190]

I have advice for those confronted with this tactic: Calm down, focus on what you need most, watch what is really happening, take the long view, and adjust your reactions and tactics. Faux irrationality works only if the pretender's adversaries allow it to. So far, this tactic has left some of Mr. Trump's adversaries rockin' and rollin', largely because they've misunderstood the dance they've been invited to: It ain't rock 'n' roll.

Contrast Trump's usual charge that the *Times* spews out "fake news" with his comments about the paper when he had lunch at the *Times*: "I have great respect for the *New York Times*. Tremendous respect. It's very special . . . I will say, the *Times* is, it's a great, great American jewel. A world jewel. And I hope we can all get along well."

I do not have access to the inner workings of President Trump's mind, and, in any event, I am not a psychiatrist. He may be psychologically troubled or he may be pretending for negotiating advantage. But if he is in the second group, he is not alone; many skilled commercial and diplomatic negotiators do that. Machiavelli argued in 1517 that sometimes it might be "a very wise thing to simulate madness."[191]

Richard Nixon wanted the North Vietnamese to see him as mad and, if angered, ready to press the nuclear trigger. Nixon reportedly told H. R. Haldeman, his chief of staff:

I call it the Madman Theory, Bob. I want the North Vietnamese to believe I've reached the point where I might do anything to stop the war. We'll just slip the word to them that, "for God's sake, you know Nixon is obsessed about communism. We can't restrain him . . . and Ho Chi Minh himself will be in Paris in two days begging for peace.[192]

I found negotiating for information as an investigative reporter much harder than negotiating for money as a lawyer or mediator. In commercial mediation, what does a party generally do to end the problem? Pay money. The sources an investigative reporter is negotiating with to get information may be putting at risk their job, security clearance, employability, home, marriage, peace of mind, even freedom. Reporting can be much harder.

Reporters struggle to get the information. But then what happens? Do papers report it in an unbiased way?

CHAPTER FIFTY-THREE

The Gray Lady Bumps into the Gold Standard

We must take positions. Our weakness in the West is born of . . . so-called "objectivity." Objectivity does not exist—it cannot exist! . . . The word is a hypocrisy which is sustained by the lie that the truth stays in the middle. No, sir: Sometimes truth stays on one side only.

—ORIANA FALLACI

Well, I don't know about objectivity, but I know for certain that it's always possible for a professional journalist who understands what he or she's up to to be fair, and that's the key word. . . .

—JIM LEHRER

SAN FRANCISCO, 2017–2020

Some readers—even some reporters—may feel there is no difference between news analysis and editorial opinion. They are wrong.

Here is what the public editor of the *Times*, Clark Hoyt, wrote:

I agree that journalism that is mere stenography is of little use to readers and is often even misleading. News reporters should provide context. They should challenge false assertions by authority. They should write articles giving their expert analysis.

But it may be one step too far to have the same reporter write a column with voice and opinion—explicit or implicit—and news articles that are supposed to be completely impartial. That is taking a big risk with the trust of readers already inclined to believe that the news media, including The Times, are biased.[193]

The editor in chief of news at the Canadian Broadcasting Corporation, Jennifer McGuire, said it more crisply:

If you are a journalist and make a living as one, you are still obligated to draw a line between opinion and analysis.[194]

This distinction lives at all levels of Western journalism. Consider the standards that the Associated Press holds its journalists to in the stories that follow. Contrast those with the standards the *Times* allows its journalists.

The AP describes itself this way:

The Associated Press is an independent, not-for-profit news cooperative headquartered in New York City. Our teams in over 100 countries tell the world's stories, from breaking news to investigative reporting. . . . More than half the world's population sees our content every day . . . via 15,000 news outlets worldwide. . . .

Since the AP serves so many outlets around the world, it has to provide stories that are, at least facially, neutral.

What follows is a comparison of selected *Times* stories with AP stories, supposedly about the same event.

Conservative Political Action Conference, Maryland

Here is coverage of a speech given by President Trump at the Conservative Political Action Conference on February 24, 2017. The *Times* story appears first, the AP story second.

The *Times*:

Trump's Blistering Speech at CPAC Follows Bannon's Blueprint
    OXON HILL, Md.—Stephen K. Bannon brought the battle plan. President Trump brought the fight.
    . . . Mr. Trump delivered a visceral gut punch *of a speech that executed almost all of the tactics that define the* forever-war philosophy *of the Trump-Bannon West Wing.*

. . . Speaking to the Conservative Political Action Conference on Friday, Mr. Trump launched what was easily the most blistering attack on the media and corporate elites of his already bellicose and eventful presidency. *His speech also included a promise to throw undocumented immigrants "the hell out of the country" and a recitation of his law-and-order campaign promises.* It represented a not-entirely friendly takeover of CPAC, an establishment Republican group. . . .

The symbiotic political and personal relationship between [Bannon and Trump]—the rumpled near-recluse and the compulsively public and image-conscious president—is driving much of the momentum and dysfunction *of the White House, aides say.*

And while Mr. Bannon described the president as "maniacally focused" on fulfilling his campaign promises, Mr. Trump often loses focus, *as he did during numerous digressions from his scripted remarks on Friday. [Emphasis supplied.]*[195]

The AP:

Trump Blasts Media, Anonymous Sources, After WH Uses Them
Trump's appearance at CPAC represented a triumph for both speaker and audience—*each ascendant after years when they were far from the center of the political universe.*

Elizabeth Connors of New York recalled past gatherings as collections of the "downtrodden." Today, she said, "it's energized" after years in which "we've been just pushed down. . . ."

Nicholas Henderson of Coeur d'Alene, Idaho, was there in his "Make America Great Again" hat and pronounced Trump's speech rousing. "He touched on a lot of things we'd already heard before, which is reassuring, tells us he's still committed to those promises he made during the campaign," Henderson said . . .[196] *[Emphasis supplied.]*

The *Times* said the speech represented a "not entirely friendly take-over of CPAC." The AP said that Trump's appearance was a "triumph for both speaker and audience" and quoted two attendees who applauded the speech.

Trump Signs Executive Order

The *Times* and *AP* both covered Trump's signing an executive order to reverse regulations relating to the coal industry on March 28, 2017.

The *Times*:

> *Trump Signs Executive Order Unwinding Obama Climate Policies*
> *WASHINGTON—President Trump, flanked by company executives and miners, signed a long-promised executive order on Tuesday to nullify President Barack Obama's climate change efforts and revive the coal industry, effectively ceding American leadership in the international campaign to curb the dangerous heating of the planet.*
>
> *Mr. Trump made clear that the United States had no intention of meeting the commitments that his predecessor had made to curb planet-warming carbon dioxide pollution, turning denials of climate change into national policy. . . .*
>
> *"C'mon, fellas. You know what this is? You know what this says?" Mr. Trump said to the miners. "You're going back to work."*
>
> *Throughout the presidential campaign, Mr. Trump vowed to roll back Mr. Obama's major climate change policies, a set of ambitious E.P.A. regulations to curb greenhouse pollution from coal-fired power plants. He made clear that American leadership in the global campaign against climate change would take a back seat to his commitment to energy industry jobs.*[197]

The AP:

> *Trump, in Break from Other World Leaders, Digs in on Coal*
>
> *WASHINGTON—Declaring an end to what he's called "the war on coal," President Donald Trump signed an executive order Tuesday that eliminates numerous restrictions on fossil fuel production, breaking with leaders across the globe who have embraced cleaner energy sources.*
>
> The order makes good on Trump's campaign pledge to unravel former President Barack Obama's efforts to curb global warming, *eliminating nearly a dozen measures in an effort to boost domestic energy production, especially oil, natural gas and coal.*

Environmental activists, including former Vice President Al Gore, denounced the plan. But Trump said the effort would spark "a new energy revolution" and lead to "unbelievable" American prosperity.

"That is what this is all about: bringing back our jobs, bringing back our dreams and making America wealthy again," Trump said during a signing ceremony at the Environmental Protection Agency headquarters, where he was flanked on stage by more than a dozen coal miners.

Throughout the election, Trump accused the former president of waging "a war" against coal as he campaigned in economically depressed swaths of states like West Virginia, Pennsylvania and Ohio.

The miners "told me about the efforts to shut down their mines, their communities and their very way of life. I made them this promise: We will put our miners back to work," the president said. "My administration is putting an end to the war on coal."

But Trump's promise runs counter to market forces, including U.S. utilities converting coal-fired power plants to cheaper, cleaner-burning natural gas. And Democrats, environmental groups and scientists said the executive order ignores the realities of climate change. . . .

In all cases, business groups had complained to Trump—a self-celebrated business tycoon—that the rules were overly burdensome and expensive.

The American Petroleum Institute, the chief lobbying arm of the oil and gas industry, said Trump's new "common-sense" regulations will help continue a domestic energy boom that "benefits American consumers, workers and the environment." *[Emphasis supplied.]*[198]

The *Times* has only one sentence quoting Trump, and there is no support reported in the article for his side while the AP gave six paragraphs to Trump and his supporters.

Trump's Views on NATO

Here's a comparison of how the two covered President Trump's changing views on the North Atlantic Treaty Organization (NATO) on April 12, 2017:

The *Times*:

Trump's Previous View of NATO Is Now Obsolete

WASHINGTON—As a candidate, President Trump disparaged NATO as a musty relic of old thinking, an alliance focused on long-gone adversaries rather than new-era threats, a burden that drained American resources on behalf of ungrateful partners who did not pay their share. In a word: "obsolete."

That was then. After 82 days in office, Mr. Trump officially pronounced NATO rehabilitated, taking credit for transforming it into a modern, cost-sharing, terrorism-fighting pillar of American and European security. "I said it was obsolete," the president noted on Wednesday as he hosted NATO's secretary general. "It's no longer obsolete."

Never mind that the alliance has changed very little if at all in the last three months, and that whatever modest changes have been made were in train long before Mr. Trump entered the doorway of the White House. After weeks of being lobbied, cajoled and educated by the leaders of Britain and Germany, not to mention "my generals," as he likes to call his national security team, Mr. Trump has found fresh virtue in a venerable organization. . . .

Mr. Trump's about-face on NATO was only part of a day of flip flops at the White House. . . . *[Emphasis supplied.].*[199]

The AP:

Trump Reverses Himself on NATO, China, Russia and More

WASHINGTON—President Donald Trump hasn't been in the White House for 100 days, yet he's already reversed himself on many of his key campaign promises.

In several interviews this week, the president has forged new positions on topics ranging from NATO to Chinese currency manipulation. They come as other campaign promises lag, including Trump's vow to build a concrete wall along the length of the southern border and have Mexico pay for it.

"One by one we are keeping our promises—on the border, on energy, on jobs, on regulations," Trump tweeted Wednesday evening. "Big changes are happening!"

Here are some of the areas where a president who prides himself on his flexibility has been willing to dispense with past positions:

NATO:

Trump cemented his shift in posture toward the 28-nation military alliance. . . .

As a candidate, Trump had dismissed NATO as "obsolete," saying the post-World War II organization wasn't focused on combating the growing threat from terrorism and complaining that too many members weren't paying their fair share toward defense.

He struck an entirely different tone Wednesday, one he had been warming up to during frequent telephone conversations with his world counterparts.

"I said it was obsolete. It's no longer obsolete," Trump said of NATO at a news conference. . . .

Trump still insists that NATO members meet a 2014 agreement to boost defense spending to 2 percent of gross domestic product within a decade. He has backup on this point from an important ally: [NATO Secretary General Jens] Stoltenberg. . . . [200] *[Emphasis supplied.]*

Compare these two sentences in particular:
The *Times:*

"After weeks of being lobbied, cajoled and educated by the leaders of Britain and Germany, not to mention "my generals," as [Trump] likes to call his national security team, Mr. Trump has found fresh virtue in a venerable organization."

The AP:

"[Trump] struck an entirely different tone Wednesday, one he had been warming up to during frequent telephone conversations with his world counterparts."

Note that the *Times* characterizes Trump's change of heart as one in a series of "*flip flops,*" while the AP calls Trump a president who "*prides himself on his flexibility.*"

More examples of the coverage by the *Times* and the AP appear in the notes.[201]

CHAPTER FIFTY-FOUR

Bring the Jury In

When you go into court, you are putting your fate into the hands of twelve people who weren't smart enough to get out of jury duty.
—Norm Crosby

The penalty for laughing in a courtroom is six months in jail; if it were not for this penalty, the jury would never hear the evidence.
—H. L. Mencken

If a man could say nothing against a character but what he can prove, history could not be written; for a great deal is known of men of which proof cannot be brought.
—John Boswell, *The Life of Samuel Johnson*

It's time to bring the jury in. Please step up and sit again in that wide-bottomed oak chair with the eight wobbly slats in the back. Yes, I know the seat looks hard. And, yes, the slats look painful. And no, the chair isn't padded. But thousands of citizens have been dragooned into this chamber, impressed as jurors, and made to sit in that chair, without benefit of cushion, for days—even weeks and months. You can do it. This won't take long, I promise.

On the whiteboard I have printed in black marker the question presented by this case. Have a look at it, please: *Did the* New York Times *Washington Bureau suppress the Watergate story, or try to suppress it?*

We are finally here, Dear Juror.

His Honor, the Judge, will instruct you that this is a civil matter, not a criminal matter. So the test you use here is *more probably than not*—not beyond a reasonable doubt. If you imagine a seesaw in a playground, the seesaw does not have to touch the ground or grass. It just has to tip more in the direction of one side's being true than the other.

I'm not going to be able to tell you that somebody has confessed to this suppression. Or that we have a videotape or audiotape of the suppression. (We do know there was an audiotape of the briefing of the *Times* Washington news editor, Robert Howard Phelps. But Mr. Phelps said he couldn't tell us where the tape is now.) We do have Mr. Phelps's confession. But it is a confession of negligence, not actual suppression, and it is *suppression* we are concerned with.

I'm aware that your chair—unlike the judge's chair, and even the judge's clerk's chair—has no cushion. With that in mind, I'm going to make out the case for suppression briskly.

Here is the case: *Was there a meeting between Patrick L. Gray and Robert M. Smith?*

Very likely. Smith says he ran back from the restaurant to the Washington Bureau and led Phelps to Phelps's small private office. Phelps sat down on the narrow flowered couch. Smith put a Bureau tape recorder on the polished dark wood end table.

Just as Phelps was sitting down and Smith was closing the door, someone tried to come into the office. Smith says he shooed them away and then Scotch-taped a "Do Not Disturb" sign to the door. He turned on the tape recorder and handed Phelps a reporter's notebook from the Bureau supply cabinet.

Then, Smith says, he began recounting what had just happened as he paced up and down the little room.

Phelps confirmed the meeting, the tape, the notes. Phelps even added details such as Smith's telling him that Gray had given him Donald Segretti's name and Smith's trying to remember "Segretti-spaghetti" since he couldn't take notes in the French restaurant. That's a lot of detail from two different people, one of whom—Smith—didn't want the information attributed to Gray because of a binding promise that he had made.

Pat Gray's son, Ed, reports that his father's diary confirms the lunch. Pat Gray also wrote in *In Nixon's Web* that he and Smith "had become quite friendly."[202] Please squirm around a bit in that hard chair and reflect for just a second. If you think there was no meeting, please raise your hand.

I see no hands.

On to Question Two: Did Phelps, news editor of the *Times* Washington Bureau, leave his private office with the information about Watergate in hand?

Dear Juror, Phelps says he did. Smith says he did. And in his hands, he was holding the notebook in which he had just taken notes of Smith's briefing and a tape of the briefing. He walked about twenty-five steps through the Bureau to his chair at the gray metal news desk. He passed through a room that had three dozen first-rate reporters. He didn't approach even one of them. He didn't give any of them the notebook. He didn't give any of them the tape. No one says he did; Phelps says he did not. This is supported by the testimony of Bill Kovach, who was brought to the Washington Bureau of the *Times* to head its investigative unit as it tried to match the scoops of Woodward and Bernstein.

"Bob Phelps never said to me, 'Patrick Gray might be a good guy to hook up on or anything,'" Kovach told journalist Charles Kaiser in Kaiser's Hillman Foundation blog post from 2009. Kovach continued:

> *[H]e never mentioned any tape, he never mentioned Bob Smith. . . .*
>
> *I can't imagine how he—37—years after the fact, when he's writing his memoirs—remembers this interview with L. Patrick Gray, and it could have been dynamite. And didn't remember it three or four months later to tell me.*
>
> *Why the hell would you ask someone to run the investigative operation—and we were still trying to catch up with Watergate at the time—and not tell him that?[203]*

Why the hell, Dear Juror? *Is Phelps's explanation of his failure credible? Can anyone believe it?* Do you believe it? Please recall Phelps's testimony. Remember that he wrote about this in his book:

> *. . . Those three beats—Woodward later called the October 10 article "probably our most important story"—cemented the* Post's *lead. From then on Watergate was rightly regarded as Woodward and Bernstein's story.*
>
> *It didn't have to be that way. For a short time, we had our own leak in the FBI, but my dereliction and long-laid plans by Robert M.*

Smith, our Justice Department reporter, to attend law school held us back from printing anything.

Here is what happened . . .

[Phelps then recounts that I wrote three page-one stories about Gray. He goes on:]

. . . Naturally, then, Bob wanted to sound out Gray on Watergate.

On August 16, he had lunch with Gray at Sans Souci, a posh restaurant popular with officials and the media. As Bob recalls, he was amazed when Gray opened up about Watergate. He dropped the name Segretti.

. . . Smith couldn't take notes, but he remembered Segretti, whose name had not yet appeared in the Watergate stories, by using the mnemonic "spaghetti—Segretti."

In response to Smith's questions, Gray hinted, without saying directly, that the White House and former attorney general Mitchell were involved in Watergate. Smith needed no mnemonic to remember those points.

Because he had to leave for Yale Law School the next day, Smith didn't have time to check out Gray's leads. He did the next best thing. Within minutes of returning from the lunch, with the conversation still fresh in his mind, he spoke into a recorder sitting at my desk in my little office while I debriefed him.

There we were, with leads from the acting director of the FBI that a man named Segretti, former attorney general Mitchell, and the White House, perhaps Nixon himself, were involved in Watergate, long before the Post's *revelations. Clearly we couldn't rush into print. We thought Gray might be trying to use us, as public officials regularly do, for some political or personal purpose. . . .*

But Smith, the reporter in the best position to follow through with Gray, was off to. . . the start of a career that would take him to San Francisco, London, and Paris as an internationally respected mediator . . .

We never developed Gray's tips into publishable stories. Why we failed is a mystery to me. In fact, while I can still picture the debriefing, my memory is fuzzy on the crucial point of what I did with the tape. Betty and I flew to Alaska the next week and vacationed there for a month.

If I followed my usual practice, I would have given the tape to one of the assistant editors or to one of the Watergate reporters. Some logical recipients on the staff have died; none of the others remembers the tape.

Regardless, there is no point in placing blame on any member of the staff.

I could have screwed up completely and tossed the tape into a drawer and never thought about it again. That is inconceivable. Certainly one of the first questions I would have asked on returning from Alaska would have been about the tape.

The fact is that I bear major responsibility for our failure to follow up on our best opportunity for an early Watergate breakthrough. We had more than a month to work on Segretti even after I returned from vacation, before Woodward and Bernstein heard of the man and before the Post *published the story on the massive spying operation on October 10.*

I should have circulated Smith's debriefing to all our Watergate reporters. It would never have been lost with all those ears hearing it. What is clear is that Gray's mention of a big fish like Mitchell seemed more important than that of a minnow like Segretti. Mitchell was more likely to lead to the biggest fish of all, the president. . . .

Since Felt disclosed that he was Deep Throat, I have speculated over a situation in which the two top FBI officials were both leaking on Watergate, Felt to the Post *and Gray to the* Times, *each for his own interest, Felt perhaps in revenge for not getting appointed director, or, as Woodward thought, to protect the FBI, and Gray perhaps to protect his legacy after he found out the White House involvement in the cover-up.*

Patrick Gray does say in the book that he and Smith "had become quite friendly" but does not disclose what they had talked about.

Felt and Gray leaks have dovetailed? Would they have found each other out? Hollywood could make a drama—maybe a comedy—out of the possibilities. What I am certain of is that Gray would never have been able to mislead Bob Smith if he had tried.

Phelps blames himself, but not just himself. He blames everyone:

> . . . . *From the top editors down we all shared in the blame. . . . The basic reason for our poor performance was institutional. Our reporters and editors were assigned to Washington to cover national and foreign affairs, not crimes.*
>
> *Moreover, controlling us all at the bureau was a reluctance to take any risk that would damage the* Times' *credibility. . . .*
>
> *Significantly, I didn't devote myself sufficiently to the story. I spent too much time on other news and other problems. . . .*[204]

Let me repeat, Dear Juror:

> *Why we failed is a mystery to me. In fact, while I can still picture the debriefing, my memory is fuzzy on the crucial point of what I did with the tape. . . . If I followed my usual practice, I would have given the tape to one of my assistant editors or to one of the Washington reporters. . . . I could have screwed up completely and tossed the tape into a drawer and never thought about it again.*
>
> *"That,"* Phelps continues, *"is inconceivable." [Emphasis supplied.]*

"I lead the bafflement brigade," Phelps told Charles Kaiser in a telephone interview. "I have no recollection at all; and that baffles me. It is enough to make you question your sanity, of course."[205]

But we don't have to seriously consider the insanity defense, do we, Dear Juror?

What is inconceivable is Phelps's effort to make the tape the "crucial point." What is the man talking about? This is what the French and we lawyers call a *canard*—a red herring. Here is a guy in a room surrounded by two dozen of the best reporters in the country. He has just debriefed a reporter, by his own admission, on the story of the century, with information that the scandal reached all the way to the office of the president. He has heard all this. An audio recorder has captured all this. He had taken notes on all of this. And he is trying to make the centerpiece of why the *Times* did nothing *the location of an audiotape?*

Phelps adds *canard* to *canard*:

Our credibility was too precious to sacrifice, even for a beat of such proportions. As a guardian of that credibility—the Times had become my substitute for religion—I was not going to commit the cardinal sin of betrayal.[206]

That betrayal would, I take it, consist of telling a reporter or two about the information I had given him. Phelps has tried somehow to convert this absolute failure to religious virtue, or at least the avoidance of cardinal sin. He does offer this, though: Sy Hersh—the investigative reporter of My Lai and Abu Ghraib fame—"nearly quit when Max Frankel rejected his proposals for Watergate stories."

Finally, note please, Dear Juror, that Phelps gives us, as part of his excuse, that he and his wife were taking a trip to Alaska *a week later.* One week in an industry in which time is measured in hours or minutes, sometimes seconds. Stories can be followed up six times in one week.

So:

Is the testimony of Phelps as to the disappearance of tape, notes, and memory believable?

Is his total inaction believable?

Is his going off on vacation a week later a credible excuse?

Is his needing verification by a second source to corroborate Gray (when he did utterly nothing to get a second source) believable?

All of this brings us, Dear Juror, to the final question:

Did Robert Howard Phelps, Washington news editor of the New York Times, *acting alone, or at somebody's direction, suppress the Watergate story?*

CHAPTER FIFTY-FIVE

Watergate in a Time of Disappearing Ink

Carl Bernstein: [On Watergate] The American System worked. . . . The press did its job as an independent entity trying to obtain the best obtainable version of the truth. . . .

—*WASHINGTON POST*, JANUARY 2007

Actually, I didn't like the Watergate trials 'cause they interrupted The Munsters.

—STEPHEN COLBERT, IN AN INTERVIEW WITH *ROLLING STONE*, OCTOBER 2006

THE PRESENT

Did Watergate make a lasting impact on American government?

I am not a political scientist. I also admit: I don't want to be publicly flogged on Twitter by President Trump. But I would argue that Watergate was different in magnitude, but not in kind and not in ongoing impact. As contrarian as this makes me sound, Watergate did *not* shake the heavens and the earth, the oceans and the dry land. The Republic totters onward.

It has had more of an effect on the media. What did *All the President's Men* manage to do that has lasted nearly half a century?

Andrew Kohut, director of the Pew Research Center, said in a 2005 *New York Times* article, "The public values the watchdog role of the press, but not as much as it once did." Over time, he continued, the public "came to see the press as a watchdog that barked too much, and sometimes was out of control."

In a *New York Times* Op-Ed titled: "The Journalism Watergate Inspired Is Endangered Now," Alicia Shepard wrote:

> *As important as Watergate was in political history, it was equally important in journalistic history. Watergate marked the birth of a different kind of reporting—more aggressive and much less respectful of the establishment.*
>
> *. . . . An entire generation went into journalism because of the two men—and the influence of the book and movie about them, "All the President's Men."*
>
> *Several other changes came about: the advent of celebrity journalism in which reporters become the story, a greater acceptance of anonymous sources, a far more skeptical attitude of reporters toward government and a sharp rise in investigative reporting.*
>
> *The reporting duo played a key role in romanticizing investigative reporting. . . .*[207]

Alan Brinkley, a historian at Columbia University, argued, "[Watergate] created a model of journalism that is easily abused and debased. . . . It created generations of people trying to replicate that role by digging in more and more unsavory ways. As much as Watergate is a model . . . that we admire, you can also see in it the origins of the distrust we have today."[208]

So there you have it: Bob and Carl are to blame for distrust of the media? When I read that, I thought that maybe—*just maybe*—I left for law school at just at the right time. But, whatever they may be responsible for, Bob and Carl are not responsible for the new digital media. At one and the same time, it is digital media that shore up trust in reporting and destroy that trust. As Woodward told Nick Tabor of the *Daily Intelligence* in July 2016:

> *One of the difficulties with in-depth reporting now is obviously the internet.*
>
> *As glorious as it is, it has created a culture of impatience and speed—"Give it to me in 140 characters," or "Give me the sound bite"—and things get shortened and in the shortening process get*

distorted or get totally politicized, and I think the idea should be the facts.

. . . . In the '70s, when Carl and I were working on the Nixon case, we could work for two or three weeks on a story. We would do a draft. It would go to the editors. We'd have a meeting: "What about this?" "Get more sources." "Check this." "Are you sure?" And there wasn't that 24/7 pressure of, "Is somebody else going to get the story?" It was, "Let's do this as comprehensively as we can."[209]

Economics also has had a great impact on reporting today. Alicia Shepard lamented this in her *New York Times* piece about investigative reporting:

Some terrific reporting that made a difference in government and in people's daily lives has come from expensive reporting that can take six months to a year before anything is published. . . .

But today, resource-intensive investigative reporting is in trouble. How could it not be?. . .

When newspapers can't even cover daily journalism, how are they going to invest in long-term, expensive investigative reporting? How can they possibly justify spending weeks or months on a project when they can't afford to cover city government or local schools in the way they should?

Today, several nonprofits are attempting to fill the void, but only ProPublica.org is making a dent, and it's ever so small.[210]

ProPublica is a not-for-profit outfit that does investigative journalism.

Leonard Downey Jr., former executive editor of the *Post*, addressed this in "Forty Years After Watergate, Investigative Journalism Is At Risk" in the *Post*:

Perhaps the surest sign of the endurance and importance of Watergate-legacy investigative reporting is the questioning of whether the news media should have more aggressively and quickly exposed the underlying causes of recent national crises.

Could the rationale and military plans for the invasion of Iraq have been more vigorously scrutinized in the run-up to the war?

Was enough done to examine risky Wall Street manipulations before the 2008 financial meltdown?

Investigative nonprofits are being started all the time. But many of the fledgling sites are struggling to survive. Foundations that provide seed money seldom are interested in helping with long-term sustainability. Fundraising and membership drives must compete with other causes. . . .[211]

Do these changes mean there is more or less chance for the suppression of news? On the one hand, with far fewer and smaller newspaper outlets, there is more chance of suppression. But on the other, we have many more accessible sources of news now than we did during the Watergate era. Unfortunately, many of these have far less trained, less expert, and less professional journalists than the journalists of former days, and generally they have far more limited sources and resources.

What happens in that cacophony, when the American press misunderstands the American people—and when the American people don't trust the press? When a number of Americans—and not a small number, including the president—revile the press? For the result, disconnect is too subtle a word.

The attitude of the White House toward the media changes. In 2015, in *Columbia Journalism Review*, Susan Milligan summed up the relationship this way:

Evidence suggests that the relationship between the president and the press is more distant than it has been in a half century.

John F. Kennedy held frequent press conferences—23 a year, according to Martha Joynt Kumar, a presidency and media scholar— and also had an ongoing relationship with Ben Bradlee, then Newsweek's Washington bureau chief.

Jimmy Carter would play softball with the press corps.

Bill Clinton attended an off-the-record dinner with African-American reporters at the home of then-Newsday White House correspondent William Douglas. By 2014, White House reporters' ability to question the president was largely limited to the 44 exchanges Obama had with the media, just five of them in solo press conferences.[212]

The relationship between the media and the public has also changed. According to a 2016 Gallup report, more than two-thirds of the American public have less than a "fair amount of trust" in the mass media.[213] I was fortunate. In my era, Clark Kent ruled. The public still saw the press as the good guys.

But those were the days when misbehavior wasn't rampant. No one had spread false stories about Weapons of Mass Destruction in Iraq. There were no internet garbage sources. No "citizen journalism." No hardball. No recklessly competitive television. No digital sites chasing revenue with "clickbait." Fewer bottomless toolboxes of axes to grind. Not so blurry a line (among laypeople and professionals) between objectivity and advocacy.[214] There was no Facebook, and there were no Twitter attacks. It was, in a way, a time of innocence.

Turning to today:

If you think news is fake, you are wrong. But if you think it's true, you are also wrong.

Finally, why do you suppose the *Times*, bursting with resources and illimited in curiosity, has never itself looked into the mysterious vanishing of its early, critical Watergate leak from the FBI?

CHAPTER FIFTY-SIX

Modern Times: Journalism by Citizens; The Digital Dance Is a Foxtrot; Understanding Today's Media

In an age in which the media broadcast countless pieces of foolishness, the educated man is defined not by what he knows, but by what he doesn't know.

—NICOLAS GOMEZ DAVILA

[T]ruth is stranger than Photoshop.

—CHRIS HANRETTY, PROFESSOR OF POLITICS,
UNIVERSITY OF LONDON

THE PRESENT

Digital machinery has changed the speed of news and its imagery. The internet has changed the population of the media, opening the field up to bloggers and "citizen journalists." The power to define and publish a news event has been transferred to any citizen with a cellphone and a Twitter account. Inked-stained wretches survive in smaller and smaller numbers. And without the stains—or ink.

The citizen journalist is no journalist at all. Unless you accept that, there is such a thing as a citizen plumber, citizen *chocolatier*, and citizen physician. Aleks Krotoski wrote in the *Guardian*:

What effect has the internet had on journalism? "First-hand witnesses cannot see the big picture," says Yves Eudes, a reporter with French broadsheet Le Monde. "They're not trained to understand whether what they're seeing is relevant to the big picture or to see what really happens. They're trained to see what they want to see. If you only rely on Twitter or Facebook, you might end up howling with the wolves."[215]

A million would-be scribes can hack, and a million hacks can try to scribe, but without something new and authentic to say, they will fail. This is true no matter what technology they use. They will fail so long as professional reporters keep coming up with facts and analyzing those facts—and the facts everyone else has—in intelligent and imaginative ways.

The government is partially to blame for some of the failures of journalism: First, it can keep information secret, punish those who share it, and jail those who print it. Secondly, it can lie so repeatedly, so matter-of-factly, and so ritually that even an honest press cannot make readers see or, ultimately, value, what is true. It becomes harder and harder to make out what is *fake news*.

Sixty-two percent of Americans get their news on social media.[216] In the digital domain, "news"—is supported by clicks and viewership. The search for support puts pressure on news outlets to produce "clickbait"—fluffy material with fetching headlines.

In 2016, Mathew Ingram, a technology writer, described the competition for clicks and its consequences in a *Fortune* article, "Here's Why Trust in the Media Is at an All-Time Low":

> *Instead of a handful of newspapers, TV channels, and trusted journalists, we now have what amounts to the biblical Tower of Babel: Hundreds of thousands, if not millions of news sources, many of which are simply repeating whatever they think might get readers or viewers to click . . .*
>
> *The lack of centralized gatekeepers—or rather, the outsourcing of the gatekeeper function of mainstream media—also means there is no consensus on who is telling the truth, and that is a genie that is not going back into the bottle any time soon.*[217]

The Reuters Institute for the Study of Journalism even declared in 2010 that "mass media is passé." It said:

Today, it is all about personal media. . . .

. . . [A] lot of tips or leads these days are from the web or what's "trending" in social networks like Twitter, Facebook or its popularity rating on Digg or based on search volume patterns in search engines like Google or Bing. . . . This is radically changing the industry's concept of what a scoop or breaking news is. Journalists are forced to accelerate the traditional journalistic process because people now want real time information.

The click economy has driven even traditional, mainstream media outlets to focus on quick hits and "viral" stories, even if they have little truth to them. And even if those stories are later corrected, only a tiny number of people will see or share the correction. . . .

At the same time, this phenomenon is being fueled by the rise of a new ecosystem for the distribution of news, an ecosystem with Facebook at the center, like a spider at the center of a web. . . .[218]

Advances in technology have created worldwide competition and led to more pressure to satisfy advertisers. This threatens accuracy and integrity. Many news outlets now rely on a trick called "native advertising" or "sponsored content"—advertisements designed to mimic the style and tone of a publication. The point is to disguise advertisements as editorial content. In addition to using doubtful advertising methods, news outlets set up paywalls to try to offset the loss of hard-copy subscribers and hard-copy advertisements.

On the other hand, the digital world helps reporters to do their job. It lets them use social media to post questions and track down sources, and use search engines to learn more about a topic. Twitter can suggest other ways to look at stories, other people to interview, and new off-shoots or topics. But these changes have not affected the essentials: defining what is news, circumventing censorship, and writing well and evocatively.

Whatever role tweeting may play in journalism, it is not likely to end the dependence of Washington reporters on their sources. Sources can tweet like mad and bypass reporters, but how many of those sources have access to important pieces of information and are willing to risk tweeting them? Twitter may nibble at the frosting, but it is unlikely to undo the dependence on live sources for the cake. French restaurants and parking garages will continue to have a role.

The new media had an impact—an impact as huge as the transatlantic fiber optic cables. As Dan Rather said in a *Huffington Post* article: "From the streets of Cairo and the Arab Spring, Occupy Wall Street, from the busy political calendar to the aftermath of the tsunami in Japan, social media was not only sharing the news but driving it."[219]

The issue is whether these new media fundamentally and permanently changed Watergate-style reporting.

Is it still bedrock? Or has it become fossil?

EPILOGUE

Memoir is a falsification.

—Ana Akhmatova

Hope is such a bait, it covers any hook.

—Oliver Goldsmith

The places where I lawyered and mediated—and reported—were far, far from Roxbury. In Roxbury, it had been cold or hot. Sweaty or snowy or slushy. There had been a couple of slivers of the year when things were pleasant.

The day had begun in Roxbury with the lamplighter. He would lean his little ladder against the cross bars near the top of the streetlights and open one of the panes of clear glass, then pull on a chain to close the gas supply and turn off the lights. The kosher butcher would open his door, take rabbinically certified meat from the cooler, and arrange it in the display cases. The baker would fill his display cases with warm, crispy kaiser rolls and rows of black-and-white cakes. My grandfather's pool hall would think about opening. The ice cream counter at the drugstore, in front of the hard red-topped metal stools, would be swabbed, and the hot fudge reheated.

Telegraph Hill in San Francisco was nothing like that. First off, the weather was often pleasant. My wife, Cathy, and I had a little house up the hill rising steeply from North Beach. Our butcher was Italian, not Jewish, and always gave the very best veal to Cathy. (I suspected he was always generous with the veal, giving us more than a fair weighing of the scale would have. He probably would have given Cathy the whole shop if she had asked for it.)

Cathy would not have liked me to say she had been a model in New York, but she was. She was beautiful—tall, blonde, elegant, always on the edge of a genuine smile.

I am short, chubby, Eastern European, inelegant, and given to ration my smiles to—well, Cathy, hot fudge sundaes, and toddlers trying to jog behind their parents. In a way atypical of Americans, my smiles seem to demand a reason.

Just as Roxbury had been the Black and Jewish ghetto, North Beach was the old Italian section of San Francisco, near the Bay with its Saints Peter and Paul Church guarding Washington Square Park and the Italian-American Athletic Club. Some of the old Italian restaurants and delicatessens survive, though these days there are more Chinese merchants. Above North Beach, on Telegraph Hill, the Art Deco Lillian Coit Memorial Tower rises two hundred or so feet in unpainted, reinforced concrete. A tall Plain Jane tower loomed up the hill over our small Plain Jane house.

It was from that little house, on a usual pleasant Saturday morning in North Beach that Cathy and I were strolling—unafraid of hurled rocks and sneak thieves—near Washington Square Park and the Italian restaurants when a wiry fellow in his mid-twenties approached us. He looked unsteady. He looked us over, then looked directly at Cathy and said, "You could have done better."

I was instantly furious. Cathy was instantly anxious: What foolish thing might I do?

Younger then, I had vivid memory of my days at the Army's Infantry Officer Candidate School at Fort Benning in Georgia, where insults might lead to the base hospital. We walked on. He walked away, not in a straight line. But I knew that he was right. She might have done a lot better. It was long after Cathy and I met that I found out she had been dating a multimillionaire when we met. When the millionaire learned that Cathy had moved into my Georgetown house, he offered her, literally, everything—anything—to come back. She didn't.

So there we were, years later, strolling in North Beach. Like many reporters, that guy (unsteady as he was) had told the truth. And, like many reporters, by doing that he had offended.

It was in early 2017 that President Trump called journalists "among the most dishonest human beings on earth."[220] He was dead wrong. It may be useful for a politician to create a lying enemy to rally people against.

Such a creation is even sweeter if this enemy has offended you, as Trump felt the media had. So did many of his supporters.

In New Haven, when I was studying to become professionally unloved—a lawyer—I was also studying, with growing puzzlement, the *Times*'s anemic Watergate coverage. One day, I approached the concrete steps of the law school with the disappointing newspaper in my hands. I paused and looked up at the stone sculptures over the arch. Below the arch, in front of me, were two wooden doors. One door was supposed—in some other era—to be for professors, the other for students.

In the sculpted stone above the professor's door, I saw an image of students being taught by an energetic professor. The students were sleeping. Over the students' door, enthusiastic students were looking at an indifferent professor.

I also saw a teaching assistant carved sitting in the stone. Folklore has it that the TA is looking at pornography.

The sculptures made me smile. Then I remembered the newspaper in my hand. I stopped smiling. My cynicism—hard earned—came to life. It reminded me that there is little in the media—print, video, audio, digital—that shouldn't be read skeptically. Respect for the First Amendment doesn't mandate respect for the foolish or untrue.

There is no question about the usefulness of a digital report that summarizes each media outlet's coverage of the major stories in a couple of sentences. And then displays them side-by-side.

If I'm right, the failure of the *Times*—or the paper's refusal—to cover Watergate was the result of conscious bias, but what we are seeing now is different. It is reflexive, unconscious bias. The *Times* should have done better then. As you read it—and its competitors—ask: Shouldn't they be doing better?

Media coverage is a symptom and a cause of the divide in America. Normally, the media could play a healing role. But the White House could not trust the *New York Times*. And the *New York Times* could not trust the White House. And millions of Americans swear they can't trust either one. The awful result is a wound that journalists have inflicted on themselves and on us—a wound that prevents the press, including the *New York Times*, from having a role in bridging the divide.

I'll let the *New York Times* have the last word. This is what Peter Baker wrote in July 2019 in an article on page one labeled News Analysis:

> *WASHINGTON—President Trump woke up on Sunday morning, gazed out at the nation he leads, saw the dry kindling of race relations and decided to throw a match on it. It was not the first time, nor is it likely to be the last. He has a pretty large carton of matches and a ready supply of kerosene.*

This was not an editorial. It was an article. Who is Baker? He is not a member of the paper's Editorial Board—the part of the paper that is permitted, and paid, to voice opinions. No, he is the *Times's* chief White House reporter.

The Spike—How to Read a Newspaper Like an Inside Dopester

The inside-dopester is competent in the way that . . . the mass media . . . have taught him to be. . . . Ideology demands that, living in a politically saturated milieu, he knows the political score as he must know the score in other fields . . . such as sports.

—David Riesman

There were so many insiders that, it seemed, there were no outsiders....
—David Grann in the New Yorker

If you don't read the newspaper, you're uninformed. If you read the newspaper, you're mis-informed.

—Mark Twain

The Spike was the dangerously sharp needle on the desk in front of the editor. The editor impaled on it the stories that, for one reason or another, weren't going to make it into the paper.

Early on in my career, I developed a dozen hints for people who read newspapers and want to understand them better:

1. Watch Out for Bias

You must understand the bias of the reporter, the editor, and the publication.

In its Style section in October 2015, the *New York Times* praised entrepreneurs "harnessing goodness through technology." The article was headlined "The Transformers" and written by Laura Arrillaga-Andreessen, not a *Times* staffer. The article went on to praise Airbnb. When I did the tiniest bit of research, I learned that Ms. Arrillaga-Andreessen is the wife of Marc Andreessen, a substantial investor in Airbnb. According to *Tech-Crunch*, her husband contributed almost half to the $112-million investment Airbnb raised in 2011.[221]

Ms. Arrillaga-Andreessen went on in her article to mention that Airbnb was being challenged by a hotel industry spending "billions to combat it."

This conflict was brought to the attention of the public editor of the *Times*, and she responded to a concerned reader in the paper. The public editor asked the editor of the section, Deborah Needleman, whether she had a problem with the story as it had appeared. Ms. Needleman answered that she thought Ms. Arrillaga-Andreessen "is a separate person from her husband with her own career and credentials. . . . Laura . . . is, separately from her husband, a billionaire [making her through marriage a billionaire twice over] and for that reason I failed to consider any monetary conflict in her case." Ms. Needleman said that she would have included a disclosure but would have again commissioned Ms. Arrillaga-Andreessen to do the piece.

Because I was once a federal prosecutor, I remain interested in defenses. I can surmise only that this must be the too-rich-to-be-unethical defense: If you have enough money, and your husband happens to as well, you are excused from any possible conflict. We live in an age when women have gained great independence, matrimonial and otherwise, but is it credible that a wife would have no interest in her husband's investments—perhaps the family investments?

2. Who Says So?

The constant process of editorial selection defines what the paper is telling you is important in the world—what you should know about. Everything in a newspaper doesn't have to be gray and serious, but in October 2015, an article from Lisbon in the *New York Times* about tuk-tuks filled more than half a page. (Tuk-tuks are three-wheeled, hooded vehicles drawn by one or more people, fitted with a small engine.) The piece pronounced "Three-wheeled outsiders arrived in droves and make themselves at home."

Many of us could have lived without knowing that tuk-tuks are occupying central Lisbon, and half a page is a lot in a tight news budget. Some editor made that quixotic call. Why?

3. The Bazaar

Sometimes the marketplace drives what's in the paper. Again, in October 2015, the *Times* ran a piece about the risk of cancer from eating certain processed or red meats. The piece reported, though, that experts had concluded the increase in risk is so small that most people should *not* be greatly worried. Given the shortage of news space, the question is why this story got into the paper at all. Perhaps it did because other parts of the media were reporting the story. The argument might be made that the risk ought to be put in perspective.

But then there are stories that tell readers *nothing at all*.

4. Inside Baseball

When reading the front page of a newspaper, ask why those stories are important enough to be there. Again, in October 2015, a lengthy front-page piece—it was more than a full page long—said nothing. It offered a portrait of Carly Fiorina's time as CEO of Hewlett-Packard. She was one of many candidates running for the Republican nomination for president. The reporters discovered—probably to no one's surprise—that different people had different views of Ms. Fiorina's stewardship at HP. Readers were left at the end of five columns scratching their heads. The story could have been summed up in a single paragraph: There are them that liked her, and them that didn't, with a crisp indication of those who liked her and those who did not.

On October 24, 2015, the *Times* told its readers that the most important thing for them to know about their world that day was about watching police. It reported that the acting director of the FBI had said that observing police closely leads to a *rise* in crime. The paper acknowledged that this was an "unsettled theory." It was not only unsettled. It was also self-serving. Presumably, the FBI and the police don't welcome increased scrutiny of what they're doing. A few paragraphs could have summed up the report.

5. Lede & Kicker

If you are trying to read the paper in a hurry, you must read the lede (the first paragraph, or "graf"), of course. I'd suggest you then go to the "kicker"—the last paragraph or two. The kicker may provide the point of the piece, and may give you the writer's own impression, often with a quote the reporter has chosen as significant.

6. Selective Style

In October 2015, the *Times* ran a piece headed "Politics Rears Its Well-Coiffed Head," describing itself as "a lesson to be learned in the morphing hairstyles of politicians."[222] A *cataclysmic* piece of political news? I suppose the editors of the Style section are entitled to cover manes any way they like, but I have to add this: Readers didn't get to see Bernie Sanders's tresses.

7. What Makes Reporters Tick?

Some say the illness begins when reporters are young. My bureau chief at *Time* magazine could always tell who in a group of children was going to become a reporter. A fight would break out in the street. Some of the kids pushed through the crowd and tried to help one side or the other, or perhaps break up the fight. One youngster, though, would push through the crowd, but not enter the space of the combatants. Instead, the youngster would work his way back out of the crowd onto the street, and yell, at full volume, "Johnny and Jerry are fighting! Johnny and Jerry are fighting!"

(Some other child might go to a merry-go-round and, astride the silver horse, try to read the tiny print on the back of the ticket for the ride. That child will be a lawyer.)

8. Inside Dopester

David Riesman, a commentator on American society, put forward a theory involving a personality type he called "the inside-dopester." The dopester is a savvy figure who delights in knowing, and talking about, the "inside story" of political deal-making and horse-racing, but does that as an amoral observer—and only for the social status that knowing confers.

The *Times* obviously believes the "inside dopester" is alive and well. It came to offer, for a fee, the "inside story" behind the story. *The Story behind the Story* is the chance to meet the reporter and find out what really happened—or ask how the reporter got the story. Sometimes, the inside story is worth knowing, but much of the time if it is worth knowing, shouldn't it have been in the piece that appeared in the paper? Of course, this separate, "inside" peek does bring the paper more income.

9. Dopester, or Dope?

In November 1970, I traveled as a correspondent from Washington to Fort Bragg, North Carolina, home of the Green Berets. I was trying to find out what the Special Forces were really doing: Were they unseating governments here and there, like chessmen on a board? Getting the story was hard, even though I knew a little about the Army. Since I was a Reserve infantry lieutenant, I could even get into the Officers' Club. Oddly—or perhaps not—George W. Petrie, a Green Beret first lieutenant, turned up in civvies at my motel room door and told me he might be able to answer my questions. He did answer all my questions about the Son Tay prison camp raid—in which US Army Special Forces attempted to free seventy to one hundred American prisoners of war—but would only hint, not talk, about other Special Forces operations.

I wondered whether I was getting played. Clearly, the Green Berets wanted this story out, but was the version of a single soldier credible? And how the devil had he found me? I had to make a judgment call, fast—at a time when I had the flu and was running a 102-degree fever.

I decided Petrie was trustworthy. And here's a little more of the "inside story": I called the National Desk and asked them to please read the piece I had written right then, and ask me any questions they had, and not call me later. I explained that I was sick and needed to sleep.

At 11:00 p.m., an editor called and woke me. He wanted to check a trivial point. I was still running 102.

10. Outside Pressures

At a few papers, reporters do have great freedom. I once did a piece from Washington about Occidental Petroleum having allegedly bribed

government officials in Venezuela. I wrote the story and sent it to New
York. The phone on my desk rang. I picked it up to hear an angry Armand
Hammer, the CEO of Occidental Petroleum. Hammer made his views on
my story appallingly clear. From his powerfully delivered point of view, all
such stories came from unreliable sources. "This information," he ranted,
"is coming from disgruntled former employees."

I did not reply with the obvious: *Where in the world do you think we're
going to get this kind of information?* Instead, I offered him the chance to
say whatever he wanted in response to the assertions. He declined, but
said that if I persisted with the piece, he was going to call Arthur Sulzberger, the *Times*'s publisher. I told him he had every right to call Arthur,
known as Punch, if he wanted to, but as far as I was concerned, the piece
was going to run. I don't know whether Hammer called Punch, but I
never heard from Punch. The piece ran the next day.

There are times when even the boldest and most honest newspaper
might consider staying its hand—like the time my colleague Tad Szulc
found out about the Bay of Pigs invasion in advance. The *Times* ultimately printed Tad's story but deleted both the fact that the invasion was
imminent—and that the CIA was involved. The *Times*'s managing editor,
Turner Catledge, replaced all references to the CIA with the term *United
States officials.*

The question was: If the *Times* knew about the invasion, wasn't there
every likelihood that Fidel Castro did too? Would it have been better
if the *Times* had reported the invasion as imminent? Publicly, President
John F. Kennedy appeared furious about disclosure of preparations for
the raid, but, as reported by the *Times*, he told Catledge privately: "If you
had printed more about the operation, you would have saved us from a
colossal mistake."[223]

The *Times* did report later:

> *The climate for the invasion—anticipated and promised by the Cuban
> rebels for many weeks—was created to a large extent by events of last
> week. Since last Thursday a major wave of sabotage swept Cuba. Sat-
> urday, three B-26 aircraft bombed three air bases on the island. Begin-
> ning in the middle of last week informants in Cuban groups made it*

known confidentially that "important events" were to be expected over the weekend.

Second, the United States had failed to neutralize the Cuban Air Force, as the B-26 attacks of April 15 missed many intended targets. The Cuban Air Force, therefore, was able to bombard the rebels as they invaded. Lastly, the rebels, who were far outnumbered by Cuban forces, were not able to stir up local Cubans to join their insurgency, which was necessary for the invasion to have a chance of succeeding.[224]

11. More Outside Pressure: Miss Cranberry Arrives

There may be non-military—even non-governmental—operations that prove challenging to young reporters. One of these, back at the *Boston Herald*, involved the interview of Ms. (in those days, Miss) Cranberry. At least, I think it was Cranberry. The question bedeviling me was how to interview Miss Cranberry, the attractive young model wearing a sash. Someone led her across the newsroom and seated her at my metal desk, I was starstruck by her fruit-enhanced charm. How was I to interview her?

I had been instructed to do a "cut line" (caption) for her elevation to queen of whatever the harvest was. I shyly struggled through information for the cut line. Then Miss Cranberry was led off to the Photo Department. I knew this cut line (and photo) were certain to run in the paper, since fruit and vegetable producers and large-scale canners, bottlers, and greengrocers advertised in the paper.

The Miss Cranberry press release bore in thick black pen *JFR MUST*. *JFR* were the initials of the paper's advertising director.

12. The Pressure to Compete

Like everyone else, reporters have different motivations. Some want awards, some promotions and raises, some fame, some the joy of being first, and nearly all the Pulitzer Prize. Many are driven by a combination of those things. These desires can produce distortions.

I began my career as a correspondent for *Time* magazine and worked in bureaus in New York, the Caribbean, and Chicago. I am proud of a few reports I did at *Time*. I remember one that involved the mayor of New York and small neighborhood parks. It began:

"When John Vliet Lindsay wrapped his hand around Falleco Silen's $2.98 football, it was curtains for the Dead End Gang. . . ." The city was ousting the gang from its trash-strewn touch-football field because Mayor Lindsay was commandeering the field for a pocket park.

In the New York Bureau of *Time*, I envied the young correspondent who was a star. For example, Brigitte Bardot—"BB"—was arriving from France, and the correspondent I admired was sent to the airport. He reported that BB and Roger Vadim, her husband, kissed for a precise number of seconds—let's say forty-eight.

Think about it: How did this correspondent know when to begin timing this kiss? The idea would not have occurred to me. I asked myself: Why can't *I* do that kind of thing?

A month or so later, the *Time* bureau chief discovered that the correspondent had made up some of his reporting. Apparently, he had not even spoken with people he had claimed to interview. People had called *Time* to say so. That helped me understand why I couldn't match his "reporting," and where journalistic pressure to compete could lead. But I continued to feel that pressure.

ACKNOWLEDGMENTS

Carly Wipf, my assistant, kept me and the book going—indefatigably and with an enthusiastic editor's eye—to the end. I cannot fathom why she wants to be a reporter.

Eric Fox spared the schoolmaster's rod but dispensed wondrous syntactical and analytic advice. "It's an important book," he would fib as the chapters showed themselves.

Susanne Kirk, an editor for decades at the hallowed Scribner, watched with unflagging humor and reassurance as the drama of a book critical of the *Times* (with its feared *Book Review*) and the first-glance (but wrong) impression of pro-Trumpism took rebellious shape, found a big-time agent, and then a publisher. From one end to the other, Mississippi watched Susie shaking her head and laughing, as she pressed me to finish. "It's a good book," she fibbed as more chapters appeared.

Sarah Wallace Rosenbloom is an extraordinary, old-fashioned ("What do you like to read?") librarian reared in Texas, who has managed, or help manage, libraries from the London School of Economics to a city in Iowa. Her "Baker Street Irregulars" of head librarians everywhere kindly provided, with their digital skills, research—gift-wrapped in encouragement.

Former colleagues at the *New York Times* made inestimable contributions, all with the usual NFA guarantee—*not for attribution*. I honor that pledge, and them.

Not least, Emilio spent many hours on his mat next to my computer desk—all the while bravely risking a bushy tail dangerously close to a desk chair on wheels. He calmed me with the placid snoring of a ragdoll when he expertly judged that I needed calming and urgently encouraged me to hasten when mealtime approached.

All errors of substance or style are mine alone.

NOTES

PROLOGUE

1. Here's how a publicity release for an appearance by Phelps described him:

Phelps got his start in 1941 . . . as a reporter for the . . . *Citizen* in Ambridge, PA. After a stint with the United Press wire service, he joined the U.S. Navy, where he served as an enlisted combat correspondent based out of Okinawa during World War II. After the war, he worked at *The Providence Journal* before landing a job as a copy editor for *The New York Times*. . . .

As the news editor of the *Times'* Washington bureau from 1965 to 1974, Phelps coordinated the paper's reporting on such seminal moments as the riots at the 1968 Democratic National Convention, the Pentagon Papers, and Watergate.

In 1974, Phelps left the *Times* and took a job as the executive editor of the *Boston Globe*, where he supervised the Pulitzer Prize–winning coverage of school desegregation.

CHAPTER TWO

2. Alfred Kazin, *The Past Breaks Out*, New York, Houghton Mifflin Company, 1987.

CHAPTER FIVE

3. The *Kirkus Review* discussed the book this way in its June 1, 1949 issue:

Covering the new laws against prostitution necessitates covering the whorehouses and discussing the situation with the madames . . . ; assigned to a political junket with Premier Schuman, he learns of the qualities of wine, old cemeteries, and macaroons; with President Auriel, he eats his way through native feasts . . . and learns what it is like to fly with the French Air Force; he follows the course of M. Villa's attempts to grow hair and the abortive aeronauting of a fanatic balloonist; he bruises himself on the Iron Curtain and comes out the loser; he meets a spy in Warsaw. [And, of course, he visits the heart of Andorra.]

4. Michael Berenbaum, *The World Must Know: The History of the Holocaust as Told in the United States Holocaust Memorial Museum*, 2nd ed., Washington, DC: John Hopkins University Press, 2006.

CHAPTER SIX

5. Duralex, *Duralexusa*, n.d.

CHAPTER SEVEN

6. Wolcott Gibbs parodied Backward Reels in the *New Yorker*, November 21, 1936:

Puny in spite of these preparations, prosy in spite of the contributions of Yale poets Archibald McLeish & John Farrar, was the first issue of Time on March 3, 1923. Magazine went to 9,000 subscribers; readers learned that Uncle Joe Cannon had retired at 86, that there was famine in Russia, that Thornton Wilder friend Gene Tunney had defeated Greb.

CHAPTER EIGHT

7. Charles Hamilton, *Adam Clayton Powell, Jr.: The Political Biography of an American Dilemma*, Maryland, Cooper Square Press, 2001.

8. Evelyn Waugh, *Scoop*, Milwaukee, Chapman & Hall, 1938.

9. I was a US Army Reserve infantry lieutenant and knew a little about pistols. But I did not pack one. I did tell my girlfriend; she wept. I promised to be careful. But the International Red Cross ended up canceling the plane. The result: No Biafra, no rabies, and pretty soon no girlfriend. She must have thought: *If you can't take me to my favorite French restaurant in Georgetown, the least you can do is be a war correspondent.*

CHAPTER NINE

10. "The Right War at the Right Time," *Time*, May 14, 1965.

11. David Halberstam, "Foreign Correspondents," *New York*, March 1985.

CHAPTER TEN

12. "Topics of The Times; A Salisbury Scoop," *New York Times*, July 11, 1993.

13. Eric Pace, "Harrison E. Salisbury, 84, Author and Reporter, Dies," *New York Times*, July 7, 1993.

CHAPTER ELEVEN

14. His Latvian name is pronounced *keys*.

15. Jimmy Breslin, "It's an Honor," *New York Herald Tribune*, November 26, 1963.

16. "The Reporters: Homer Bigart," PBS, 2003.

17. Gene Roberts and Hank Klibanoff, *The Race Beat*, New York, Random House, 2008, 184.

CHAPTER TWELVE

18. Robert D. McFadden, "Michael Kaufman, Times Reporter Who Roamed World, Is Dead at 71," *New York Times*, January 15, 2010.

19. "A bulletin of second-guessing issued occasionally from the southeast corner of The Times News Room." Here are some of its objects of praise and lamentation. The first few words are Bernstein's comment, followed by the offending or meritorious material in quotes, and then any further explanation by Bernstein:

Insex. "Elm Beetle Infestation Ravishing Thousands of Trees in Greenwich." (Aug. 26 1st edition) Keep your mind on your work, buster. The word you want is "ravaging."

Hasn't happened since Lazarus. "Move On to Revive Townsend Harris." (Aug. 19; proof)

Inviting leads. . . . "Brazil looked last week like a tightrope walker who had just missed a bad fall and still had a long way to travel." (Aug. 22; Brendan Jones) . . . "The attempt by the Russian bear to snuggle close to the British lion has brought out a strain of Missouri in many Britons."

Coke. "Cleansing with soap and water is sufficient for spilled coke and soda pop.". . . Coke is not only a fuel and a short name for cocaine, but also—as the Coca-Cola people keep reminding us at the drop of a Pepsi-Cola bottle—a registered nickname for Coca-Cola. As such it should be capitalized. Better yet, don't use it.

Trophies of a head-hunter. "Nobody Wants to Cast the First Watermelon." . . . "Colonel Fills Boss' Shoes, and Coat, Pants and Hat."

It shouldn't happen. The head said, "Ibn Saud Appoints Son Prime Minister of Nation." First, it wasn't Ibn Saud, who is quite dead, but his son, King Saud. Second, it wasn't Saud's son who was appointed but his brother." [Winners and Sinners, 1954, Ted Bernstein]

CHAPTER THIRTEEN

20. Until, that is, Rosenthal betrayed him. Rosenthal had long promised Gelb that he would make him his deputy. In "Friendships, Feuds and Betrayal in the Newsroom" (*Nieman Reports*, Spring 2004), Phelps wrote:

"My heart dropped," Gelb recalls. "I couldn't believe that Abe, with whom I had worked as closely as a brother since we started together on the metropolitan desk in 1963, would wait until the last possible moment to spring this news—first, that he was moving to the top, and, second, that he was not designating me as his deputy."

21. Sam Roberts, "Arthur Gelb, Critic and Editor Who Shaped The Times, Dies at 90," *New York Times*, May 20, 2014.

22. Ibid.

23. Ibid.

24. Peter Kihss, "Falling Masonry Kills a Lawyer 14 Floors Down," *New York Times*, July 29, 1982.

CHAPTER FOURTEEN

25. Exceptions were granted, but as Ingram continued:

[Dana] Milbank [a Washington Post columnist] noted that, since dozens of senior correspondents didn't meet the new standards either, "they all serve at the pleasure of Press Secretary Sarah Sanders" and "therefore, in theory, can have their credentials revoked any time they annoy Trump or his aides." (The White House press secretary told the Post the move was a result of security concerns, not a desire to crack down on specific journalists.)

CHAPTER FIFTEEN

26. From oysters to the Maginot Line: from A. J. Liebling, "A Good Appetite," in *Just Enough Liebling: Classic Work by the Legendary* New Yorker *Writer*, New York, North Point Press, 2004.

"The Proust madeleine phenomenon is now as firmly established in folklore as Newton's apple or Watt's steam kettle.

The man ate a tea biscuit, the taste evoked memories, he wrote a book. This is capable of expression by the formula TMB, for Taste > Memory > Book.

Some time ago, when I began to read a book called The Food of France, by Waverley Root, I had an inverse experience: BMT, for Book > Memory > Taste. Happily, the tastes that The Food of France re-created for me—small birds, stewed rabbit, stuffed tripe, Côte Rôtie, and Tavel—were more robust than that of the madeleine. . . . (The quantity of brandy in a madeleine would not furnish a gnat with an alcohol rub.)"

Liebling lamented the decline of the true trencherman, even in France. He once described the liver as the "seat of the Maginot mentality."

27. Lynda Roscoe Hartigan, "James Van Der Zee," Smithsonian American Art Museum, n.d.

28. James Van Der Zee, *The World of James Van Der Zee: A Visual Record of Black Americans.* New York, Grove Press, 1969.

29. Robert M. Smith, "Harlem Photographer Sees Lifework Hauled Away," *New York Times,* April 8, 1969.

30. "[A] small but dynamic show, with shots that range from 'mortuary' views of bodies in their coffins to cornerstone layings, which to him symbolized Harlem's solidity. And so did the wonderful luxury of his 1934 portrait of one Josephine Becton in her flower-bedecked living room, accompanied by a piano, a silver tea service and a large open Valentine's heart full of chocolates." (From review of *Harlem Guaranteed,* a selection of 30-some photographs, Grace Glueck, *New York Times*)

31. Martin W. Sandler explained in his book, *America Through the Lens: Photographers Who Changed the Nation*:

People had much less need for professional studio portraits, and Van Der Zee's fortunes declined dramatically. In order to support himself, he was forced to shoot passport photos and to search for other photography jobs. At the same time, the glory days of Harlem came to an end.

32. Joseph Lelyveld, John Kifner, and Robert M. Smith, "The View from Kent State: 11 Speak Out," *New York Times,* May 11, 1970.

33. "Vietnam War Casualties Officer Deaths by Rank," American War Library, 2008. Accessed April 19, 2020.

34. Robert M. Smith, "Kent State Study by F.B.I. Differs from Ohio Finding," *New York Times,* October 31, 1970.

CHAPTER SIXTEEN

35. Irving, Washington, Rip Van Winkle and *The Legend of Sleepy Hollow: Two Stories,* New York, Peter Pauper Press, 1955 [originally published 1820].

36. McCandlish Phillips, "5th Ave. Weather: Sunshine And Gaels," *New York Times,* March 18, 1970.

37. McCandlish Phillips, "Bird Accused of Cursing Wins Case by Eloquence of Silence," *New York Times,* July 1, 1960.

38. McCandlish Phillips, "Lindy's Serves Cheesecake, Bagels and Humor for Last Time," *New York Times,* September 22, 1969.

39. From Robert M. Smith, "Harvard Vote Bars Strike; Radcliffe Head Besieged," *New York Times,* April 29, 1969:

More than 100 Harvard and Radcliffe students marched from the middle of Harvard Yard to the Radcliffe Administration building and invaded the office of Dr. Mary I. Bunting, Radcliffe's president, to protest in a noisy, 10-minute session the disciplining of 22 Radcliffe girls.

It was a confrontation marked by restraint on the part of some of the Radcliffe girls, or Cliffies as they are called. Many of them carried green book bags and urged a "real dialogue."

. . . Many of the girls urged that Dr. Bunting not be screamed at but be given a chance to respond to questions. Some of the boys agreed, but others kept arguing that it was no use talking with her. They either urged leaving her white second-floor office with its teal desk and tiered bookshelves or just kept shouting at her.

Finally, one of the girls turned to the group behind her. "Hey, you guys," she called, "will you let us girls run one thing?". . .

There were 128 of the demonstrators as they came out of the yard, and they were about evenly divided between girls and boys.

Halting traffic in Harvard Square briefly, they marched up Garden Street, chanting . . . Television crews and newsmen dogged their heels or ran ahead during the march.

When they reached the quiet green of Radcliffe Yard, a few girls were studying lazily on the grass. It was a hot spring day—81 degrees— and the dogwoods near Fay House, the administration building, were in vivid white blossom.

CHAPTER SEVENTEEN

40. James Reston, "Now, About My Operation in Peking," *New York Times*, July 26, 1971.
41. Gay Talese, *The Kingdom and the Power*, New York, Random House, 2007, 19.
42. Ibid.

To Krock's staff he added many new men and, as was soon obvious, a special breed of man, an almost Restonian species: they were lean and tweedy journalists, usually quite tall, educated at better universities and brighter than they first seemed to be.

They were deceptively aware and low-pressured, slow nodders and ponderous puff-ers of pipes, very polite and altogether disarming. Most of them had been reared in the Midwest or South, or at least they affected the easy manner of small-town America, contrasting noticeably with the many fast-talking, city-sharp men who had emerged from crowded urban neighborhoods and worked on The *Times'* staff in New York. . . .

His writing expressed faith in the nation's future, was gentle with the Establish-ment—he did not rock the boat. He wrote interestingly, often humorously without being excessively cutting or clever.

[H]is America was a land in which the citizens seemed not so disenchanted, the police not so brutal, the United States' bombing of Vietnam not entirely unjustified, the politicians in Washington not so self-serving, the age of Jefferson not so long ago or lost in essence.

43. Stephen Kinzer, *The Brothers: John Foster Dulles, Allen Dulles, and Their Secret World War*, New York, Times Books, 2013.
44. In "All the News That's Fit to Buy" (*The Nation*, December 8, 2005), Alexander Cockburn wrote:

In his *Secret History of the CIA*, published in 2001, Joe Trento describes how in 1948 CIA man Frank Wisner was appointed director of the Office of Special Projects, soon renamed the Office of Policy Coordination (OPC). This became the espionage and counterintelligence branch of the CIA, the very first in its list of designated functions being "propaganda."

Later that year Wisner set an operation code-named Mockingbird to influence the domestic American press. He recruited Philip Graham of the *Washington Post* to run the project within the industry.

Trento writes that "one of the most important journalists under the control of . . . Mockingbird was Joseph Alsop [*The Washington Post*]. . . . Other journalists willing to promote the views of the CIA included Stewart Alsop (*New York Herald Tribune*), Ben Bradlee (*Newsweek*), James Reston (*New York Times*). . . .

45. In an article titled "The CIA and the Media," on Carlbernstein.com, Carl Bernstein has written:

The Agency's relationship with the *Times* was by far its most valuable among newspapers, according to CIA officials. From 1950 to 1966, about ten CIA employees were provided *Times* cover under arrangements approved by the newspaper's late publisher, Arthur Hays Sulzberger. The cover arrangements were part of a general *Times* policy . . . to provide assistance to the CIA whenever possible.

. . . . It was agreed that the actual arrangements would be handled by subordinates. . . . The mighty didn't want to know the specifics; they wanted plausible deniability.

A senior CIA official who reviewed a portion of the Agency's files on journalists for two hours on September 15th, 1977, said he found . . . five instances in which the Times had provided cover for CIA employees between 1954 and 1962. . . .

The CIA employees who received *Times* credentials posed as stringers for the paper abroad and worked as members of clerical staffs in the *Times'* foreign bureaus. . . .

CIA officials cite two reasons why the Agency's working relationship with the *Times* was closer and more extensive than with any other paper: the fact that the *Times* maintained the largest foreign news operation in American daily journalism; and the close personal ties between the men who ran both institutions.

46. John Stacks, *Scotty: James B. Reston and the Rise and Fall of American Journalism*, Lincoln, NE, Bison Books, 2003.

CHAPTER EIGHTEEN

47. From Eric Alterman, "The Journalist and the Politician," *Columbia Journalism Review*, February 14, 2013:

Arthur Krock, one-time bureau chief and columnist for the *New York Times*, is an abject lesson in the temporality of insider influence. Once upon a time, he bestrode Washington as a journalistic colossus. . . .

Krock, who died in 1974, is also occasionally remembered for his tendency to seek favors from the wealthy, none more so than Joseph Kennedy. But the publication by the historian, David Nasaw, of the first full-scale biography of Kennedy, *The Patriarch*, sheds new light on the impressive scale of the degree to which Kennedy was able to purchase the favors of the journalist and his newspaper via decades worth of bribery (and flattery) of the *Times*.

Nasaw writes how correspondence between Krock and Kennedy "reveals something quite disturbing, if not corrupt, about Krock's willingness to do Kennedy's bidding, to advise him or write a speech for him, then praise it in his column."

As Nasaw explains, "For the next quarter century, while working as Washington bureau chief and as columnist, Arthur Krock would serve as Kennedy's unofficial, clandestine press agent, speechwriter, political adviser, informant, and all-purpose consultant." Whenever Kennedy had something he needed help saying, Krock helped him say it, often putting the news columns of the *Times* at his disposal as well. . . .

48. Robert M. Smith, "The Slippery Slopes; When One Question Leads to Another," *New York Times,* August 22, 1973.
49. Robert M. Smith, "4 More Leaving Kissinger's Staff," *New York Times,* May 22, 1970.
50. From Seymour Hersh, "Kissinger Linked to Order to F.B.I. Ending Wiretaps," *New York Times,* June 9, 1974.

Henry A. Kissinger's National Security Council office was directly responsible for ordering the Federal Bureau of Investigation to end the 17 so-called "national security" wiretaps on newsmen and officials that began in 1969. . . .

CHAPTER NINETEEN
51. Originally, stringers were freelance reporters paid by inches of type produced; editors would use strings to measure the inch count.
52. Hersh's relentless pursuit of stories is legendary, the stuff of journalistic myth and metaphor. Author Thomas Powers, capturing the essential Hersh, said he had a "professional style notoriously similar to the single-minded ferocity of the wolverine . . . known among fur trappers of yesteryear for its ability to tear its way through the log wall of a cabin for a strip of bacon."

CHAPTER TWENTY-TWO
53. It is one of life's ironies that I was covering, among other things, the Pentagon.
54. Fragging is "the murder or attempted murder of strict, unpopular, or just aggressive officers and NCOs." Robert D. Heinl Jr., "The Collapse of the Armed Forces," *Armed Forces Journal,* June 7, 1971.
55. David Halberstam wrote this in a letter to Sy Hersh. He assumed that Hersh was having trouble with the editors at the *Times.*

Hersh, Seymour, *Reporter,* New York, Knopf Doubleday Publishing Group, 2018, 229.
Halberstam had left the paper in 1969.

CHAPTER TWENTY-THREE
56. Scott W. Jacobs, "Student Activists Denied Jobs in Government, Media," *Harvard Crimson,* May 14, 1970.
57. From David Schultz, "House Un-American Activities Committee," The First Amendment Encyclopedia, John Seigenthaler Chair of Excellence in First Amendment Studies, Middle Tennessee State University:

From its inception in 1938 until it was dissolved in 1975, the House Un-American Activities Committee (HUAC) took a prominent role in the investigation of communist activity in the United States. Although its supporters claim that this committee of the U.S. House of Representatives performed an important function, its critics contend that its abuse of power trampled important First Amendment rights, such as freedom of expression and freedom of association.

From Marc-Georges Pufong, "McCarthyism," The First Amendment Encyclopedia, John Seigenthaler Chair of Excellence in First Amendment Studies, Middle Tennessee State University:

The term *McCarthyism . . .* evolved to describe the practice of publicly accusing government employees of political disloyalty or subversive activities and using unsavory investigatory methods to prosecute them.

58. From Robert M. Smith, "U.S. Cane Cutters in Cuba Scored as 'Missiles'," *New York Times,* March 17, 1970:

Senator James O. Eastland told the Senate today that he believed the Americans who recently went to Cuba as sugar cane cutters "are being indoctrinated and trained to attack and destroy our institutions and government."

. . . . The Mississippi Democrat, chairman of the Senate Subcommittee on Internal Security, called the cane cutters "missiles in human form". . . .

Mr. Eastland said: "It is . . . a very clear and present danger that these militant revolutionaries will return to implement the Communist purpose of causing chaos, confusion, and outright revolution."

Administration sources indicated that some persons in the Government, apparently concentrated in one agency that was not identified, shared Senator Eastland's anxiety. . . .

CHAPTER TWENTY-FOUR

59. Robert D. McFadden, "Winston Moseley, Who Killed Kitty Genovese, Dies in Prison at 81," *New York Times,* April 4, 2016.

60. Sometimes my sources did chime in too late. There was the time a recondite section of the Tax Code had been played with in a particularly manipulative way so as to favor some folks, and a source called to tell me about the change. I had begun to write the story, when the source called again. The trucks had begun to pull away from the printer with the old section instead of the new. Treasury called the trucks back to reload them with the new (tinkered with) forms. I wrote the story but used as the lead the trucks being called back to the Treasury printer.

CHAPTER TWENTY-FIVE

61. She also wrote *Toys in the Attic, Another Part of the Forest, The Children's Hour,* and *The Little Foxes.*

62. Ellen Schrecker, "Hearing Regarding Communist Infiltration of the Hollywood Motion-Picture Industry," in *The Age of McCarthyism: A Brief History with Documents,* Boston, Bedford Books of St. Martin's Press, 1994, 201–2.

63. From Ruth Graham, "The Bizarre True Story of the Group That Seduces Philip in This Season of *The Americans,*" *Slate,* April 6, 2016: "EST was part of the Human Potential Movement of the 1970s, which emphasized human agency and personal growth as a response to generational ennui."

The program had its many supporters and many detractors. (Erhard was born John Paul Rosenberg.)

64. James Reston, *Deadline: A Memoir,* New York, Random House, December 8, 1991.

CHAPTER TWENTY-SIX

65. Joseph P. Flood, "The Path Less Traveled," *Harvard Crimson,* April 19, 2002.

CHAPTER TWENTY-SEVEN

66. Robert Smith Aff., U.S. v. N.Y. Times, No. 71 Civ. 2662 (S.D.N.Y. June 17, 1971). Alternative source: Affidavit of Robert Smith, June 17, 1971, reprinted in 1 *New York Times Company v. United States: A Documentary History* 420 (James C. Goodale ed. 1972). https://heinonline.org/HOL/P?h=hein.trials/adwl0001&i=584.
ADDED

67. Jake Kobrick, *The Pentagon Papers in the Federal Courts,* second edition. Federal Judicial Center, 2019, 46-47.

68. Robert M. Smith, "F.B.I. Is Said to Have Cut Direct Liaison With C.I.A.," *New York Times,* October 10, 1971.

69. Emanuel Perlmutter, "I.R.S. Gets Data on Phone Calls By Times's Washington Staff," *New York Times,* February 9, 1974.

70. Carrie Johnson, "The Secret Burglary That Exposed J. Edgar Hoover's FBI," NPR, January 7, 2014.

71. From Matthew Cecil, *Hoover's FBI and the Fourth Estate: The Campaign to Control the Press and the Bureau's Image,* University of Kansas Press, 2014:

Journalists quickly understand that gaining and maintaining access to authoritative sources equates to successful practice because it demonstrates an understanding of the necessities of journalism. . . . Sociologist Gaye Tuchman wrote after her own newsroom observations. "The higher the status of sources and the greater the scope of their positions, the higher the status of reporters.". . . Maintaining access to those sources clearly demonstrates mastery of the craft to other journalists . . .

The structure of news "beats" likewise feeds the power imbalance.

Reporters are essentially asked to embed themselves in an organization, becoming entirely reliant on that organization for access to information. Yet at the same time, reporters are somehow expected to remain connected to their news organization and abide by its policies and ethical principles . . .

The FBI held even greater powers of persuasion based on its role as a federal investigative and law enforcement agency. During the early days of U.S. involvement in World War II, for example, President Roosevelt placed Hoover and the FBI in charge of federal censorship. Starting with that temporary authority, Hoover used the exigencies of war to expand his efforts to monitor and even investigate journalists. . . .

CHAPTER TWENTY-EIGHT

72. Robert M. Smith, "White House Inscrutable On Nixon's Cram Course," *New York Times,* February 12, 1972.

73. Tina Kelley, "Ron Ziegler, Press Secretary to Nixon, Is Dead at 63," *New York Times,* February 11, 2003.

74. Todd S. Purdum, "The Nation; The Nondenial Denier," *New York Times,* February 16, 2003.

75. The *Times* Washington Bureau had some interesting people—though not as interesting as Rewrite, and more upscale. Less than a year later Gene somehow wrangled me off Rewrite and sent me to Washington—probably out of pity for my dining choices and possibly to get some training from Johnny (R. W.) Apple, a remarkable political reporter

whose *Times* obituary described him as having "Falstaffian appetites." The obit mentioned that "to the end of his life, Mr. Apple kept a small black bag packed with essentials, including a personal pepper mill." Apple was the quintessential Washington hand. At one point, Gene decided to dispatch me to South Dakota with a presidential aspirant. The idea was this: *"The kid needs to learn about politics—whether he likes it or not—so send him to South Dakota. How badly can he screw up there?"* "I have no winter coat," I confided to Apple. Apple told me to go to Eddie Bauer, buy a proper winter coat, and put it on my expense account. Salaries might be modest in Washington, but expenses were without known limit.

76. Timothy Crouse, *Boys on the Bus*, New York, Random House, 1972.

CHAPTER TWENTY-NINE

77. Robert Phelps, *God and the Editor: My Search for Meaning at the* New York Times, Syracuse University Press, 2009.
78. "US Paper Missed Watergate Scoop," BBC, May 26, 2009.
79. "Morning Report," Radio New Zealand, May 27, 2009.
80. Ed Pilkington, "Watergate Under the Bridge: How the *New York Times* Missed the Scoop of the Century," *The Guardian*, May 25, 2009.
81. "The *New York Times*' Dejó Escapar El Watergate," *El Periódico*, May 26, 2009.
82. Dan Amira, "Bob Woodward Unimpressed by the *Times*' Watergate Scoop," *New York*, May 27, 2009.

CHAPTER THIRTY

83. Vernon Loeb, "Soviets Knew Date of Cuba Attack," *Washington Post*, April 29, 2000.
84. Tad Szulc, "Anti-Castro Units Land in Cuba; Report Fighting at Beachhead; Rusk Says U.S. Won't Intervene," *New York Times*, April 17, 1961.
85. David W. Dunlap, "The C.I.A. Readies a Cuban Invasion, and *The Times* Blinks," *New York Times*, December 26, 2014.
86. Gabriel Sherman, "Risen Gave *Times* A Non-Disclosure On Wiretap Book," *New York Observer*, January 23, 2006.
87. David Folkenflik, "'*New York Times*' Editor: Losing Snowden Scoop 'Really Painful,'" NPR, June 5, 2014.
88. Laura Poitras, "How We Broke the NSA Story," *Salon*, June 11, 2013.

CHAPTER THIRTY-ONE

89. From Robert M. Smith, "The Slippery Slopes; When One Question Leads to Another," *New York Times*, August 22, 1973:

Slippery Slopes

NEW HAVEN—Those who place the ultimate blame for Watergate on Richard Nixon's childhood go back too far. Those who place it in the tendency of White House power to corrupt don't go back far enough. The origins of moral relativism lie somewhere between, in a quasi-mystical, demeaning, aggrandizing, relativizing, inflating, mind-sharpening, boring, stimulating, feared and corrupting experience known as law school. It is at law school that life begins to be lived on the Slippery Slope.

Law school students are introduced to the Slippery Slope fairly quickly. The first slide usually takes this format:

Professor: (Bored condescension.) Mr. Smith, do you believe that the police should torture people?

Smith: (What is he getting at?) No, sir.

Professor: Do you believe that the police should ever torture suspects?

Smith: (Pause.) No, sir.

Professor: (Volume goes up half a notch.) You're sure of that, are you?

Smith: (Longer pause.) Yes, sir. I don't think it would be right.

Professor: (Sotto voce) Not right, huh? (Back to courtroom tone.) Picture this situation, Mr. Smith. A suspect is known to have an atomic weapon. He is also known to have planted this weapon somewhere in the labyrinthine tunnels below Manhattan. It is known that the device will detonate in one hour. The police have tried unsuccessfully, after reading the suspect his Miranda warning, to learn from him where he has planted the weapon. It is known that he is very sensitive to electric shocks. Would you allow the police to give him a few quick jolts to find out where the bomb is, or would you prefer no torture—not even a teensy-weensy electric shock—and the certainty that, say, three million people will perish?

Smith: (How much time is left in this class?) Well . . .

Professor: Now, Mr. Smith. You aren't quite sure that the police should never torture suspects, are you? It's really a question of drawing a line somewhere, isn't it? In short, it's like the rest of life—it's all a question of where you want to draw the line.

From the Slippery Slope the student is led to Cost Ben analysis. Cost Ben helps the student to decide where the line should be drawn. The instruction takes this form:

Professor: What's the benefit involved in torturing the suspect, getting the information and deactivating the bomb?

Smith: Three million lives.

Professor: Good. What's the cost?

Smith: (The values I came in here with.) The pain inflicted on the suspect. Possible encouragement to the police to torture in the future. A weakening in the public ethic against torture. A dehumanization of the policemen who did the torturing . . .

Professor: Now, Mr. Smith. Don't you think the public would want the police to torture in such a situation? Don't you think the police can be restrained by efficient management and control?

When you jettison all that fuzzy-minded-social-science-garbage (pronounced as one word) and do a tough-minded, a practical Cost Ben analysis, isn't it fairly clear that they ought to torture in that, and perhaps other, situations?

If you start at the top of the hill marked Presidency, take the first road that says Slippery Slope, climb into the long black Cost Ben limousine and take your foot off the brake, you will soon reach: Watergate.

CHAPTER THIRTY-THREE

90. While Johnson is often credited with the phrase "ink-stained wretch," it is not clear that he used it. He did define lexicographer as: A writer of dictionaries; a harmless

drudge, that busies himself in tracing the original, and detailing the signification of words.

91. Thought to be, that is, outside of Washington, where journalists were adored with the reverence reserved for the maître d' of the Palm restaurant. (It was at the Palm that a prominent lawyer, Paul Porter of Arnold & Porter, choked to death on a piece of lobster.)

See Joseph Califano, "Washington Lawyer: Williams, Connolly & Califano," in *Inside: A Public and Private Life,* New York, PublicAffairs Press, 2004, 219.

92. Nan Robertson, a former *Times* reporter, wrote in her memoir *The Girls in the Balcony: Women, Men and* The New York Times (New York, Random House, 1992):

There were forty women reporters to three hundred and eighty-five men reporters, and eleven of those women were in family/style. Of twenty-two national correspondents, not one was a woman . . . There were no women on the editorial board, which had eleven members. There were no women columnists . . . Almost all the lower-paying, lower-ranking jobs were confined to women.

93. From "The Times Settles Sex-Bias Suit Filed by Female Workers in U.S. Court," *New York Times,* November 21, 1978:

The settlement took effect on January 1, 1979. It was to run for four years and change "existing equal-opportunity goals for putting women into positions ranging from entry level to top management." It would also create "an annuities fund of $232,000 to compensate [the women who brought the suit] for the historic costs of social discrimination and awards them $100,000 to cover their legal fees."

94. Irvin Molotsky, "Eileen Shanahan, 77, Former Times Reporter," *New York Times,* November 3, 2001.

CHAPTER THIRTY-FOUR

95. World Intellectual Property Organization, Berne Convention for the Protection of Literary and Artistic Works, 1982.

96. Mike Holderness, Benno Pöppelmann, and Michael Klehm, *The Right Thing: An Authors' Rights Handbook for Journalists*, Brussels, International Federation of Journalists, 2011.

CHAPTER THIRTY-FIVE

97. Robert M. Smith, "More State Banks on 'Problem List,'" *New York Times,* January 23, 1976.

98. Ibid:

While the Senator's request had asked for the names of "problem" banks, Dr. Burns [Arthur F. Burns, the Federal Reserve Board's chairman] refused to provide the names. The information was requested by the Senator last July in connection with the committee's consideration of hearings dealing with "problem" banks and their treatment by the bank regulatory agencies.

In his response, Dr. Burns said that "the term 'problem bank' is imprecise and, as generally applied, merely refers to banks that require more than usual supervisory and management attention."

"It should be noted," Dr. Burns continued, "that the term . . . encompasses a wide range of possible weaknesses with varying degrees of severity."

Here is an excerpt from an article I wrote two weeks later, "Reserve Says List of Banks Under Surveillance Grows" (*New York Times*, February 4, 1976):

Attention has been focused on the question of "problem banks"—a term that Leavitt [Brenton C. Leavitt, director of the Federal Reserve's Division of Banking Supervision and Regulation] said was misleading because it overstated the seriousness of the situation . . .

99. Robert M. Smith, "The Lockheed Letter: How and Why of Bribery," *New York Times*, February 8, 1976.

100. Gretchen Morgenson, "At Student Loan Giant Navient, Troubled Past Was Prologue," *New York Times*, January 21, 2017.

101. In his autobiography, Sy wrote that the Washington Bureau "didn't work out" for him. Hersh wrote:

"I resigned immediately, without saying why. . . . I would never work for a newspaper again."

CHAPTER THIRTY-SIX

102. Robert M. Smith, "Hammer Accused of Foreign Bribes," *New York Times*, October 9, 1975.

103. Robert M. Smith, "Haughton Expects U. S. Curb On Payments," *New York Times*, September 3, 1975.

104. Many years later—long after my career at the *Times*—Stanley Sporkin came to mind again.

I was in Jakarta, and worried. I was walking around a large, lush, oval park in the oppressive heat. I was the lawyer for a large American company, and rebels had seized millions of dollars of its equipment. The rebels wanted money to give it back. What to do? Could my client pay? Should it pay? If it did, what would Stanley, or his successor, think? It wouldn't be paying officials of the government. These were officials of a group that wanted to replace the government—and it wouldn't be paying to get business, but to get its own equipment back. Still. . . .

As I walked, I noticed there was only one other person in the park. He was walking like me, around the large oval, perspiring in the heat. Like me, he was dressed in a tropical suit. I engaged him in conversation. He was from an international relief organization. Like me, he was worried. If he released the aid funds his headquarters had authorized, what part of the money would go to corrupt officials?

105. Robert M. Smith, "S. E. C.'s Tough Guy," *New York Times*, October 5, 1975.

CHAPTER THIRTY-SEVEN

106. From Philip Nobile, "An Exclusive Report on How the *New York Times* Become Second Banana," *Esquire*, May 1975:

Robert Smith suffered from job frustration, too. He covered the Justice Department part time and excelled on investigative stories even though acting the detective was displeasing to him. Smith's youthful Boy Scout heart belonged to diplomatic reporting. He often counseled with Phelps about his stalled career. Smith settled on Yale Law School as a means to expand opportunities.

In 1969, Smith was an untried kid on the rewrite desk in New York. During the Harvard riots that year he went up to Cambridge for backup purposes. National editor Gene Roberts, also on the scene, was impressed by the rookie's performance. On a ruse, he decided to keep Smith occupied by assigning him to interview Harvard's incommunicado president Nathan Pusey. Roberts was well aware that even Reston had failed to get Pusey's attention. But nobody let Smith in on the joke. He dogged the poor fellow day and night. When the president stepped out on his porch to retrieve the morning milk, Smith was standing there. When he dined on campus, Smith was sitting at the next table. Harvard called The Times to have their fanatic pulled off. Smith was angry that Pusey finally chose to be questioned on Meet the Press instead of in The Times. But who do you suppose appeared in the Meet the Press studio to interview the president?

"If you want to know why The Times messed up Watergate," confided a knowledgeable bureau man, "ask Bob Smith." Yet Smith, thirty-four, refuses to speak on or off the record. A reliable Timesman, however, surmises that Smith could have saved the paper single-handedly. According to the Timesman, Smith was close to breaking Watergate long before The Post.

Roberts and Frankel had been concerned about stories falling through the cracks in Washington. They were anxious to have three or four uncommitted horses like Neil Sheehan in the bureau to saddle up for difficult situations. Smith seemed to match the description—he once obtained an unobtainable sealed grand jury presentment against the late Rep. Hale Boggs.

"Bob is the world's most traditional and moral man," states the reliable Timesman. "Going to the bathroom probably involves a philosophical decision. He was tormented by his persistence and agonized about going through life as a royal pain in the ass. But he was the fastest source man I've ever met." So fast that he beat Woodstein to Segretti by two months. On one of his last days at The Times, in August of 1972, he took a government official to lunch and pumped him on Watergate. "I'll give you one hint," the official said reluctantly, "remember this name— Donald Segretti." Smith feared to write it down in a public place. For the rest of the meal he repeated to himself—Segretti-cigarette, Segretti-cigarette. All he could do then was leave a memo on the strange encounter. "This was merely one of a hundred different clues," the Timesman concludes, "that would have been followed up if Smith remained." (Smith, as it turns out, is returning to the bureau after graduation from Yale this spring.)

Actually, I did not sit there saying to myself *Segretti-cigarette, Segretti-cigarette.* That is not a mnemonic. I sat there saying *Segretti-spaghetti, Segretti-spaghetti.* But I told Gene Roberts the story after getting his pledge to keep it secret and used "cigarette" to give him the essence of what had happened, but to ensure that if he broke his promise and leaked the story, I would know he had. He leaked it. I think Gene may have been trying to toot my horn, when I couldn't whisper—let alone toot—about what happened.

107. Both of these changed in 1986.

108. Phelps wrote of Gelb's City Room in "Friendships, Feuds and Betrayal in the Newsroom," *Nieman Reports,* March 2004:

[Rosenthal and Gelb] had grown into journalistic Siamese twins. Often, Gelb writes, "I felt as though Abe and I were two halves of the same person."

No wonder, then, that Gelb, on tour in Venice in 1969, was shocked when Rosenthal called with the news that he was becoming managing editor and that Seymour Topping would be his assistant managing editor.

"My heart dropped," Gelb recalls. "I couldn't believe that Abe, with whom I had worked as closely as a brother since we started together on the metropolitan desk in 1963, would wait until the last possible moment to spring this news—first, that he was moving to the top, and, second, that he was not designating me as his deputy. . . . I felt betrayed."

109. From Jack Shafer's obit on Rosenthal ("A. M. Rosenthal (1922–2006)," *Slate*, May 11, 2006): "Was Rosenthal a beast? When Sulzberger yanked him in 1986 and sent Max Frankel in, he offered this prayer: 'Make the newsroom a happy place again.'"

From Joseph C. Goulden's book *Fit to Print: A.M. Rosenthal and His Times* (New York, Lyle Stuart, 1988): "Rosenthal is a shouter, a curser, a whiner; he keeps a 'shitlist' in his head and can hold grudges for years. He is a small man physically, but his rages are so violent that he intimidates persons half again his size."

110. Max Frankel, *The Times of My Life and My Life with The Times*, New York, Penguin Random House, 2000.

111. (later himself executive editor).

CHAPTER FORTY

112. The *Times'* theory was that the attorney general was not supposed to be political. Other countries separate the roles of justice minister and chief prosecutor. The *Times* would later pillory William Barr for conflating the two roles.

Charlie Savage, "Is an Attorney General Independent or Political? Barr Rekindles a Debate," *New York Times*, May 1, 2019.

CHAPTER FORTY-ONE

113. Civiletti's old Baltimore law firm was Venable, Baetjer and Howard. When he returned to it, the firm became Venable, Baetjer, Howard & Civiletti.

114. Philip Taubman, "Benjamin Richard Civiletti," *New York Times*, July 20, 1979.

115. So is lying. One of the forms lying takes is trial balloons. In this variant, an official leak is something that is batted around by government officials to gauge whether it will be popular. They wait for the reaction to the leaked story and then decide whether to act. Pity the wretched reporter who doesn't know he or she is being taken for a ride in a hot-air balloon.

116. When I was a reporter, my sources came from different levels of government and life. They were a gallimaufry, and they were subject to all sorts of restrictions. I once had a source in the government—where doesn't matter—who lost his job because of a traffic offense. Well, it wasn't quite that. He told me what happened as he was being fired. He had been asked on the government employment application whether he had ever been arrested for anything other than traffic offenses, and he answered no. It turned out he had been arrested for what might, or might not, be regarded as a traffic offense—for

blocking traffic in a major American city. He had sat in front of the cars with other people. They were protesting the Vietnam War. When the government found out about the arrest—long after the war—they didn't agree that this was a traffic offense, and my source was fired. Not, obviously, because he was my source. But if the government had learned he was a source of mine, firing might have been the least of his problems.

117. From the regulations of the Office of Professional Responsibility, U. S. Department of Justice:

The Office of Professional Responsibility . . . shall be headed by a Counsel. . . .

(a) The Counsel shall:

(1) Receive, review, investigate and refer for appropriate action allegations of misconduct involving Department attorneys. . . .

(3) Report to the responsible Department official the results of inquiries and investigations . . . and . . . make recommendations for disciplinary and other corrective action. . . .

118. In his book *Living the Policy Process* (Oxford, Oxford University Press, 2008, 122), Heymann discusses "Changing the Setting that Another Player Faces by a Fait Accompli." The accompli he talks about is "a leak to the press, thereby precluding the possibility of the players taking, or failing to take, an action without facing public or congressional scrutiny or opposition."

119. "About McGruff," National Crime Prevention Council, 2017. Accessed August 1, 2019.

120. Robert F. Diegelman, "Federal Financial Assistance for Crime Control: Lessons of the LEAA Experience," *Crim. L. & Criminology 994* (1982).

121. Garrett O'Keefe, *Media Campaigns and Crime Prevention—An Executive Summary*, University of Denver, 1982.

122. Ibid.

CHAPTER FORTY-THREE

123. "'You've Got to Find What You Love,' Jobs Says," *Stanford News,* June 14, 2005.

CHAPTER FORTY-FOUR

124. Jeremy Alderton, *Aldertons a Cockney Rhyming Slang Dictionary*.

125. Joke: in cockney slang, "rum and coke."

126. Brian Mott, "Traditional Cockney and Popular London Speech," MS, Universitat De Barcelona, Barcelona, Spain, 2011.

127. James Mancari, "Woodward and Bernstein Stress the Constants of Journalism," *Long Island Report,* March 23, 2012.

128. Joseph E. Herzberg and members of the *New York Herald Tribune Staff, Late City Edition,* New York, Holt, 1969.

CHAPTER FORTY-FIVE

129. Jonathan Moules, "FT Global MBA Ranking 2019," *Financial Times,* January 27, 2019.

130. Alex Williams, "The Growing Pay Gap between Journalism and Public Relations," Pew Research Center, August 11, 2014.

131. Alex Williams, "How Poorly Are Journalists Paid? Depends on Where You Live," *Poynter,* June 26, 2015.

132. CareerCast.com, "The Worst Jobs of 2016," *CareerCast,* 2016.

133. *Numbers, Facts and Trends Shaping Your World,* Pew Research Center, 2018.

134. Elizabeth Grieco, Nami Sumida, and Sophia Fedeli, "At Least 36% of Largest US Newspapers Have Had Layoffs since 2017," Pew Research Center, July 23, 2018.

135. Amy Mitchell and Jesse Holcomb, "State of the News Media 2016," Pew Research Center, June 15, 2016.

136. In "The Reconstruction of American Journalism," Leonard Downie Jr., and Michael Schudson reported that even in 2009: "In most cities, fewer newspaper journalists were reporting on city halls, schools, social welfare, life in the suburbs, local business, culture, the arts, science, or the environment, and fewer were assigned to investigative reporting. Most large newspapers eliminated foreign correspondents and many of their correspondents in Washington. The number of newspaper reporters covering state capitals full-time fell from 524 in 2003 to 355 at the beginning of 2009. A large share of newspaper reporting of government, economic activity, and quality of life . . . disappeared."

137. "Some Papers March On, Crippled by Cutbacks," *New York Times,* August 4, 2019.

138. Ibid.

139. "Sizing Up the Damage to Local Newspapers," *New York Times,* August 4, 2019.

140. Kent Hoover, "Only Lawyers Valued Less Than Business Executives, Pew Survey Finds," *Business Journals,* June 12, 2013.

141. Liz Spayd, the public editor of the *Times,* wrote about the feelings of *Times* readers ("One Thing Voters Agree On: Better Campaign Coverage Was Needed," New York Times, November 19, 2016). The Times described Spayd as "at the intersection of Times readers and Times journalists."

She wrote:

Since the election, I have been on the phone with many *Times* readers around the country . . . to discuss their concerns about the *Times'*s coverage of the presidential election. The number of complaints coming into the public editor's office is five times the normal level. . . .

My colleague . . . who oversees the letters to the editor, says the influx from readers is one of the largest since Sept. 11. Many people . . . are venting about the *Times'*s coverage.

Readers complain heatedly and repeatedly about the forecasting odometer from The Upshot that was anchored on the home page and predicted that Hillary Clinton had an 80 percent chance or better of winning. They complain that The Times's attempt to tap the sentiments of Trump supporters was lacking. *And they complain about the liberal tint the* Times *applies to its coverage, without awareness that it does.* [Emphasis supplied.]

142. Kevin Lerner, "(MORE) Guided Journalists during the 1970s Media Crisis of Confidence," *Columbia Journalism Review,* May 10, 2018.

143. Federica Cocco, "New York *Times* Profits Jump 66% amid 'Trump Bump'," *Financial Times*, May 3, 2018.

144. The *Times* reported that it "had reached an agreement with the Mexican billionaire Carlos Slim Helú for a $250 million loan. . . ." Slim invested the money in the form of six-year notes with warrants convertible into common shares. The notes carried a 14 percent interest rate.

The *Times* announcement described Slim as "one of the wealthiest people in the world." It said he "controls phone companies and has major investments in retailing, construction, banking, insurance, railroads and mining." It said the estimate of his fortune was $60 billion.

Eric Dash, "Mexican Billionaire Invests in Times Company," *New York Times*, January 19, 2009.

CHAPTER FORTY-SIX

145. Did you know there is a Sweet Honesty Cologne? One user describes it as: "a feminine baby powder for adult women." You will understand that I haven't tried it.

CHAPTER FORTY-SEVEN

146. I confess, I'd approached the J-School with a little skepticism from the outset. Back in 1964, the Journalism School accepted me and set a response date for the acceptance of the admission. Well before that deadline they wrote me again. They said I had not responded in a timely fashion, and they were canceling the offer of admission. Their excuse: "a journalist's high regard for deadline. . . ." I called, surprised and angry. The School immediately backed off and reinstated the admission.

147. A. J. Liebling, *The Wayward Pressman*, San Francisco, Greenwood Press, 1972.

CHAPTER FORTY-EIGHT

148. L. Patrick Gray and Ed Gray, *In Nixon's Web: A Year in the Crosshairs of Watergate*, New York, Times Books, 2008.

149. Todd S. Purdum, "L. Patrick Gray III, Who Led the F.B.I. During Watergate, Dies at 88," *New York Times*, July 7, 2005.

150. Robert M. Smith, "Gray Plans Wide Change In F.B.I. Policy and Style," *New York Times*, May 12, 1972.

151. A public relations person called to ask how Gray or the PR apparatus at the FBI had managed to get favorable stories on the same day on the front page of both the *Times* and the *Post*. The PR guy—the soul of honeyed words—praised me for having been taken.

152. L. Patrick Gray and Ed Gray, *In Nixon's Web: A Year in the Crosshairs of Watergate*, New York, Times Books, 2008.

153. Michael Calderone, "NY *Times* Sat on Watergate Tip; Gray Responds," *Politico*, May 25, 2009.

154. Edward Gray, "Taking Issue," *American Journalism Review*, May 28, 2009.

CHAPTER FORTY-NINE
155. Robert Miraldi, *Seymour Hersh: Scoop Artist,* Lincoln, Potomac Books, 2013.
156. Charles Kaiser, "Above the Fold: The One That Got Away, How The *New York Times* Let a Watergate Lead Slip through Its Fingers," The Sidney Hillman Foundation, May 27, 2009.
157. *Robert Phelps, God and the Editor: My Search for Meaning at the* New York Times, Syracuse, NY, Syracuse University Press, 2009.
158. Charles Kaiser, "Above the Fold: The One That Got Away, How The *New York Times* Let a Watergate Lead Slip through Its Fingers," The Sidney Hillman Foundation, May 27, 2009.

CHAPTER FIFTY
159. Carl Jensen, "Bob Woodward," in *Stories That Changed America: Muckrakers of the 20th Century,* New York, Seven Stories Press, 2000, 246.
160. Clark MacGregor, the Nixon campaign manager, called Ben Bradlee, the editor of the *Washington Post,* to complain. MacGregor reported: "They knock on doors late at night and telephone from the lobby. They hounded five women." Bradlee's response: "That's the nicest thing I've heard about them in years!" "And he meant, maybe, ever."
161. Benjamin Mullin, "Read Carl Bernstein and Bob Woodward's Remarks to the White House Correspondents' Association," *Poynter,* April 30, 2017.
162. Kate Dailey, "Women of Watergate," BBC News, June 19, 2012.
163. David W. Dunlap, "The Holy Grail for Reporters: Presidential Secrets," *New York Times,* March 11, 2017.
164. Richard Pérez-Peña, "2 Ex-Timesmen Say They Had a Tip on Watergate First," *New York Times,* May 24, 2009.

CHAPTER FIFTY-ONE
165. Trump wasn't the first to attack the press. There were the rants of Spiro Agnew, Nixon's vice president. See, e.g., Lance Morrow, "1969–1971: Agnew Helps Create Modern Era of Attack Politics," *Time,* September 30, 1996, quoting Agnew: "A spirit of national masochism prevails, encouraged by an effete core of impudent snobs who characterize themselves as intellectuals."

And Will Bunch, "William Safire, 'Nattering Nabobs' and the Power of Words," *Philadelphia Inquirer,* September 27, 2009, quoting Agnew: "In the United States today, we have more than our share of the nattering nabobs of negativism. They have formed their own 4-H Club—the 'hopeless, hysterical hypochondriacs of history.'

Of course, Agnew didn't write those lines; they were written by William Safire, Agnew's speechwriter. Safire became a *Times* columnist in 1973, after the paper decided it needed a conservative on the editorial page. Unlike its effort to hire a conservative reporter, The *Times*'s effort to hire a conservative columnist succeeded. But unhappily for him, Safire lacked an on-staff tweeter. Trump's reach extends farther as a result. His charge that the media are "enemies of the American People" reached his twenty-five million Twitter followers.
166. Carl Bernstein, "Trump Press Attacks Worse Than Nixon," CNN, February 19, 2017.

167. Kristine Phillips, "Trump Called the Press 'the Enemy.' Reince Priebus Says He Meant It," *Washington Post*, February 19, 2017.

168. What's also unusual is the absence of a trace of good will. In 1988, President Reagan said to the White House press: "I hope my epitaph [with you] will be: 'He gave as good as he got.' And I think that will make for a healthy press and a healthy presidency."

169. Andrew Marantz, "Is Trump Trolling the White House Press Corps?," *New Yorker*, March 13, 2017.

170. Patrick J. Sloyan, "Trump Sets a New Bar for Presidential Paranoia," *Columbia Journalism Review*, March 20, 2017.

171. The paper's dislike of Trump was more than evident during his campaign. Even the *Times* Book Review joined in. It asked the novelist, Chimamanda Ngozi Adichie, to write a short story about the 2016 election (Chimamanda Ngozi Adichie, "'The Arrangements' A Work of Fiction," *New York Times*, June 28, 2016). The short story appeared four months before the election. Illustrated with sexualized cartoons of Melania Trump, it scathingly assailed Trump's personal life and behavior:

Americans were so emotionally young, so fascinated by what Europeans knew to be world-weary realities. They were drawn to Donald's brashness and bluster and bullying, his harsh words, even the amoral ease with which untruths slid out of his mouth. She viewed these with a shrug—he was human, and he had his good points, and did Americans truly not know that human beings told lies? But they had followed him from the beginning, breathlessly and childishly.

She hoped Donald would not open her bedroom door tonight; this was the kind of day that he would come, exuberant and expansive from victory. It had been almost two months. The last time, he kissed her, eager and dramatic and sweaty as he often was—he hated her initiating things, "aggressive women make me think I'm with a transsexual," he'd told her years ago . . .

Two years later—before the midterm elections—the Book Review struck again. It featured five crime and spy novelists to postulate the "next chapter" in the Trump presidency (Zoë Sharp, "Five Novelists Imagine Trump's Next Chapter," *New York Times*, October 23, 2018).

The Russian waited until they were a few steps past before he drew the gun. He sighted on the center of the president's back, and squeezed the trigger.

The Makarov misfired. . . . The Russian tasted failure. He closed his eyes and waited to pay the cost. It did not come. He opened his eyes. The Secret Service agent stood before him, presenting his Glock, butt first. "Here," the agent said politely. "Use mine. . . ."

172. The conservative *New York Post* (not itself known for impartiality) went after the *Times* on the issue of favoritism (Michael Goodwin, "Media More Interested in Hating Trump Than Reporting News," *New York Post*, January 24, 2017).

"Trump repeats an election lie," The Times declared, a glaring accusation about the president insisting to the congressional leaders that illegal voters gave Clinton her popular-vote victory. In eight years of lickspittle cover-ups, The Times never called Obama dishonest, let alone a liar. They were enchanted by what books he read and how many almonds he ate each night.

But all Republicans, and Trump especially, start out by being treated like dirt, and it's downhill from there. Other outlets raced to echo The Times "liar" charge and made much ado about other chaff, including press secretary Sean Spicer's complaints about a "negative" drumbeat from the press.

The first one is usually reserved for the Associated Press, but this time it went to the *Post*'s Daniel Halper. The second question went to the Christian Broadcasting Network and the third to Univision. Spicer was mocked as a crybaby. . . . In his maiden briefing, he threw out the playbook by which organizations got to ask questions.

This was more than a symbol. Like Trump taking action on his jobs agenda, this was Spicer's down payment on the plan to democratize access and end the practice of giving special privileges to major liberal organizations.

173. Jordan Fabian, "W.H.'s Dunn Calls Fox News 'Opinion Journalism Masquerading as News,'" *The Hill*, October 8, 2009.

174. From Peter Baker and Maggie Haberman, "Ever a Showman, Donald Trump Keeps Washington Guessing," *New York Times*, March 1, 2017. As far as I know, Mr. Baker claims to have neither the qualifications of a mind-reader nor a psychiatrist.

Also on page one:

Previous presidents usually measured their words to avoid a media feeding frenzy, but Mr. Trump showed again over the weekend that he *feeds off the frenzy*. Uninhibited by the traditional protocols of his office, he makes the most incendiary assertions based on shreds of suspicion. —Peter Baker and Maggie Haberman. March 5, 2017. [Emphasis supplied.]

While a "feeding frenzy" calls to mind sharks, Haberman and Glenn Thrush perhaps decided another predator might be more frightening. From March 28, 2017, page one, in the second paragraph:

Mr. Pence, a Hill-wise former Indiana congressman who is typically a palliative presence in an *administration of piranhas*. . . . [Emphasis supplied.]

Also on page one:

What Investigation? G.O.P. Responds to F.B.I. Inquiry by Changing Subject

[Sean] Spicer [former White House press secretary] also evaded questions about Mr. Trump's associates by repeatedly returning to what he said were Hillary Clinton's ties to Russia, *even though Mrs. Clinton's presidential campaign was hurt by Russian operatives' hacking*."—Michael D. Shear (White House correspondent), March 20, 2017. [Emphasis supplied.] (Note the date.)

The *Los Angeles Times* had contradicted that charge.

Although a blockbuster new U.S. intelligence report concludes that Russian President Vladimir Putin sought to help Donald Trump win the presidency, *it didn't weigh in on whether Moscow's covert cyberhacks and other activities made a difference in Trump's upset victory over Hillary Clinton*."—Noah Bierman and Brian Bennett, January 7, 2017. [Emphasis supplied.]

175. Julie Hirschfeld Davis and Maggie Haberman, "In One Rocky Week, Trump's Self-Inflicted Chaos on Vivid Display," *New York Times*, March 18, 2017.

176. Michael D. Shear, Maggie Haberman, and Glenn Thrush, "In 77 Chaotic Minutes, Trump Defends 'Fine-Tuned Machine,'" *New York Times*, February 17, 2017.

177. Baker, Peter, "'I Inherited a Mess,' Trump Says, Defending His Performance," *New York Times*, February 16, 2017.

178. Julie Hirschfeld Davis et al., "Trump's Tax Plan: Low Rate for Corporations, and for Companies Like His," *New York Times*, April 25, 2017.

179. There was also the caption below a photo on page one illustrating the lead story on April 27, 2017: "President Trump on Wednesday. He stands to benefit financially from his plan to cut tax rates, though aides would not discuss how much he would save." A story on page A17 the same day (Alan Rappeport, "The 7 Key Elements of the White House Tax Plan," *New York Times*, April 27, 2017) explained various provisions of the complicated plan. Some purportedly do help the rich, but the story went on:

The number of tax brackets for individuals is reduced from seven to three . . . That lowers the top rate by nearly 5 percentage points, easing the tax burden on most Americans, including the rich. And . . . Mr. Trump's plan would double the standard deduction. That is intended to put more money in the pockets of the average taxpayers who do not itemize their deductions. [Emphasis supplied.]

The following day, on page A19, under a photo of the president and his wife this caption ran: ". . . Mr. Trump could benefit substantially from provisions in his tax overhaul proposal."

I called a former senior editor of the *Times* to talk about this descriptive phrase, and he said, "It doesn't say Trump is doing this *because* he wants to save personally." No, it didn't say that, but it did imply it. The paper's headline-writing editors seemed also to be on the bias bandwagon. Consider this page-one headline from a May 17, 2017 article by Michael Schmidt:

Trump Appealed to Comey to Halt Inquiry into Aide Ex-F.B.I. Chief Noted Request in Memo: 'I Hope You Can Let This Go'

180. Michael Schmidt, "Trump Appealed to Comey to Halt Inquiry into Aide Ex-F.B.I. Chief Noted Request in Memo: 'I Hope You Can Let This Go,'" *New York Times*, May 17, 2017.

181. David Folkenflik, "Trump Won. The Media Lost. What Next?," BBC, November 9, 2016.

182. A. J. Liebling, "Horsefeathers Swathed in Mink," *New Yorker*, November 14, 1947.

183. James Hohmann, "The Daily 202: Why Trump Won—and Why the Media Missed It," *Washington Post*, November 9, 2016.

184. Timothy Crouse wrote in his book *Boys on the Bus* (New York, Random House, 1972):

Any self-respecting journalist would sooner endorse incest than come out in favor of pack journalism. . . . If there was a consensus, it was simply because all the national political reporters lived in Washington, saw the same people, used the same sources, belonged to the same background groups, and swore by the same omens.

They arrived at their answers just as independently as a class of honest seventh-graders using the same geometry text—they did not have to cheat off each other to come up with the same answer. . . .

185. Contrast the sensitivity of today's *Times* reporters and editors with the humor and honesty of those who put out its first edition. Page four of the Wednesday, September 17, 1851 *New York Daily Times* included this report:

Grand Lodge of Odd Fellows

Baltimore, Wednesday, Sept. 17, 1851

The Grand Lodge of Odd Fellows, at the morning session, transacted nothing of the slightest public interest.

And:

Long Island Vegetables.—The State of Long Island is some on tomatoes. We were shown the other day, a tomato raised by Mr. Frederick Rowland of Hempstead, one of these vegetables which measured 22½ inches around it, and weighed 2 pounds 3 ounces. Who can beat it?

Page one of that first edition displayed the paper's progressive bent in column six:

A Bloomer Costume made its appearance in Sixth-avenue day before yesterday. A crowd of "Conservatives" manifested their hostility to this progressive movement by derision. "New ideas" are compelled to wage fierce battle in this world before they obtain recognition and favor. Two bloomers appeared in Broadway and two in Washington square yesterday.

186. Even if the reporting of the *Times* about Trump is, in a factual sense, not incorrect, it often presents no other side and no context. The tone alone leaves no one in doubt as to the partiality. Take, for one example this bomber run (to use their sort of language) by White House correspondents Peter Baker and Maggie Haberman ("A Portrait of the White House and Its Culture of Dishonesty," *New York Times*, April 18, 2019):

The White House that emerges from more than 400 pages of Mr. Mueller's report is a *hotbed of conflict infused by a culture of dishonesty*—defined by a president who lies to the public and his own staff, then tries to get his aides to lie for him. . . . *[A]t one juncture after another, Mr. Trump made his troubles worse, giving in to anger and grievance . . .* [Emphasis supplied.]

187. Twitter, June 9, 2019.

188. Three-quarters of them are digital only.

189. "Coining the term 'bully pulpit,'—a mix of TR's favorite expression 'bully,' meaning good, with a speaking platform, or pulpit—Roosevelt used the presidency as a vehicle to sell his views to the nation."

Michael P. Cullinane, *Perspectives on Presidential Leadership,* New York, Routledge, 2014.

CHAPTER FIFTY-TWO

190. Patrick J. Sloyan, "Trump Sets a New Bar for Presidential Paranoia," *Columbia Journalism Review,* March 20, 2017.

191. Niccolò Machiavelli, *Discourses on Livy,* book 3, chapter 2.

192. H. R. Haldeman. *The Ends of Power.* New York: Times Books, 1978.

CHAPTER FIFTY-THREE

193. Clark Hoyt, "The Blur Between Analysis and Opinion," *New York Times,* April 13, 2008.

194. Jennifer McGuire, "Opinion vs. Analysis." CBC News, June 5, 2013.

195. Glenn Thrush, "Trump's Blistering Speech at CPAC Follows Bannon's Blueprint," *New York Times*, February 24, 2017.

196. Nancy Benac, "Trump Blasts Media, Anonymous Sources—after WH Uses Them," Associated Press, February 24, 2017.

197. Coral Davenport and Alissa Rubin, "Trump Signs Executive Order Unwinding Obama Climate Policies," *New York Times*, March 28, 2017.

198. Matthew Daly and Jill Colvin, "Trump, in Break from Other World Leaders, Digs in on Coal," Associated Press, March 28, 2017.

199. Peter Baker, "Trump's Previous View of NATO Is Now Obsolete," *New York Times*, April 13, 2017.

200. Jill Colvin and Ken Thomas, "Trump Reverses Himself on NATO, China, Russia and More," Associated Press, April 12, 2017.

201. **A Speech to Congress:**

Here is a comparison of coverage on Trump's address to Congress in late February, 2017: The *Times* (Glenn Thrush and Maggie Haberman, March 1, 2017):

In Speech, Trump Tests a New Tactic: Toning It Down

WASHINGTON—*President Trump loves the song "My Way," bristles at the slightest alterations in his daily routine, and lashes out when the world won't accept him on his own terms.*

Then, when that doesn't work, he tries something completely different.

Mr. Trump's well-received address to Congress on Tuesday night, a conciliatory speech in which the word "we" outnumbered the word "I" by three to one, represented precisely that kind of shift. Just last week, Mr. Trump shouted himself hoarse branding the news media "enemies of the American people" at a time when he was working on an address that invoked the better angels of his own nature, national unity and an "end to trivial fights."

This does not represent a pivot, it is not a fundamental change of approach, and it does not mean that Mr. Trump plans to abandon his tweet-first-and-ask-questions-later style.

But it is a recognition by the White House, from Mr. Trump on down, that what it had been doing was not quite working and that a softer sales tactic was needed to sell the same hard-edge populist agenda he campaigned on, people close to Mr. Trump said. . . .

Newt Gingrich, the former House speaker and a Trump ally and adviser, said, "The thing people don't get about Trump is how quickly he learns—he moves fast—so he's going to be using different approaches." . . .

Republican Senate and House members were cheered by the president's optimistic message. But in private, they are becoming increasingly anxious. . . .

Aware that Mr. Trump would be speaking to the largest television audience since his inaugural, his messaging team . . . took pains to soften his often incendiary language.

And they were pleased with the contrast between his slashing, improvisational speech to the Conservative Political Action Conference last Friday and his dignified delivery on Tuesday. . . .

Two people briefed on how Tuesday's speech to Congress was crafted said the lack of details was an intentionally evasive maneuver, using phrases that allowed different groups to read in what they wanted. It buys the president more time to change the narrative that his White House is short-staffed and in disarray.

But none of a dozen people in Mr. Trump's orbit said they had expected him to sustain the tone of measured magnanimity in the speech.

The question of when, or whether, Mr. Trump will ever move away from his brash, in-your-face style to a more sedate and conventional approach has been dogging the former real estate developer since the earliest days of his presidential campaign.

There have been nearly as many false pivots as real crises: Mr. Trump was expected to adopt a kinder-gentler attitude after an "Access Hollywood" recording of him making lewd comments about women surfaced last fall, but after a short statement of contrition he went back on the attack. . . . [Emphasis supplied.]

The AP (Erica Werner, March 1, 2017):

Trump Speech Leaves GOP Encouraged, But Still Divided

WASHINGTON—President Donald Trump's first speech to Congress left Republicans encouraged and enthusiastic Wednesday, yet still confronting thorny divisions on health care, taxes and more.

Trump's disciplined and optimistic tone was what GOP lawmakers wanted to hear after a rocky first month that provoked daily anxiety on Capitol Hill with each new presidential tweet. Republicans welcomed Trump's presentation and his call for "a new chapter of American greatness."

"It's just one speech, but I think what we see is a guy who comes from outside the political process now weaving his way through into becoming an effective leader," said Sen. David Perdue, R-Ga.

Vice President Mike Pence said on MSNBC Wednesday morning that Trump showed Congress and the nation his "broad shoulders, big heart, reaching out, focusing on the future."

And House Speaker Paul Ryan declared the speech a "home run."

Yet even though Trump offered some specifics on health care and appeared to embrace a key element of a leadership-backed plan emerging in the House, his comments did little to settle an extremely difficult debate over Republicans' top legislative priority. . . .

And Trump's failure to say anything about Medicare and Social Security, the massive entitlements that are eating up the budget, left some Republicans complaining that he was ducking political reality . . . [Emphasis supplied.]

Compare how the two news organizations spent the first half-dozen paragraphs describing the event. The *Times* says Trump invoked the "better angels of his nature" for the speech as a strategy to soften his image and win back public approval. The AP simply reported the event and included several quotes that praised the speech.

Charges Against a Former National Security Adviser

Finally, here are two articles on Trump's allegations against Susan Rice, former national security adviser:

The *Times* (Maggie Haberman, Matthew Rosenberg, and Glenn Thrush. April 5, 2017):

Trump, Citing No Evidence, Suggests Susan Rice Committed Crime

WASHINGTON—President Trump said on Wednesday that Susan E. Rice, the former national security adviser, may have committed a crime by seeking to learn the identities of Trump associates swept up in surveillance of foreign officials by United

States spy agencies, repeating an assertion his allies in the news media have been making since last week.

Mr. Trump gave no evidence to support his claim, and current and former intelligence officials from both Republican and Democratic administrations have said they do not believe Ms. Rice's actions were unusual or unlawful. The president repeatedly rebuffed attempts by two New York Times reporters to learn more about what led him to the conclusion, saying he would talk more about it "at the right time."

The allegation by a sitting president was a remarkable escalation—and, his critics say, the latest effort to change the story at a time when his nascent administration has been consumed by questions about any role his associates may have played in a Russian campaign to disrupt last year's presidential election.

Since March 4, when Mr. Trump posted on Twitter that President Barack Obama had "wiretapped" him at Trump Tower during the campaign, the president and his allies have repeatedly sought evidence trying to corroborate that claim, despite flat denials from James B. Comey, the director of the F.B.I., and other senior intelligence officials.

Wednesday's interview revealed how Mr. Trump seizes on claims made by the conservative news media, from fringe outlets to Fox News, and gives them a presidential stamp of approval and also increases their reach.

Last week, some Republican television commentators asserted that Ms. Rice had improperly leaked the names of Trump associates picked up in surveillance of foreign officials. On Sunday, a conservative writer and conspiracy theorist reported, without identifying his sources, that Ms. Rice had been the one to seek identities of the Trump associates.

Other conservative outlets picked up the report, and the Drudge Report website, which has been supportive of Mr. Trump, featured the story prominently. White House officials then accused mainstream news outlets of not giving the story proper coverage. . . .

"The allegation is that somehow the Obama administration officials utilized intelligence for political purposes," Ms. Rice said. "That's absolutely false.". . .

It is not the first time Mr. Trump has made a provocative allegation without providing supporting evidence. One of the most notorious instances of this was his years long claim that Mr. Obama was not born in the United States. . . .

Mr. Trump's March 4 Twitter message came after reports in conservative news outlets—including Breitbart, the website once run by the president's chief strategist, Stephen K. Bannon—claiming that there had been surveillance of some kind against Mr. Trump when he was a candidate.

Mr. Trump was widely criticized for the intemperate post, and he began to ask his advisers about how he might be able to investigate the issue. . . .

Representative Adam Schiff of California, the top Democrat on the Intelligence Committee, cast Mr. Trump's comments as part of a broader effort by the president to distract from the investigations into Russia's interference in the election. The committee is running one of the investigations.

"He began by accusing President Obama of a crime without any evidence," Mr. Schiff said. "He's now moved on to accusing Susan Rice of a crime without any evidence, and this is sadly how this president operates."

It *"would be a terrible way to do business,"* Mr. Schiff added. *"It's a worse way to run a country."* [Emphasis supplied.]

The AP (Julie Pace, April 5, 2017):

Trump Tells Newspaper Obama Aide Might Have Broken the Law

President Donald Trump on Wednesday said his predecessor's national security adviser might have committed a crime when she asked government analysts to disclose the names of Trump associates documented in intelligence reports.

Trump made the accusation in an interview with The New York Times and would not say if he reviewed new intelligence to support his claim. He told the Times he would say more "at the right time."

"I think it's going to be the biggest story," Trump said. "It's such an important story for our country and the world. It is one of the big stories of our time."

Susan Rice, former President Barack Obama's national security adviser, is the latest target for Trump and his embattled defenders. Rice has firmly denied that she or other Obama officials used secret intelligence reports to spy on Trump associates for political purposes.

"Absolutely false," Rice declared Tuesday.

Trump on Wednesday disagreed. When the Times asked him if Rice broke the law, he said, "Do I think? Yes, I think."

The White House has seized on the idea that the Obama administration improperly surveilled the Republican during and after the November election—an accusation Democrats say is just another red herring thrown out to distract attention from investigations of Russian interference in the campaign on behalf of Trump.

White House spokesman Sean Spicer cast Rice's handling of intelligence in the waning days of Obama's term as suspicious, although he did not detail what he found to be inappropriate.

"The more we find out about this, the more we learn there was something there," Spicer said. . . .

Still, the White House has appeared to find other ways to promote the idea that Obama officials were conducting improper surveillance of Trump's team. . . .

The U.S. routinely monitors the communications of foreigners. The identities of Americans who talk with those foreigners, or who are discussed in conversations between two non-U.S. persons, are masked in intelligence reports.

Rice became a favorite target of conservatives after the 2012 attacks on a U.S. diplomatic outpost in Benghazi, Libya. . . . Even Republicans who have been critical of White House efforts to muddy the Russia investigations have said it is imperative to get to the bottom of her handling of Trump-related intelligence.

"When it comes to Susan Rice, you need to verify, not trust," said Sen. Lindsey Graham, R-S.C. [Emphasis supplied.]

The *Times* spends a good portion of the article discrediting Trump's claims by criticizing his dependence on "fringe outlets" and Fox News, saying he "seizes" on their claims. Most notable, though, are the "kickers" (the endings of the two articles):

The *Times:*

"He began by accusing President Obama of a crime without any evidence," Mr. Schiff said. "He's now moved on to accusing Susan Rice of a crime without any evidence, and this is sadly how this president operates."

It "would be a terrible way to do business," Mr. Schiff added. "It's a worse way to run a country."

The AP:

"When it comes to Susan Rice, you need to verify, not trust," said Sen. Lindsey Graham, R-S.C.

CHAPTER FIFTY-FOUR

202. L. Patrick Gray and Ed Gray, *In Nixon's Web: A Year in the Crosshairs of Watergate,* New York, Times Books, 2008.

203. Charles Kaiser, "Above the Fold: The One That Got Away, How the *New York Times* Let a Watergate Lead Slip through Its Fingers," The Sidney Hillman Foundation, May 27, 2009.

204. Robert Phelps, *God and the Editor: My Search for Meaning at the* New York Times, Syracuse, NY, Syracuse University Press, 2009.

205. Charles Kaiser, "Above the Fold: The One That Got Away, How the *New York Times* Let a Watergate Lead Slip through Its Fingers," The Sidney Hillman Foundation, May 27, 2009.

206. Robert Phelps, *God and the Editor: My Search for Meaning at the* New York Times, Syracuse University Press, 2009.

CHAPTER FIFTY-FIVE

207. Alicia Shepard, "The Journalism Watergate Inspired Is Endangered Now," *New York Times,* June, 13 2012.

208. Anne Kornblut, "The News Media Is Still Recovering from Watergate," *New York Times,* June 5, 2005.

209. Nick Tabor, "The *Washington Post'*s Bob Woodward [:] What's Wrong (and Right) With the Media," *Daily Intelligence,* July 24, 2016.

210. Alicia Shepard, "The Journalism Watergate Inspired Is Endangered Now."

211. Leonard Downie Jr., "Forty Years After Watergate, Investigative Journalism Is at Risk," *Washington Post,* June 7, 2012.

212. Susan Milligan, "The President and the Press," *Columbia Journalism Review,* April 2015.

213. Art Swift, "Americans' Trust in Mass Media Sinks to New Low," *Gallup,* September 14, 2016.

214. For example, I was astonished by the journalistic missteps in Judith Miller's Weapons of Mass Destruction stories in the *Times.* Terry McDermott reviewed Miller's book, *The Story: A Reporter's Journey in the Times* on April 7, 2015 ("Review: Judith Miller's 'The Story: A Reporter's Journey'"):

In late 2002 and through 2003, Judith Miller, an investigative reporter at The New York Times, wrote a series of articles about the presumed presence of chemical and

biological weapons and possible nuclear matériel in Iraq. They all included careful quali-
fiers, but their overwhelming message was that Saddam Hussein posed a threat . . .

During the war, she writes, she was the sole reporter embedded with the military
team charged with finding Iraq's weapons of mass destruction. It failed, meaning so had
she. . . .

CHAPTER FIFTY-SIX
215. Aleks Krotoski, "What Effect Has the Internet Had on Journalism?" *The Guardian*,
February 19, 2011.
216. Amy Mitchell and Jesse Holcomb, "State of the News Media 2016," Pew Research
Center, June 15, 2016.
217. Mathew Ingram, "Here's Why Trust in the Media Is at an All-Time Low," *Fortune*,
September 15, 2016.
218. Jennifer Alejandro, "Journalism in the Age of Social Media," Reuters Institute for
the Study of Journalism, 2010.
219. Dan Rather, "I've Discovered Facebook," *Huffington Post*, December 16, 2011.

EPILOGUE
220. Julie Hirschfeld Davis and Matthew Rosenberg, "With False Claims, Trump
Attacks Media on Turnout and Intelligence Rift," *New York Times*, January 21, 2017.

AFTERWORD
221. Alexa Tsotsis, "Airbnb Bags $112 Million in Series B from Andreessen, DST and
General Catalyst," *TechCrunch*, July 24, 2011.
222. Vanessa Friedman, "Justin Trudeau Takes an Image, and Wins With It," *New York
Times*, October 21, 2015.
223. David W. Dunlap, "1961: The C.I.A. Readies a Cuban Invasion, and The Times
Blinks," *New York Times*, December 26, 2014.
224. Tad Szulc, "Anti-Castro Units Land in Cuba; Report Fighting at Beachhead; Rusk
Says U.S. Won't Intervene," *New York Times*, April 17, 1961.

BIBLIOGRAPHY

"About McGruff." National Crime Prevention Council, 2017. Accessed August 1, 2019.

Adichie, Chimamanda Ngozi. "'The Arrangements': A Work of Fiction." *New York Times*, June 28, 2016.

Jeremy Alderton, *Aldertons a Cockney Rhyming Slang Dictionary*, aldertons.com.

Alejandro, Jennifer. "Journalism in the Age of Social Media." Reuters Institute for the Study of Journalism, 2010.

Alterman, Eric. "The Journalist and the Politician." *Columbia Journalism Review*, February 14, 2013.

Amira, Dan. "Bob Woodward Unimpressed by the Times' Watergate Scoop." New York, May 27, 2009.

Attwood, William. *The Man Who Could Grow Hair*. London, Wingate, 1950.

Baker, Peter. "'I Inherited a Mess,' Trump Says, Defending His Performance." *New York Times*, February 16, 2017.

———. "Trump's Previous View of NATO Is Now Obsolete." *New York Times*, April 13, 2017.

Baker, Peter, and Maggie Haberman. "A Conspiracy Theory's Journey From Talk Radio to Trump's Twitter," *New York Times*, March 5, 2017.

Baker, Peter, and Maggie Haberman. "A Portrait of the White House and Its Culture of Dishonesty." *New York Times*, April 18, 2019.

———. "Ever a Showman, Donald Trump Keeps Washington Guessing." *New York Times*, March 1, 2017.

Bierman, Noah, and Brian Bennett. "U.S. intelligence report doesn't say whether Russian hacking helped elect Donald Trump," *Los Angeles Times* , January 7, 2017.

Benac, Nancy. "Trump Blasts Media, Anonymous Sources—After WH Uses Them." Associated Press, February 24, 2017.

Berenbaum, Michael. *The World Must Know: The History of the Holocaust as Told in the United States Holocaust Memorial Museum*. 2nd ed. Washington, DC, John Hopkins University Press, 2006.

Bernstein, Carl. "The CIA and the Media," Carlbernstein.com.

Bernstein, Carl. "Trump Press Attacks Worse Than Nixon." CNN, February 19, 2017.

Breslin, Jimmy. "It's an Honor." *New York Herald Tribune*, November 26, 1963.

———. "Society Carey." *In The World According to Breslin*. New York: Ticknor & Fields, 1984, 110.

Bunch, Will. "William Safire, 'Nattering Nabobs' and the Power of Words." *Philadelphia Inquirer*, September 27, 2009.

Calderone, Michael. "NY Times Sat on Watergate Tip; Gray Responds." *Politico*, May 25, 2009.

Califano, Joseph. "Washington Lawyer: Williams, Connolly & Califano." In *Inside: A Public and Private Life*. PublicAffairs Press, 2004, 219.

CareerCast.com. "The Worst Jobs of 2016." CareerCast, 2016.

Cecil, Matthew. *Hoover's FBI and the Fourth Estate: The Campaign to Control the Press and the Bureau's Image.* Lawrence University of Kansas Press, 2014.

Cocco, Federica. "*New York Times* Profits Jump 66% amid 'Trump Bump'." *Financial Times,* May 3, 2018.

Cockburn, Alexander. "All the News That's Fit to Buy." *The Nation,* December 8, 2005.

Colvin, Jill, and Ken Thomas. "Trump Reverses Himself on NATO, China, Russia and More." Associated Press, April 12, 2017.

Crouse, Timothy. *Boys on the Bus.* New York: Random House, 1972.

Cullinane, Michael P. *Perspectives on Presidential Leadership.* New York: Routledge, 2014.

Dailey, Kate. "Women of Watergate." BBC News, June 19, 2012.

Daly, Matthew, and Jill Colvin. "Trump, in Break from Other World Leaders, Digs in on Coal." Associated Press, March 28, 2017.

Dash, Eric. "Mexican Billionaire Invests in Times Company." *New York Times,* January 19, 2009.

Davenport, Coral, and Alissa Rubin. "Trump Signs Executive Order Unwinding Obama Climate Policies." *New York Times,* March 28, 2017.

Davis, Julie Hirschfeld, and Maggie Haberman. "In One Rocky Week, Trump's Self-Inflicted Chaos on Vivid Display." *New York Times,* March 18, 2017.

Davis, Julie Hirschfeld et al. "Trump's Tax Plan: Low Rate for Corporations, and for Companies Like His." *New York Times,* April 25, 2017.

Davis, Julie Hirschfeld, and Matthew Rosenberg. "With False Claims, Trump Attacks Media on Turnout and Intelligence Rift." *New York Times,* January 21, 2017.

Diegelman, Robert F. "Federal Financial Assistance for Crime Control: Lessons of the LEAA Experience." *Crim. L. & Criminology* 994 (1982).

Downie, Leonard, Jr. "Forty Years After Watergate, Investigative Journalism Is at Risk." *Washington Post,* June 7, 2012.

Downie, Leonard, Jr., and Michael Schudson. "The Reconstruction of American Journalism." *Columbia Journalism Review,* December 2009.

Dunlap, David W. "1961: The C.I.A. Readies a Cuban Invasion, and The Times Blinks." *New York Times,* December 26, 2014.

———. "The Holy Grail for Reporters: Presidential Secrets." *New York Times,* March 11, 2017.

Duralex. Duralexusa, n.d.

Fabian, Jordan. "W.H.'s Dunn Calls Fox News 'Opinion Journalism Masquerading as News.'" *The Hill,* October 8, 2009.

Flood, Joseph, P. "The Path Less Traveled." *Harvard Crimson,* April 19, 2002.

Folkenflik, David. "'New York Times' Editor: Losing Snowden Scoop 'Really Painful.'" NPR, June 5, 2014.

———. "Trump Won. The Media Lost. What Next?" BBC, November 9, 2016.

Frankel, Max. *The Times of My Life and My Life with* The Times. New York: Penguin Random House, 2000.

Friedman, Vanessa. "Justin Trudeau Takes an Image, and Wins with It." *New York Times,* October 21, 2015.

Goodale, James C. *New York Times Company v. United States of America: A Documentary History*. New York: Arno Press, 1972, p. 420.

Glueck, Grace. "Art in Review: James VanDerZee Betye Saar," *New York Times*, Oct. 25, 2002.

Goodwin, Michael. "Media More Interested in Hating Trump Than Reporting News." *New York Post*, January 24, 2017.

Goulden, Joseph C. *Fit to Print: A.M. Rosenthal and His* Times. New York: Lyle Stuart, 1988.

Graham, Ruth. "The Bizarre True Story of the Group That Seduces Philip in This Season of The Americans." *Slate*, April 6, 2016.

Gray, Edward. "Taking Issue." *American Journalism Review*, May 28, 2009.

Gray, L. Patrick, and Ed Gray. *In Nixon's Web: A Year in the Crosshairs of Watergate*. New York: Times Books, 2008.

Grieco, Elizabeth, Nami Sumida, and Sophia Fedeli. "At Least 36% of Largest US Newspapers Have Had Layoffs since 2017." Pew Research Center, July 23, 2018.

Haberman, Maggie, and Glenn Thrush. "Amid White House Tumult, Pence Offers Trump a Steady Hand," *New York Times*, March 28, 2017

Haberman, Maggie, and Glenn Thrush. "In Speech, Trump Tests a New Tactic: Toning It Down," *New York Times*, March 1, 2017.

Haberman, Maggie, Matthew Rosenberg, and Glenn Thrush. "Trump, Citing No Evidence, Suggests Susan Rice Committed Crime," *New York Times*, April 5, 2017.

Halberstam, David. "Foreign Correspondents." New York, March 1985.

Haldeman, H. R. *The Ends of Power*. New York: Times Books, 1978.

Hamilton, Charles. *Adam Clayton Powell, Jr.: The Political Biography of an American Dilemma*. Maryland: Cooper Square Press, 2001.

Hartigan, Lynda Roscoe. "James Van Der Zee." Smithsonian American Art Museum, n.d.

Heinl, Robert D., Jr. "The Collapse of the Armed Forces." *Armed Forces Journal*, June 7, 1971.

Hersh, Seymour. "Kissinger Linked to Order to F.B.I. Ending Wiretaps." *New York Times*, June 1974.

———. *Reporter*. New York: Knopf Doubleday Publishing Group, 2018.

Herzberg, Joseph E. *Late City Edition*. New York: Holt, 1969.

Hess, John. *My Times: A Memoir of Dissent*. New York: Seven Stories Press, 2003.

Heymann, Philip. *Living the Policy Process*. 1st ed. Oxford: Oxford University Press, 2008.

Hohmann, James. "The Daily 202: Why Trump Won—and Why the Media Missed It." *Washington Post*, November 9, 2016.

Holderness, Mike, Benno Pöppelmann, and Michael Klehm. "The Right Thing: An Authors' Rights Handbook for Journalists." Belgium: International Federation of Journalists, 2011.

Hoover, Kent. "Only Lawyers Valued Less Than Business Executives, Pew Survey Finds." *Business Journals*, June 12, 2013.

Hoyt, Clark. "The Blur Between Analysis and Opinion." *New York Times*, April 13, 2008.

Ingram, Mathew. "Here's Why Trust in the Media Is at an All-Time Low." *Fortune*, September 15, 2016.

Irving, Washington. *Rip Van Winkle and The Legend of Sleepy Hollow: Two Stories*. New York: Peter Pauper Press, 1955 [originally published 1820].

Jacobs, Scott W. "Student Activists Denied Jobs in Government, Media." *Harvard Crimson*, May 14, 1970.

Jensen, Carl. "Bob Woodward." In *Stories That Changed America: Muckrakers of the 20th Century*. New York: Seven Stories Press, 2000, 246.

Jobs, Steve. "You've Got to Find What You Love." *Stanford News*, Palo Alto, California, June 14, 2005.

Johnson, Carrie. "The Secret Burglary That Exposed J. Edgar Hoover's FBI." NPR, January 7, 2014.

Kaiser, Charles. "Above the Fold: The One That Got Away, How The *New York Times* Let a Watergate Lead Slip through Its Fingers." The Sidney Hillman Foundation, May 27, 2009.

Kazin, Alfred. *The Past Breaks Out*. New York: Houghton Mifflin Company, 1987.

Kelley, Tina. "Ron Ziegler, Press Secretary to Nixon, Is Dead at 63." *New York Times*, February 11, 2003.

Kihss, Peter, "Falling Masonry Kills a Lawyer 14 Floors Down." *New York Times*, July 29, 1982.

Kinzer, Stephen. *The Brothers: John Foster Dulles, Allen Dulles, and Their Secret World War*. New York: Times Books, 2013.

Kobrick, Jake. *The Pentagon Papers in the Federal Courts*, second edition. Federal Judicial Center, 2019.

Kornblut, Anne. "The News Media Is Still Recovering from Watergate." *New York Times*, June 5, 2005.

Krotoski, Aleks. "What Effect Has the Internet Had on Journalism?" *The Guardian*, February 19, 2011.

Lelyveld, Joseph, John Kifner, and Robert M. Smith. "The View From Kent State: 11 Speak Out." *New York Times*, May 11, 1970.

Lerner, Kevin. "(MORE) Guided Journalists during the 1970s Media Crisis of Confidence." *Columbia Journalism Review*, May 10, 2018.

Liebling, A. J. "A Good Appetite." In *Just Enough Liebling: Classic Work by the Legendary New Yorker Writer*. New York: North Point Press, 2004.

———. "Horsefeathers Swathed in Mink." *New Yorker*, November 14, 1947.

———. *The Wayward Pressman*. San Francisco: Greenwood Press, 1972.

Loeb, Vernon. "Soviets Knew Date of Cuba Attack." *Washington Post*, April 29, 2000.

Machiavelli, Niccolò. *Discourses on Livy*, book 3, chapter 2.

Mancari, James. "Woodward and Bernstein Stress the Constants of Journalism." *Long Island Report*, March 23, 2012.

Marantz, Andrew. "Is Trump Trolling the White House Press Corps?" *New Yorker*, March 13, 2017.

McDermott, Terry. "Review: Judith Miller's 'The Story: A Reporter's Journey.'" *New York Times*, April 7, 2015.

McFadden, Robert D. "Michael Kaufman, Times Reporter Who Roamed World, Is Dead at 71." *New York Times*, January 15, 2010.

———. "Peter Kihss, Reporter for 49 Years, Is Dead at 72." *New York Times*, December 30, 1984.

———. "Winston Moseley, Who Killed Kitty Genovese, Dies in Prison at 81." *New York Times*, April 4, 2016.

McGuire, Jennifer. "Opinion vs. Analysis." CBC News, June 5, 2013.

Milligan, Susan. "The President and the Press." *Columbia Journalism Review*, April 2015.

Miraldi, Robert. *Seymour Hersh: Scoop Artist*. Lincoln, NE: Potomac Books, 2013.

Mitchell, Amy, and Jesse Holcomb. "State of the News Media 2016." Pew Research Center, June 15, 2016.

Molotsky, Irvin. "Eileen Shanahan, 77, Former Times Reporter." *New York Times*, November 3, 2001.

Morgenson, Gretchen. "At Student Loan Giant Navient, Troubled Past Was Prologue." *New York Times*, January 21, 2017.

"Morning Report." Radio New Zealand, May 27, 2009.

Morrow, Lance. "1969–1971: Agnew Helps Create Modern Era of Attack Politics." *Time*, September 30, 1996.

Mott, Brian. "Traditional Cockney and Popular London Speech." MS, Universitat De Barcelona, Barcelona, Spain, 2011.

Moules, Jonathan. "FT Global MBA Ranking 2019." *Financial Times*, January 27, 2019.

Mullin, Benjamin. "Read Carl Bernstein and Bob Woodward's Remarks to the White House Correspondents' Association." *Poynter*, April 30, 2017.

"The *New York Times*' Dejó Escapar El Watergate." *El Periódico*, May 26, 2009.

Nobile, Philip. "An Exclusive Report on How the *New York Times* Became Second Banana." *Esquire*, May 1975.

Numbers, Facts and Trends Shaping Your World. Pew Research Center, 2018.

O'Keefe, Garrett. *Media Campaigns and Crime Prevention—An Executive Summary*. Report, University of Denver, 1982.

Overholser, Geneva, and Kathleen Hall Jamieson. *The Press*. Oxford: Oxford University Press, 2005.

Pace, Eric. "Harrison E. Salisbury, 84, Author and Reporter, Dies." *New York Times*, July 7, 1993.

Pace, Julie, and Eileen Sullivan. "Trump Tells Newspaper Obama Aide Might Have Broken the Law," Associated Press, April 5, 2017.

Pérez-Peña, Richard. "2 Ex-Timesmen Say They Had a Tip on Watergate First." *New York Times*, May 24, 2009.

Perlmutter, Emanuel. "I.R.S. Gets Data on Phone Calls by Times's Washington Staff." *New York Times*, February 9, 1974.

Phelps, Robert. "Friendships, Feuds and Betrayal in the Newsroom." *Nieman Reports*, March 2004.

———. *God and the Editor: My Search for Meaning at the* New York Times. Syracuse, NY: Syracuse University Press, 2009.

Phillips, Kristine. "Trump Called the Press 'the Enemy.' Reince Priebus Says He Meant It." *Washington Post*, February 19, 2017.

Phillips, McCandlish. "Bird Accused of Cursing Wins Case by Eloquence of Silence." *New York Times*, July 1, 1960.

———. "5th Ave. Weather: Sunshine And Gaels." *New York Times*, March 18, 1970.

———. "Lindy's Serves Cheesecake, Bagels and Humor for Last Time." *New York Times*, September 22, 1969.

———. *What Every Christian Should Know About the Supernatural.* Illinois: Scripture Press Publications, 1987.

Pilkington, Ed. "Watergate Under the Bridge: How the *New York Times* Missed the Scoop of the Century." *The Guardian*, May 25, 2009.

Poitras, Laura. "How We Broke the NSA Story." *Salon*, June 11, 2013.

Pufong, Marc-Georges. "McCarthyism." In *The First Amendment Encyclopedia.* John Seigenthaler Chair of Excellence in First Amendment Studies, Middle Tennessee State University.

Purdum, Todd S. "L. Patrick Gray III, Who Led the F.B.I. During Watergate, Dies at 88." *New York Times*, July 7, 2005.

———. "The Nation; The Nondenial Denier." *New York Times*, February 16, 2003.

Rappeport, Alan. "The 7 Key Elements of the White House Tax Plan." *New York Times*, April 27, 2017.

Rather, Dan. "I've Discovered Facebook." *Huffington Post*, December 16, 2011.

"The Reporters: Homer Bigart." PBS, 2003.

Reston, James. *Deadline: A Memoir.* New York: Random House, December 8, 1991.

———. "Now, About My Operation in Peking." *New York Times*, July 26, 1971.

"The Right War at the Right Time." *Time*, May 14, 1965.

Roberts, Sam. "Arthur Gelb, Critic and Editor Who Shaped the Times, Dies at 90." *New York Times*, May 20, 2014.

Roberts, Gene, and Hank Klibanoff. *The Race Beat.* New York: Random House, 2008, 184.

Robertson, Nan. *The Girls in the Balcony: Women, Men and The New York Times.* New York: Random House, 1992.

"RSF's 2018 Round-up of Deadly Attacks and Abuses against Journalists—Figures Up in All Categories: Reporters without Borders." RSF, December 18, 2018.

Sandler, Martin W. *America Through the Lens: Photographers Who Changed the Nation.* New York: Henry Holt and Company, 2005.

Savage, Charlie. "Is an Attorney General Independent or Political? Barr Rekindles a Debate." *New York Times*, May 1, 2019.

Schmidt, Michael. "Trump Appealed to Comey to Halt Inquiry into Aide Ex-F.B.I. Chief Noted Request in Memo: 'I Hope You Can Let This Go.'" *New York Times*, May 17, 2017.

Schrecker, Ellen. "Hearing Regarding Communist Infiltration of the Hollywood Motion-Picture Industry." In *The Age of McCarthyism: A Brief History with Documents.* Boston: Bedford Books of St. Martin's Press, 1994, 201–2.

Schultz, David. "House Un-American Activities Committee." In *The First Amendment Encyclopedia*. John Seigenthaler Chair of Excellence in First Amendment Studies, Middle Tennessee State University.

Shafer, Jack. "A.M. Rosenthal (1922–2006)." *Slate*, May 11, 2006.

Sharp, Zoë. "Five Novelists Imagine Trump's Next Chapter." *New York Times*, October 23, 2018.

Shear, Michael, Maggie Haberman and Glenn Thrush. "In 77 Chaotic Minutes, Trump Defends 'Fine-Tuned Machine.'" *New York Times*, February 17, 2017.

Shear, Michael D. "What Investigation? G.O.P. Responds to F.B.I. Inquiry by Changing Subject," *New York Times*, March 20, 2017.

Shepard, Alicia. "The Journalism Watergate Inspired Is Endangered Now." *New York Times*, June 2012.

Sherman, Gabriel. "Risen Gave Times A Non-Disclosure on Wiretap Book." *New York Observer*, January 23, 2006.

"Sizing Up the Damage to Local Newspapers." *New York Times*, August 4, 2019.

Sloyan, Patrick J. "Trump Sets a New Bar for Presidential Paranoia." *Columbia Journalism Review*, March 20, 2017.

Smith, Robert M. "F.B.I. Is Said to Have Cut Direct Liaison With C.I.A." *New York Times*, October 10, 1971.

———. "4 More Leaving Kissinger's Staff." *New York Times*, May 22, 1970.

———. "Gray Plans Wide Change In F.B.I. Policy and Style." *New York Times*, May 12, 1972.

———. "Hammer Accused of Foreign Bribes." *New York Times*, October 9, 1975.

———. "Harlem Photographer Sees Lifework Hauled Away." *New York Times*, April 8, 1969.

———. "Harvard Vote Bars Strike; Radcliffe Head Besieged." *New York Times*, April 29, 1969.

———. "Haughton Expects U. S. Curb On Payments." *New York Times*, September 3, 1975.

———. "Kent State Study by F.B.I. Differs from Ohio Finding." *New York Times*, October 31, 1970.

———. "The Lockheed Letter: How and Why of Bribery." *New York Times*, February 8, 1976.

———. "More State Banks on 'Problem List'." *New York Times*, January 23, 1976.

———. "Reserve Says List of Banks Under Surveillance Grows." *New York Times*, February 4, 1976.

———. "S. E. C.'s Tough Guy." *New York Times*, October 5, 1975.

———. "The Slippery Slopes; When One Question Leads to Another." *New York Times*, August 22, 1973.

———. "U.S. Cane Cutters in Cuba Scored as 'Missiles'," *New York Times*, March 17, 1970.

———. "White House Inscrutable On Nixon's Cram Course." *New York Times*, February 12, 1972.

"Some Papers March On, Crippled by Cutbacks." *New York Times*, August 4, 2019.

Spayd, Liz. "One Thing Voters Agree On: Better Campaign Coverage Was Needed." *New York Times*, November 19, 2016.

Stacks, John. *Scotty: James B. Reston and the Rise and Fall of American Journalism*. Lincoln, NE: Bison Books, 2003.

Swift, Art. "Americans' Trust in Mass Media Sinks to New Low." Gallup, September 14, 2016.

Szulc, Tad. "Anti-Castro Units Land in Cuba; Report Fighting at Beachhead; Rusk Says U.S. Won't Intervene." *New York Times*, April 17, 1961.

Tabor, Nick. "The Washington Post's Bob Woodward [:] What's Wrong (and Right) with the Media." *Daily Intelligence*, July 24, 2016.

Talese, Gay, *The Kingdom and the Power*. New York: Random House, 2007.

Taubman, Philip. "Benjamin Richard Civiletti." *New York Times*, July 20, 1979.

Thrush, Glenn. "Trump's Blistering Speech at CPAC Follows Bannon's Blueprint." *New York Times*, February 24, 2017.

"The Times Settles Sex-Bias Suit Filed by Female Workers in U.S. Court." *New York Times*, November 21, 1978.

"Topics of The Times; A Salisbury Scoop." *New York Times*, July 11, 1993.

"Tribune Co. to Cut 700 Jobs." Pew Research Center, November 21, 2013.

Tsotsis, Alexa. "Airbnb Bags $112 Million in Series B from Andreessen, DST and General Catalyst." *TechCrunch*, July 24, 2011.

"US Paper Missed Watergate Scoop." BBC, May 26, 2009.

Van Der Zee, James. *The World of James Van Der Zee: A Visual Record of Black Americans*. New York: Grove Press, 1969.

"Vietnam War Casualties Officer Deaths by Rank," American War Library, 2008.

Waugh, Evelyn. *Scoop*. Milwaukee: Chapman & Hall, 1938.

Werner, Erica. "Trump speech leaves GOP encouraged, but still divided," Associated Press, March 1, 2017.

Williams, Alex. "The Growing Pay Gap between Journalism and Public Relations." Pew Research Center, August 11, 2014.

———. "How Poorly Are Journalists Paid? Depends on Where You Live." *Poynter*, June 26, 2015.

World Intellectual Property Organization. Berne Convention for the Protection of Literary and Artistic Works. World Intellectual Property Organization, 1982.

INDEX